D0148237

Figuring Poesis

Studies on Themes and Motifs in Literature

Horst S. Daemmrich
General Editor

Vol. 32

PETER LANG
New York • Washington, D.C./Baltimore
Bern • Frankfurt am Main • Berlin • Vienna • Paris

Evans Lansing Smith

Figuring Poesis

A Mythical Geometry of Postmodernism

PETER LANG
New York • Washington, D.C./Baltimore
Bern • Frankfurt am Main • Berlin • Vienna • Paris

Library of Congress Cataloging-in-Publication Data

Smith, Evans Lansing.
Figuring poesis: a mythical geometry of postmodernism/ Evans Lansing Smith.
p. cm. — (Studies on themes and motifs in literature; v. 32)
Includes bibliographical references.
1. Postmodernism (Literature). 2. Postmodernism. 3. Hermeneutics.
I. Title. II. Series: Studies on themes and motifs in literature; vol. 32.
PN98.P67S66 809'.045—dc20 96-33034
ISBN 0-8204-3497-3
ISSN 1056-3970

Die Deutsche Bibliothek-CIP-Einheitsaufnahme

Smith, Evans Lansing:
Figuring poesis: a mythical geometry of postmodernism/
Evans Lansing Smith. –New York; Washington, D.C./Baltimore;
Bern; Frankfurt am Main; Berlin; Vienna; Paris: Lang.
(Studies on themes and motifs in literature; Vol. 32)
ISBN 0-8204-3497-3
NE: GT

The paper in this book meets the guidelines for permanence and durability
of the Committee on Production Guidelines for Book Longevity
of the Council of Library Resources.

Printed in the United States of America.

To the Memory of My Grandmothers, Mary Morrow and Mary White, and Especially to the Memory of My Mother,

Jane Lansing Moller

Painter, Pianist, Poet

Acknowledgments

I am grateful to the publishers for generously allowing me to quote from the poetry of David Jones (*The Anathemata*, Faber and Faber1952), Derek Walcott (*Omeros*, The Noonday Press, Farrar, Strauss, and Giroux, 1990), and James Merrill (*The Changing Light at Sandover: A Poem*, Alfred A. Knopf, a division of Random House, 1980, 1982). Without their generosity, the accumulation of detail crucial to my argument would not have been possible. In completing this book, my thanks are due to President Louis Rodriguez, Dr. Jesse Rogers, and Dr. Michael Collins, of Midwestern State University, for their roles in the allocation of funds necessary to subsidize publication. Thanks also to Dr. Michael Land for his help in printing the final manuscript. I would also like to thank Jim Hoggard, both for his enthusiasm and interest in my work, and for his permission to quote from his fine book of poetry, *Two Gulls, One Hawk*.

Preface

This book completes a trilogy focused on myth in the literature of the modernist mode, i.e., the literature of our century which employs what T.S. Eliot called the "mythical method," a sustained parallel between the realistic details of daily life in the present, and some myth from the past which gives those details "shape and significance." By modernist, I refer to those practitioners of the method writing during and before World War II; and by postmodernist, I refer to those practitioners of the method writing during and after World War II. My book is more concerned with literature than with theory; with contextualizing the presence of myth in the works, than with theoretical formulations about myth or postmodernism. I nevertheless present data which those inclined to abstraction will have to take into account in their theories about postmodernism and myth. For I take considerable pains to establish the presence of myth in the texts, and thereby to allow the individual writers to speak for themselves, in their own unique voices.

Table of Contents

Introduction

"Cycles in fact are rounder than circles
Cycles in time become globes"

James Hoggard, "Tornado's Eye"

Myths (like the apocalypse, the goddess, alchemy, the maze, and the underworld) are the fundamental elements of literature; geometrical figures (like the circle, the square, and the triangle) are the fundamental elements of larger forms, like polygons. Taken together—which the literature of postmodernism forces us to do—myths and geometrical figures form a universal grammar of the human imagination. As Arthur Schopenhauer put it, "geometrical figures are the universal forms of all possible objects of experience and are applicable to them all *a priori* " (262). The following chapters explore these universal forms, through close readings of postmodernist texts. By the term postmodern, I refer simply to that literature written since the time of the Second World War which was influenced by the "mythical method" of the great modernists writing before the War. This method forms the point of departure for postmodernism, which extends the method in an elaborately playful and dramatic manner. In this sense, the theatricality and dynamism of the postmodernist use of myth recalls the evolution of the forms of Mannerism and the Baroque, which developed out of Renaissance mythography in a way similar to the emergence of the postmodern from the modernist. One also thinks of the rapid evolution towards the breakthroughs of modernism, as post impressionist painting extended the developments of the previous generation of impressionists. In all three cases, it is a matter of the witty elaboration of intricate forms which are based upon the discoveries of immediate precursors: Borges evolved from Joyce, for example, the way Bernini evolved from Michelangelo, Rosicrucianism from the Renaissance, Matisse from Monet.

T.S. Eliot's definition of the "mythical method" is one of those keynotes of modernism, conferring "shape and significance" upon the "anarchy and futility" of the modern world, which has continued to thrive in the literature of postmodernism. The method involved a fusion of realistic detail with mythical symbolism, such as we find throughout the works of writers like D.H. Lawrence, Thomas Mann, James Joyce, and many others. Many postmodernist works written during and after the end of the Second World War are informed by the same myths which engaged their precursors: the maze, the Great Goddess, alchemy, the descent to the underworld, and the apocalypse.[1] The extent to which these myths continue to inform the literature written at the end of and after the Second World War is somewhat surprising. It has not received the attention it deserves among the critics, who seem to assume a sharp dividing line between modernism and what came after it. The daring audacity of innovative forms which characterizes the works of such authors and Borges, Grass, Carrington, and Cortázar often obscures the conventional tropes of the mythical method which continue to confer upon them the shape and significance T. S. Eliot remarked upon in Joyce's *Ulysses*. And, as we will see, these mythical tropes often occur simultaneously with a variety of geometrical figures which represent the emergence of order out of chaos.

The modernists writing before and during the War developed an elaborate vocabulary to express the nature of the conventional forms created by the mythical method, a vocabulary which the postmodernists expanded on. Thomas Mann called myths "fundamental types" ('Grundtypen') (*Doctor Faustus* 488; 647), and "timeless schema" ('zeitlose Schema') (*Joseph* 422; 493). In *The Anathemata*, the Welsh poet David Jones used such terms as "fore–types," "proto–morphs," "signa," and "figures." In his essay on the Tibetan Book of the Dead, Jung referred to these archetypal forms as "eidola," borrowing Plato's term for the pure Forms of the mind. In *The Death of Virgil*, Herman Broch called the source of these "ancient forms" the "crystalline archetype" ('kristallische Urbild') (444; 418), "the form which is the pattern of all forms" ('die Form aller Formen') (212; 201), and the "first image" ('Urbild aller Bilder') (481; 453). Borges called them "ancient forms, forms incorruptible and eternal" ('formas antiguas, formas incorruptibles y eternas') (*Labyrinths* 170; *Obras* 117), while Julio Cortázar preferred the term "figuras" to "represent systems of relations, intuitive constellations of meaning in which people, events, places relate to each other across time and space in patterns that transcend discursive, diachronic reason" (Zamora 83).

Each of the five myths discussed in the chapters below represents the process which these fundamental forms are discovered by the writer and by the reader, so that the myths can be taken as allegories of poesis and hermeneusis. In each myth, the raw materials of daily life are broken down to those elements which confer shape and significance upon life and art. In the myths of the apocalypse and alchemy, material compounds are reduced to those fundamental elements which serve as the basis of re–creation. Similarly, the myth of the Great Goddess combines the tomb, to which all things return, with the womb, which contains the seeds of new life. And, as James Hillman has shown, the descent to the underworld catalyzes the revelation of "the ideas that form and shape life" (*Dream* 51). Finally, the myth of the maze—traditionally linked to the images of the underworld, alchemy, and the Goddess—embraces the complexities of the creative and destructive process by which the fundamental forms of the mind are revealed as the basis of poetic and hermeneutic endeavors. As the following chapters demonstrate, the revelation of these elemental forms of myth in postmodernist texts is often represented in "diagrams" by which reality is "geometricized", as Charles Williams puts it in *The Descent into Hell* (24). That is to say, the fundamental elements to which the world is broken down, and from which new creation emerges, are frequently represented by geometrical figures.

The foundations for a mythical geometry of Modernism are therefore in the philosophical, mythical, Biblical, alchemical, and literary traditions, in which the basic forms of the created world are represented by Euclidean figures. Some of the oldest "multi–cultural" artifacts of humankind involve geometrical cosmograms which use such basic figures as the point, the circle, the spiral, the triangle, and the square. Joseph Campbell notes the absence of any "concept of geometrical organization" in Paleolithic art, and its sudden emergence in the high Neolithic of about 4500 B.C.E. At that time, ceramic ware characterized by "very beautiful, strictly balanced, circular organizations of abstract aesthetic forms" dramatically appears in the Halaf and Samarra styles of the high Neolithic towns of the Ancient Near East (*Flight* 140–41). These pottery designs typically involve a sequence of concentric circles inscribing a center broken into quadrants (*Flight* Fig. 10). The Samarra ware from Iraq of about 4000 B.C.E. introduces cruciform or swastika patterns swirling around the center of the inscribing circles (*Flight* Fig. 1), an archetypal image of the squared circle which may have its roots in the late Paleolithic: the oldest quadriform swastika occurs on mammoth ivory bird figurines from the Ukraine of 10, 000 B.C.E. The world wide distribution of the concentric circle, swastika, and square, and its relation to the emergence of temple architecture (like the pyramid, the stupa, and the ziggurat) in the high cultures of the Ancient Near East can be seen as resulting from the archetypal nature of geometrical symbolism, from its diffusion along trade routes, or both (Campbell, *Atlas* 2.1.28).

Equally archaic is the imagery of the line and spiral, which Brancusi used in his famous portrait of James Joyce. The spiral is the oldest of those geometrical forms found in postmodernism, attested by such artifacts as the stones inscribed with spirals at the entrance to the earthmound of Newgrange (c. 3500 B.C.E.) outside of Dublin, in which rituals associated with the death and rebirth of the sun at the winter solstice were most likely performed (Bord 25). Numerous examples of the spiral, often associated with the labyrinth, are also to be found in such Mediterranean sites as Hal Tarxien on Malta (Di Stasi 101; Gimbutas 279f.). The earliest prototype of the spiral labyrinth and the mythologies of death and rebirth takes us as far back as 16,000 to 13,000 B.C. to an Upper Paleolithic burial cite in Siberia, where among some "twenty female statuettes of mammoth ivory" surrounding the skeleton of a child was found a buckle with a "stippled design showing a spiral of seven turns with S–forms enclosing it—the earliest spirals known in the history of art" (Campbell, *Atlas* 1.1.72).

Horst and Ingrid Daemmrich have recently explored the metaphor of the spiral as a basic pattern of spatial configuration and thematic structure in a wide range of European literary works. Their analysis of writers like Richardson, Dickens, Fontane, and Mann corresponds exactly to the archetypal basis of the geometrical symbolism of the spiral. The Daemmrichs discovered that the centripetal spiral in realistic works represents a self–centred, inward–turning movement, leading to imprisonment and isolation; while the centrifugal spiral of classicism leads towards liberation and social reform (18–33). The former spiral revolves from the present to the restrictive past, from the environment to the inner consciousness, and from the human to the non–human (344–45); while the latter turns from the human towards the divine, from the individual to the community, and from the past towards the renovations of the future (344–45). The centripetal spiral represents the outer circle of realistic circumstance closing in (55, 338), while the centrifugal movement of classicism portrays the small inner circle of idealism radiating outwards to effect social reform (338). The downward and inward turning spiral of increasing confinement can parallel the penetration of the maze, as in Mann (342), and the forces which drive the centripetal spiral may be either socio–economic, in Richardson, or the intellectual habits of collective thinking, in Mann (21, 55, 339).

Generally speaking, even though the centripetal spiral contains the seeds of its reversal (as we see in Dante's *Divine Comedy*), this mode of analysis links the centripetal spiral to death, and the centrifugal spiral to life, in a way which recalls the iconographic tradition of myth. Mythic spirals generally combine the oppositions between life and death in the form of centripetal and centrifugal radiation. The spiral eyes guarding the entrance to the ancient temple of Hal Tarxien on the island of Malta, for example, connect a left spiral turning in a clockwise direction, and a right turning in a counterclockwise movement (Di Stasi 100). As Coomaraswamy as pointed out, the various turnings of the spiral combine the "paired motions of evolution and involution, birth and death, positive and negative values," so that "it will depend upon our orientation with reference to movement along it, whether we think of it as centrifugal or as a centripetal form" ("Thread" 30). Like the Daemmrichs, Coomaraswamy suggests that the direction the spiral turns may be related either to death or to life, to confinement or to liberation, and that the boundaries that separate death from life may be confused by the paradoxical perplexities of the spiral. If the centripetal turning of the wheel leads to incarnation, the soul may experience that as death, whereas the centrifugal movement promises that liberation which can only be achieved through death, which is new life to the soul.

Archaic figures like the spiral laid the foundation for the emergence of the Indo–European cosmogonies of Plato and the early Hindus, in which geometrical shapes serve as symbols as the fundamental elements of the creation. In the *Timaeus*, Plato represented the purest idea in the mind of God by the circle, which is broken to form the spiral maze of the material world. He argues that the "original of the universe contains within itself all intelligible beings," and that the Deity "framed one visible animal comprehending within itself all other animals of a kindred nature" (14). The appropriate shape for this original being was the globe, since "to the animal which was to comprehend all animals, that figure was suitable which comprehends within itself all other figures" (16). This globe revolves around its own soul in the center, just as the universe is a circle moving in a circle (16). Plato uses these geometric forms to create a symbol of that figure which contains all other figures within it: the circle for the "original" which contains all other "intelligible beings;" and the globe for that "animal which was to comprehend all animals" (16). We will return to this notion of a "figure which comprehends within itself all other figures" in the conclusion to our study, where we will use the term "hologlyph" to designate a symbolic image of that archetype which contains all other archetypes within itself.

In Plato's cosmogony, the Deity divides the essences into "seven unequal circles," which correspond to the seven planetary spheres, which revolve in spirals (20). A heavenly species, corresponding to the fixed stars, is created "after the likeness of the universe in the figure of a circle;" the earth itself circles around a pole extended through the universe, and all of these figures revolve eternally, "circling as in a dance" (21). When, however, souls fell into bodies to create mortal beings, the chaotic swirling of the elements shatters the harmony of the soul: its circles "were broken and disordered in every possible manner, so that when they moved they were tumbling to pieces" (25). Penelope Doob points out that this breaking of the circles creates a geometrical figure of great importance to postmodernism: the maze. When the chaos of the affections subsides, "the several circles return to their natural form, and their revolutions are corrected" (25). Plato then concludes his cosmogony with the fashioning by "form and number" of the four elements in their rudimentary state: all emerge from the basic form of the triangle—three from a triangle with unequal sides (scalene), and one from a triangle of equal sides (isosceles) (34). Fire is formed of the simplest solid, the pyramid, which is a combination of four equilateral triangles. Air is created as the octahedron, formed from eight equilateral triangles. Water takes the shape of an icosahedron, a combination of twenty equilateral triangles. Finally, earth is formed by six square surfaces each made up of four rectangular isosceles triangles, i.e., a cube (35–36).

It is important to note that Plato's use of geometrical figures occurs in the context of a cosmogonic myth—a myth, that is to say, which has to do with the processes of creativity within the human mind (which are then projected onto the world). The various polyhedra are used to represent the basic elements of the created world, and hence become images of poesis. Euclid of course refined these speculations in the *Elements,* of which Books 1–6 are devoted to plane geometry, and Books 11–13 to solid geometry. The *Elementa* was of particular importance to the painters of the Italian Renaissance, when geometry, optics, and mathematics facilitated the emergence of perspective. The Renaissance painters attempted to "replicate what the human eye perceives according to the tenets of Euclidean geometry, which medieval Europeans understood as synonymous with the vision of God" (Edgerton 5). They built on the 12th century revival of Euclid and other Greek geometers, when Adelard of Bath, Hermann of Carinthia, and Gerard of Cremona first translated the whole of the *Elementa* from Arabic into Latin (Edgerton 45). By 1267, Roger Bacon could argue that Europe was losing the crusades because it lacked knowledge of geometry, and that "nothing is intelligible unless it is presented before our eyes in figures" (Edgerton 45). Furthermore, Bacon argued, "the whole knowledge of things to be made certain by geometric figuring is contained in" Scripture (Edgerton 45). In 1485, Piero della Francesca possessed a copy of the *Libellus de quinque corporibus regularibus*, an "illustrated commentary on the five regular solids, the tetrahedron, hexahedron, octahedron, icosahedron, and dodecahedron, as described in Books XIII–XV of Euclid's *Elementa*, and which Plato had shown would all fit into a sphere" (Edgerton 163). Marilyn Lavin argues that Piero designed his "Baptism" of Jesus "on the basis of Euclid's Proposition 16, a formula for constructing a 15–sided figure by superimposing a pentagon on an equilateral triangle," and then dividing the circle in which the pentagon is inscribed into 15 chords of 24 degrees each (29). Samuel Edgerton traces the impact of such geometricizing of the painted surface throughout the Renaissance, beginning with Giotto and Masaccio. The first linear perspective illustrations of the five regular solids are to be found in Fra Luca Pacioli's *Divina proportione* of 1509, close to the time when Raphael's Stanze della Signatura in the Vatican "nearly succeeded in geometricizing medieval theology" (196). As the German art historian Theodor Hetzer put it, none of the other Renaissance painters "ever so successfully realized the sheer aesthetic attractiveness and metaphysical implications of Euclidean geometry in the formal structure of painting" (Edgerton 196). Meanwhile, in Germany, Albrecht Dürer wrote and illustrated several learned studies on geometry, one source perhaps of the mysterious polyhedron in the "Melancholia" of 1514. Johanness Kepler consulted one of Dürer's books (Edgerton 173), and later used the regular polyhedra inscribed in spheres to calculate distances in the planetary system (Hansen 35). It is no accident, therefore, that in the "School of Athens," Raphael shows us a philosopher in the lower–right foreground inscribing geometric figures on a board, for such figures were at the heart of Renaissance conceptions of painting and architecture.

But the use of geometrical figurations of the basic structures of the creative mind has its roots in Biblical images as well as in the philosophical and artistic traditions. When, during the Middle Ages, Meister Eckart evoked God as an intelligible sphere whose circumference is nowhere and whose center is everywhere, he was drawing upon an extensive typology of sacred geometry in Scripture. In the Old Testament we have such figures as the quadrant formed by the four rivers running out from Paradise in Genesis 2, and the complex intersections of Ezekiel's Wheels, both of which feed cabalistic speculations about the Tetragrammaton and Merkabah mysticism (Poncé 35–38). For the Angels of Ezekiel also form quaternities, the four of them each with four faces (of a man, a lion, an ox, and an eagle), standing on a "wheel in the middle of a wheel" Ezekiel 1: 4–21). Typologically, the New Testament fulfills these figures, giving us the Trinity, the Cross—a basic quaternity uniting Heaven and Earth, Eternity and Time, and the four cardinal points of the compass—and the cube, which is used to figure the Heavenly Jerusalem in Revelation. The city has three doorways in each of four sides; twelve foundations made of twelve different precious stones; it lies foursquare with the length, breadth, and height all twelve thousand furlongs; and the wall therefore totals "an hundred and forty four cubits" (Rev. 21: 12–17). These measurements rather mercifully simplify the baroque complexity of the dimensions of the tabernacle, the geometrical specifications of which occupy two full Chapters (26–27) of Exodus. The sacred geometry of the Apocalypse of John later become the basis of the Gawain poet's vision in *Pearl*, a poet who in *Sir Gawain and the Green Knight* gives us the pentangle.

A variety of geometrical figures permeate the hermetic literature of the Middle Ages, Renaissance, and so–called Rosicrucian Enlightenment at the beginning of the 17th century. The inverted cone with a ninefold spiral, reflected by the cone of the purgatorial mountain, encircled by spiraling terraces, and by the heavenly spheres, which shape Dante's *Divine Comedy,* have their roots in such basic Egyptian and Mesopotamian forms and the pyramid and the ziggurat. Hildegard von Bingen's *Scivias* replaces the Ptolemaic spheres with elliptical eggs (curiously in advance of Kepler). Hermetic speculations used upward–pointed and inverted triangles with lines intersecting the apices, as symbols of the four elements (Fabricius 14). When the triangles of the four elements are all put together, they produce the Star of David, another symbol of the philosopher's stone. Putting the Tetragrammaton in the center creates a Masonic symbol of God (Biedermann 173–74). In *De Compendiosa Architectura* of 1582, Giordano Bruno depicted the five human senses, coordinated by the mind in the center, as a downward pointed pentagon, the five sides of which serve as the bases of the five equilateral triangles which form the points of a pentagonal star (Mookerjee, *Yoga* Fig. ix.). Bruno also used triangles inscribed in circles as mystical diagrams of the universe in his *De Monade Numero et Figura* of 1591 (Mookerjee, *Yoga* Pl. 100–101), and, in his *De Imaginum* of the same year, he created a cosmogram of the universe as an upward pointed triangle inscribed with a circle which is in turn inscribed within a square, the four sides of which serve as the bases of four isosceles triangles pointed in the four directions of the compass (Mookerjee, *Yoga* Fig. viii.).

A vast array of related geometrical figures is to be found in the illustrated Hermetic texts (alchemical and cabalistic) of the Middle Ages and Renaissance, texts which have become prominent in that scholarship of the 20th century which engaged the attention of Jung, Thomas Mann, and many others. The prototypical figure is of course, a concentric network of spheres based on the Ptolemaic system, perhaps most beautifully illustrated in Robert Fludd's *Utriusque cosmi* of 1617 (Fabricius 46), in which we also find God portrayed as an inverted female triangle entering a large circle (representing the material world), which inscribes a smaller upward–pointed isosceles triangle (representing the male principle), with an apex in the center of three smaller inscribed circles, representing the *Mundus angelicus*, the *Mundus elementaris*, and the *Mundus stellaris* (Mookerjee, *Yoga* Pl. 103). But other more elaborate figures abound in the hermetic corpus. Jacob Boehme typically employed a network of circles and triangles inscribed within each other and circumscribing Solomon's Seal to represent the esoteric processes of divine creativity (Poncé 56). The characteristic hermetic task of squaring the circle is beautifully represented in Michael Maier's *Atalanta Fugiens* of 1617, which represents the creative synthesis of the four elements and the union of male and female and heaven and earth (Fabricius 198). Rembrandt's famous etching of the "Practicing Alchemist" (known as the "Faust") also depicts the adept staring into a circle with a quaternity inscribed in a center surrounded by esoteric syllables. In the *Arithmologia* of 1665, Athanasius Kircher depicts the Deity in the form of an eye within a triangle inscribed with an octagon, which is in turn inscribed by a nine pointed star made up of nine triangles (Godwin 82). In cabalistic speculations about the emanations of the En–Sof into the vessels of the Sephiroth, fantastically baroque networks of downward and upward pointing triangles inscribing and inscribed by circles become standard symbols of creation (Poncé 8–9, 159). Cabalistic tradition also produced the image of the diamond—an upward pointed and downward pointed pyramid sharing the same base, created by assigning seven letters to the center, the four cardinal points, the above, and the below, and joining them with lines (Poncé 43).

Much of this came into modernism through the writings of Yeats, Strindberg, Thomas Mann, A. E. Waite, H. D., and McGregor Mathers, and later on into postmodernism through the important work of such preeminent scholars as Dame Frances Yates and Gershom Scholem. Such figures, however, had long been a part of those strains of the literary tradition susceptible to the influence of Renaissance and Rosicrucian brands of hermeticism. Marlowe's Faustus, for example, confesses that "These metaphysics of magicians / And necromantic books are heavenly; / Lines, circles, signs, letters and characters: / Ay, these are those that Faustus most desires" (1.47–50). The affiliation between Faust and the geometrical figures of hermetic tradition would last all the way to Rembrandt's portrait of the alchemist contemplating three concentric circles inscribing four triangles, each one containing one of the letters of the name of God (INRI). Such magical figurations occur also in Shakespeare's *Tempest*, in which Prospero "makes a magic circle with his staff" before delivering his famous farewell to the hermetic arts (5.1.39). The pun on "art" linking hermeticism and literature throughout *The Tempest* is crucial, for it suggests a traditional conception of the artist as a Magus, master of an esoteric semiotics of signs, letters, numbers, and geometrical figures. Euclidean metaphors of poesis are also implied in Milton's *Paradise Lost*, in which God begins the Creation by using "golden compasses ... to circumscribe / This Universe, and all created things. / One foot he centred, and the other turned / Round through the vast profundity obscure" (7.226–29). In *The Garden of Cyrus*, Sir Thomas Browne uses the term "hieroglyphics" to refer to "the higher Geometry of nature" (185). To illustrate "how nature Geometrizeth" (187), Browne focuses obsessively on various forms of the quincunx (rhombus, pentangle, decussated quadrates), found imprinted upon natural and human objects: flowers, star fish, the anatomy of animals and men; Biblical and Babylonian agricultural and gardening systems; honeycombs, butterfly eggs, cabalistic and hermetic number symbolism; "the mystical Mathematics of the City of Heaven" (210); and even upon Roman military dispositions of its legions during battles (173). Like the pentangle, or endless knot, upon Gawain's shield, various reticulations of the quincunx form a key or hieroglyphic cipher, enabling the acute observer to "trace the Labyrinth of Truth" (210). Browne's notion of nature as the hieroglyphic script of the spirit greatly influenced Ralph Waldo Emerson, who also turned to geometrical symbolism in his essay called "Circles," in which he declared that the circle is "the primary figure" in nature, and the "highest emblem in the cipher of the world" (403).

But the use of geometrical figures to represent the processes of human or of divine creativity is universal, not unique to the Western World. A brush painting by the Zen Buddhist Sengai of 1830, for example, depicts the fundamental forms of creation as a square, a triangle, and a circle (Mookerjee, *Yoga* Pl. 99). For the Hindus as well there seems to have been formulated from very early on a network of correspondences linking basic geometrical forms with the fundamental elements of creation: the square with earth, the circle with water, the triangle with fire, the crescent with air, and the diamond with ether. These five forms then become the basic architectural elements of the Buddhist Stupa (Campbell *Mythic Image* 90). In the Kundalini yoga system, these five figures unite the five elements and the five spiritual centers of the human body known as chakras (wheels) (Mookerjee, *Kundalini* 32). The movement of the spiritual energy up through the five chakras along canal of the spinal cord was often conceived of as a spiraling ascent, analogous to Dante's movement up the purgatorial mountain. As the Daemmrichs have suggested in their study of the spiral in literature, such a movement may have psychological meaning, whether the spiral turn inwards and downwards, in a centripetal movement (344), or, as Mookerjee puts it, "inwards and upwards from the circumference of the sphere or the base of the cone into the point–experience or crest–experience at the centre of being" (*Kundalini* 33).

In the Book of Changes, known as the *I Ching*, the Chinese encoded the entire mechanism of the microcosm in the form of an octagon enclosing 64 hexagrams made up of solid and broken lines (310). A similar octagonal fancy is to be found in the notebooks of Leonardo, who puts a mirror in the center of an eight–sided maze (Corbin 101). The Oriental figure known as the Shri Yantra uses a sequence of nine concentric upward and downward pointing triangles, inscribed within a square outer frame which contains concentric circles and stylized lotus petals, all emanating from a central point, to represent the rhythms of creation and dissolution (Mookerjee, *Yoga* 31–35; Zimmer, *Myths* 143). The center of the figure represents the bindu, simultaneously the original point, at which the divine energy bursts into manifestation, and the ending point, where the creation dissolves to return to the source. The upward–pointed triangles represent the male rhythm of spiritual ascent, while the downward pointed triangles represent the female rhythm of incarnation. The square frame is "shivered" to produce the four doors of the temple aligned with the four cardinal points (Zimmer, *Myths* 140–46). A similar cosmogram of interlocking triangles is to be found among the Islamic mystics, who pictured the world as an upper triangle of light pointing downward from its base near the primordial Will, and a lower triangle of darkness pointing upward from its base at the "maximum distance from the primordial will" (Corbin, *Spiritual Body* 229). The diamond in the middle, created by the intersection of the two triangles, represents this world, a mixture of light and darkness.

Like Plato's polyhedra of the *Timaeus*, the geometrical figure of the Shri Yantra is a cosmogonic image embracing the creation and dissolution of the world. And, as in the Biblical, hermetic, and cabalistic traditions, the geometrical forms represent the basic elements of the creation and destruction of the world. As Ajit Mookerjee suggests, "Such basic geometrical figures as the point, straight line, circle, triangle, and square have a symbolic value in representing the basic energies of the universe. They can be combined in increasingly complex figures to represent particular forces or qualities embodied in some aspect of creation, evolution, dissolution" (*Yoga* 33). As such, cosmogonic mythologies establish key metaphors of the processes of human creativity, those processes which create the text (poesis), and those processes which interpret the text (hermeneutics). Both writer and reader, therefore, participate in the creation of what Eliot called shape and significance, out of the chaos and anarchy of daily life. The geometrical forms figure that special sense of order conferred upon the world and the text by the mythical allusions recur in the literature, the architecture, and in the painting of postmodernism, In the works discussed in the chapters that follow, there is a tendency towards such complex geometrical figures as the polygon and the squared circle, both of which unite all the elements into an image of totality. Jung has argued that such figurations form the mandala, a circular image of wholeness uniting a vari ety of geometrical forms. Postmodernism adapted the mandala in a self–reflexive manner, so that the mythology of geometrical forms represents the multi–faceted complexities of narrative structure, as well as the intricacies of the hermeneutic labyrinth. The analysis to follow explores the five myths adapted by the postmodernists, and then proceeds to delineate the various geometrical forms frequently associated with those myths.

Chapter 1
Forthrights and Meanders

The archaeological publications of Howard Carter in Egypt in the 1920's, Sir Arthur Evans (from 1921 to 1935) in Crete, and of Sir Leonard Wooley at the Royal Cemetery of Ur (1929 to 1934), and the publications of E. A. Wallis Budge on the Egyptian Books of the Dead in 1904, placed the mythology of the maze squarely in the center of modernist awareness.[2] Literary versions of the story occur in Virgil's *Aeneid*, Book 6, and in Ovid, but an oral tradition had certainly circulated from the time of the flourishing of Minoan culture in about 1450 B.C.E. According to such Classical authors as Herodotus, Strabo, and Pliny, Daedalus modeled his maze on the Egyptian temple of Amenemhet III (Bord 33), and it is certainly true that we find the idea of the labyrinth in the Egyptian Books of the Dead (transcribed c.1650 B.C.E.), in which the Sun God travels through the twelve chambers of the Tuat. It is to the publications of Sir Wallis Budge in 1904 that we may owe much of the modernist imagery of the maze and the underworld (170–262). But it may well be that the first labyrinth in the literary tradition is to be found in the Sumerian story of the descent of Inanna, from about 1750 B.C.E., in which the Goddess must pass through seven doorways to enter the kingdom of the dead. This material gradually entered the consciousness of the modernist culture along with the flood tablets, published first in 1872.

Penelope Reed Doob's recent study shows how the imagery of the labyrinth permeates all aspects of European culture, from the antiquity of Virgil and Ovid through the Middle Ages of Dante and Chaucer. Subsequent studies need to pick up where she left off, bringing us from the Renaissance (treading the "quaint mazes in the wanton green" with Shakespeare, navigating the "watery maze" with Andrew Marvell, or seduced by the "surging maze" of the serpent in Milton's *Paradise Lost*); to the Enlightenment (ensnared by the "labyrinths" of Belinda's ringleted hair in *The Rape of the Lock,* contemplating Pope's "mighty maze but not without a plan" in *An Essay on Man,* traversing the hedge mazes of Versailles, or entering Racine's political and psychological maze in *Phèdra*); and on through Romanticism and Ruskin's *Fors Clavigera* to Modernism.[3] For Marvell and Pope, the world and human history are labyrinthine; Milton associates the labyrinth both with rhetoric (language) and the Fall (and thereby with time and history, as Borges also will); Racine develops the political and erotic themes associated with the maze (in a way similar to both Gide and Mann), and revises the myth by having Phaedra imagine herself as guiding Hippolytus to the Minotaur.

The myth of the maze provides an archetypal mirror for the mysteries both of the creative process and of interpretation: constructing a maze becomes a metaphor for poesis (the writing of a book) and hermeneutics (reading and interpretation). These metaphors link the maze, music, dance in the works of James Joyce, Hermann Broch, Nikos Kazantzakis, and Thomas Mann. Stravinsky's ballet, "The Rites of Spring," exemplifies the modernist preoccupation with ricorso, the creative return to the archaic so characteristic of the arts of the time, evident also in the paintings of Picasso, the sculpture of Brancusi, and the films of Cocteau. It is from the work of such precursors that the postmodernists found their point of departure. In their work, the splintered circle, the octagon, and the hexagon become standard geometrical figurations of the complexities of poesis and hermeneusis. Generally speaking, the anthropological approach of the modernists has shifted to issues of epistemology in postmodernism. Questions about perception, poesis, and hermeneutics have replaced the rites of passage in Mann and Kazantzakis: the maze has moved from the bull ring and the marriage chamber to the libraries of Eco and Borges.

Jorge Luis Borges

At the same time that Mann was incorporating Kerényi's labyrinth studies in the Joseph novels, and Picasso and Kazantzakis were transforming the iconography of the Minotaur, the Goddess, and the maze, Jorge Luis Borges was at work developing his own unique variations on the theme. His career was just hitting full stride; theirs was coming to an end. His first major works were produced in the early 1940's, at the same time as the last masterpieces of modernism. Borges saw his work as a manifestation of the Baroque, verging on self–parody, a perception that supports my sense that postmodernism stands in a similar relation to modernism as the Baroque and Rosicrucian eras stood in relation to the Renaissance. It is a relation exemplified by contrasting the theatrical dynamism of Bernini's "David" with the elegant classicism of Michelangelo's.

The idea of the labyrinth is an obsession in his work, most thoroughly delineated in such stories as "The Immortal," "The Library of Babel," and "The Garden of Forking Paths" (1941). The narrator of the first story journeys through a desert, where, after being "lacerated by a Cretan arrow," he falls asleep within sight of the "pyramids and towers" of the Immortal City and dreams "of an exiguous and nitid labyrinth: in the center was a water jar" (107). (Mann and Broch also center their labyrinth with a symbolic water source). The next day he descends a stairway in a cave to a "vast circular chamber" beneath a mountainous and elaborately wrought city: "there were nine doors in this cellar; eight led to a labyrinth that treacherously returned to the same chamber; the ninth (through another labyrinth) led to a second circular chamber equal to the first," and so on through a vast "stone network" that the narrator eventually escapes climbing up a ladder (109–10). This ladder leads upward from the "blind region of dark interwoven labyrinths into the resplendent City," which itself turns out to be another "atrocious" and "complexly senseless" maze, full of "dead–end corridors, high unattainable windows, portentous doors," and "inverted stairways" (111).

The passage overall emphasizes the impenetrable, inextricable, and inexplicable nature of the maze, which Doob amply demonstrates as traditional features of its symbolism. These features may enclose the indecipherable mystery of either a divine or a demonic design; hence, the maze in "The Immortal" has a Minotaur in its center, evoked as "a chaos of heterogeneous words, the body of a tiger or a bull in which teeth, organs and heads monstrously pullulate in mutual conjunction and hatred" (111). The Minotaur, that is to say, is not only the empty center of a meaningless universe, but also of the text and its forest of "heterogeneous words" and chimerae. Hence, the story explicitly links the labyrinth to the linguistic complexities of poesis and hermeneusis.

Borges brings the text and the world together again with the metaphor of the maze in "The Library of Babel," in which the Library and the universe become indistinguishable in their impenetrability, inextricability, and inexplicability. The universe is compared to a library composed of "an indefinite and perhaps infinite number of hexagonal galleries," with a spiral stairway, and a mirror in the hallways, which replicates the infinite network of galleries and chambers (51). Within the hexagonal chambers of this infinite universe are textual mazes which reflect the "delirious divinity" (57) which seems to have constructed the architectural maze. These texts are labyrinthine permutations of the "same elements: the space, the period, the comma, the twenty–two letters of the alphabet," and the Library as a whole registers "all the possible combinations of the twenty–odd orthographic symbols," ultimately yielding "all that it is given to express, in all languages," from the "archangel's autobiographies" to the "true story" of the reader's death! (54). Both the creator of these texts, and their interpreter, are trapped within its orthographic maze.

In "The Garden of Forking Paths" (1941), the secrets of the labyrinth are revealed at the climax of the narrator's journey by train to a little village outside of London called Ashgrove, which Borges intends for his readers to recognize as Hades (the grove of ashes). Here, in an aristocratic, scholarly country home, the narrator meets a Sinologist, Dr. Stephen Albert, who has deciphered the mystery of the narrator's Grandfather, who had retired from life in order to build a labyrinth and to write a novel, endeavors always thought to have been separate, but which Albert now shows to have been aspects of one single opus. The labyrinth is the novel itself, the theme of which is the universal history of Time. The labyrinth is the book of the world (as it was for the Gnostics), and the reader gets lost in the maze of its symbols, just as the soul gets lost in the labyrinth of the material world.

This line of reasoning suggests that Borges follows a long line of speculation about the maze according to which Daedalus was an image of the "sublime Artificer of the Universe" (Boccaccio qtd. in Doob: 215), and an image of the human creator as well, whose work is a meager textual imitation of the complexities of God's cosmic labyrinth (Doob Chapter 7). The reader too becomes implicated by entering the maze: "labyrinthine art begets a hermeneutic labyrinth" (Doob 215). In the words of Borges, the maze, the book, and the world of time constitute a single structure: Ts'ui Pên finds in Stephen Albert's home that "the book and the maze were one .... the confusion of the novel suggested to me that *it* was the maze" (25). As such, the maze is "A labyrinth of symbols," but it is also "An invisible labyrinth of time" (25). That Borges should choose a garden as a metaphor for the novel is also in line with horticultural adaptations of the labyrinth from the Middle Ages and the Renaissance (Doob 103–112) to the Enlightenment gardens of Versailles (Bord 189). But Borges seems most concerned with the maze as a metaphor for time and the novel: as Stephen Albert suggests to the erstwhile Ts'ui Pên, *The Garden of Forking Paths* is composed of "an infinite series of times, in a growing, dizzying net of divergent, convergent, and parallel times. This network of times which approached one another, forked, broke off, or were unaware of one another for centuries, embraces all possibilities of time" (28).

Compare Nietzsche's dazzling portrait of the universe in a long winding sentence from his notebooks which combines the Gnostic imagery of the mirror, the maze, and the maelstrom: "And do you know what the world is to me?" Nietzsche asks. "Shall I show it to you in my mirror? This world: a monster of energy, without beginning, without end ... a sea of forces flowing and rushing together, eternally changing, eternally flooding back, with tremendous years of recurrence, with an ebb and a flood of its forms ... my *Dionysian* world of the eternally self–creating, the eternally self–destroying ... do you want a *name* for this world?" (550). Borges names it the labyrinth, and though he mentions Schopenhauer and Newton, he oddly leaves out the obvious impact of Nietzsche on his conception of the universe of time as an inextricable and multicursal maze, in which all moments branch off into opposing directions which eventually circle back to themselves in endlessly recurring cycles. As we will see in the paragraphs below, Nietzsche's linkage of the mirror and the maze in this extraordinary passage is typical of postmodernist musings on the philosophic and aesthetic symbolism of the labyrinth. We find the metaphors of the mirror and the maze conflated with the mythologies of the Goddess and the underworld in works from 1946–1959 by Jean Cocteau, Vladimir Nabokov, Günter Grass, Gabriel Garciá Márquez, and Robbe–Grillet.

Alain Robbe–Grillet

In his novel *In the Labyrinth*, Alain Robbe–Grillet uses boulevards, windows, doorways, hallways, staircases, and wallpaper as variations on the theme of the maze, through which an exhausted soldier wanders in search of a destination he has forgotten. Robbe–Grillet devotes a great deal of time to his description of Paris as an urban labyrinth of streets and doorways, as the soldier follows a young boy across the city, a pursuit which recalls Aschenbach following Tadzio in Death in Venice, or the dying Virgil led by Lysanius to the Emperor's Palace in The Death of Virgil. For this boy, like the Hermes figures in Mann and Broch, appears and vanishes in the blink of an eye, gliding "backwards across the snow–covered sidewalk," beneath "the ground floor windows one after another: four identical windows followed by a door only slightly larger, then four more windows, a door, a window, a window, a window, a door, a window, a window" (89). The passage suggest the Inanna complex, linking the maze to death and the passage through a sequence of thresholds. By putting a painting in the center of the maze, however, Robbe–Grillet's novel as a whole moves towards those issues of perception and self–reflexiveness frequently evoked in postmodernist labyrinths of Eco, Borges, and Merrill.

Robbe–Grillet also handles interiors as sequences of doorways, halls, staircases, and rooms elaborately enmeshed by either wallpaper or lines of beds and windows. The wallpaper is a maze unto itself (much like the one Nabokov portrays in *Pnin*), reproducing the same design "thousands of times up and down the walls all around the room" in which the soldier lies dying (35). Entangled amongst these labyrinthine surfaces of wallpaper, corridors, boulevards, and interior décor is a variety of geometrical figures similar to those patterns emphasized in the work of Borges, Mann, Cortázar, and Eco: conical lampposts in the street project encircling rings of light around rectangular bases (34); the filament of interior lamps (also conical on square bases) project circles of light which enclose luminous hexagons (35); numerous glasses of wine leave "a series of more or less closed arcs, occasionally overlapping" on the dusty tables of living and barroom (66); the soldier's regiment number is embroidered on "a diamond shaped tab of material" on the collar of his overcoat (41); the soldier's worn shoe leaves a "series of chevrons" imprinted in the snow, and its sole has a "cross inscribed in a circle" embedded in a "circular depression of rubber" (54). All of these figures (circle, square, cone, hexagon, diamond, and the intersecting vortices of arcs) suggest the kind of geometrical symbols of those basic forms of the mind revealed by the apocalypse, by the heroic penetration of a maze, and by the descent into Hades.

Robbe–Grillet's narrative circles constantly back upon itself, repeating earlier passages and descriptions nearly verbatim, and framing the whole with reference to a painting which hangs from the wall of a café in which the soldier takes refuge, a painting which represents the action of the novel itself, depicting the soldier himself sitting boredly at table with the boy beside him. As in Cocteau's films, or as in the stories of Borges, this maze has a mirror in its midst which repeats all surfaces ad infinitum, a portrait of the inescapable universe in which we all live and die. For the Minotaur of death awaits the soldier in the midst of a dream or hallucinatory maze similar to the infinite gallery of parallel rooms in which the old patriarch of the Buendia family dies in *One Hundred Years of Solitude*. And as in Borges, Robbe–Grillet adds a water source as the mysterious destination of the soldier, who "makes his way through the labyrinth of unlighted hallways until he reaches this infinitely distant and problematical water" (98) ("s'avancer dans le dédale des couloirs sans lumière, jusqu'à cette eau infiniment lointaine et problématique" (121)). And as in Umberto Eco's novel *The Name of the Rose*, the mirror in the center of the maze represents art itself, and the complications of hermeneutics which the reflections produce.

Vladimir Nabokov

A few years after Cocteau's films, another postmodernist practitioner of Eliot's mythical method made use of the mythic imagery of the mirror and the maze to give his work shape and significance. Timofey Pnin achieves liberation (in Vladimir Nabokov's novel of the same title of 1953) precisely by coming to the center of the maze, where, as we will see, he discovers a reflection of his soul, appropriately named Mira. Alexandroff frequently notes the Gnostic motifs in Nabokov, and connects them to a discussion of the maze in *Invitation to a Beheading* (84–86), but he does not apply these insights to *Pnin*. Nabokov also evokes the myth of the labyrinth in *Ada*, where it represents the incestuous imprisonment of desire more frequently than the intricacies of the text (153, 351, 416, 435, 473, 477, 489). And in *Pale Fire*, Charles Kinbote links both death and desire to the myth of the maze, comically describing the would–be assassin Gradus pursuing the exiled king through the "labyrinth of stacks" (281) in the Wordsmith Library (shades of Borges? anticipations of Eco?), and more tenderly comparing the King's love for the frustrated Queen Disa to "a blundering of the soul through an infinite maze of hopelessness and remorse" (210). But in *Pale Fire*, the myth of the labyrinth is also seen as an image of poesis, as John Shade sorts through the "inky maze" of early drafts of his poem (64) to guide his phrases toward "faint daylight" (64).

By far the most sustained narrative image in *Pnin* is the motif of the labyrinth, often linked to other images like the zigzag, death, noise, alienation, and the mirror. When Pnin first arrives in the Clements home (where he takes a room as a boarder), he sees "the slow scintillant downcome" of a snowfall outside "reflected in the silent looking glass" (34). Pnin's 'son' Victor (is there a word for the son of your ex–wife, conceived adulterously while she was married to you, and whom your ex then asks you to support by paying his prep school tuition?) is a painter who becomes fascinated by the cubistic "reflections" of oak trees and office buildings on the surfaces of "A polished black sedan," and by the "view of himself and of the street" reflected "in the glass of a sun–rimmed headlamp," which he compares to "that very magical small convex mirror that, half a millennium ago, Van Eyck Petrus Christus and Memling used to paint into their detailed interiors, behind the sour merchant or the domestic Madonna" (97–8). When Pnin and Victor fall asleep in Old Bill Sheppard's house, the narrator again draws our attention to an image outside in the street which mysteriously combines the mirror and the maze: an "auroral breeze wrinkled a large luminous puddle, making of the telephone wires reflected in it illegible lines of black zigzags" (110). Before Pnin entertains his guests during a "little house–heating soiree," he scrutinizes his reflection "in the cracked mirror of the medicine chest" to see if his "morning shave still held" (151); and he prepares his ambrosial Russian punch in a beautiful bowl given him by Victor, "one of those gifts whose first impact, a blazoned blur, reflecting with such emblematic force the sweet nature of the donor that the tangible attributes of the thing are dissolved, as it were, in this pure inner blaze" (153).

Two final occurrences of the motif at connect the themes of betrayal and death (analogies of the Fall) with the imagery of the mirror. First, the narrator recounts his first visit to Pnin's father, Dr. Pavel Pnin, an ophthalmologist who removes a speck of coal dust from his left eye. In the waiting room, "where the blue dab of a window in miniature was reflected in the glass dome of an ormolu clock on the mantelpiece," the narrator witnesses a brief adulterous liaison between an intertextual couple we are meant to recognize as Anna Karenina and Vronsky. The narrator, who will himself cuckold Pnin in Paris and eventually take his job from him at Waindell, later concludes the novel with an image that combines the motifs of the mirror, the maze, and death: while spending the night with the Cockerell's, the "thunder of trucks" rocking the house shocks him awake, and "through the parody of a window shade some light from the street reached the mirror and dazzled me into thinking I was facing a firing squad" (190).

These last images of the mirror spiral back to their first occurrence in the novel, one which establishes the connection between the mirror and the maze, during Pnin's hallucinatory seizure on his labyrinthine journey to a little town called Cremona to give a lecture. A very curious coincidence—though it is probably risky to attribute any detail in Nabokov to coincidence—is the fact that a Roman mosaic maze depicting "Theseus killing the Minotaur" was discovered in the 1950's in a villa on the Via Cadolini, in Cremona (Bord 80). But the association goes as far back as 1922, when W.H. Matthews published his book *Mazes and Labyrinths*, with a section on Cremona. Hence Nabokov seems to have chosen the name of the town where Pnin is to give his lecture for its association with the labyrinth. On the way to Cremona, Pnin recalls "his tussle with the wallpaper" as a sick child in St. Petersburg: while the plan of the vertical plane readily reveals itself as "a combination made up of three different clusters of purple flowers and seven different oak leaves" which is repeated "with soothing exactitude," the system which governs the horizontal axis remains elusive, and leads the feverish child into "a meaningless tangle of rhododendron and oak" (23). In Gnostic iconography, the labyrinth represents the maze of the material world, a creation of the evil powers of darkness in which the soul is imprisoned after its fall from its home in the realm of light. Quispel cites a Naaseen psalm: "wandering astray in the Labyrinth, / she vainly seeks the way out" (211; my trans.). Jonas also refers to the "labyrinthine aspect of the world: in the worlds the soul loses its way and wanders about, and whenever it seeks an escape it only passes from one world into another" (52).

Nabokov makes the connection between the soul's journey through life and the maze explicit in *Pale Fire*, when Kinbote reads a passage from Franklin Lane's notebooks which describes meeting Aristotle after death. In the passage, Lane imagines that Aristotle would take "the long ribbon of man's life and trace it through the mystifying maze of all the wonderful adventure .... The crooked made straight. The Daedalian plan simplified by a look from above—smeared out as it were by the splotch of some master thumb that made the whole involuted, boggling thing one beautiful straight line" (261). (As we will see below, Márquez also meditates upon the connection between the ribbon—Ariadne's thread—and the maze). It is therefore appropriate that Nabokov has Pnin perceive the wallpaper maze in which he is lost as a world created by evil powers from which he seeks release: "It stood to reason that if the evil designer—the destroyer of minds, the friend of fever—had concealed the key of the pattern with such monstrous care, that key must be as precious as life itself and, when found, would regain for Timofey Pnin his everyday health, his everyday world" (24).

Much of the novel, in fact, concerns Pnin's struggle to escape the maze of the foreign country (America) into which he—and his 'son' Victor—have fallen. On one occasion, Victor is caught smoking a cigar in his prep school attic, a "labyrinth" composed of a "maze of partitions" (101). As a result, Victor is "held over one precious day of Easter vacation" (Good Friday perhaps?) before his visit to his "water father" Pnin (the atonement with the Father on Easter?). The liturgical timing of this visit, therefore, links the labyrinth with those images of incarnation and redemption so important to Gnosticism and "The Beginnings of Christianity" (as Jonas puts it): escape from the labyrinth coincides with Resurrection and return to the spiritual father. In the chapter after this visit, Pnin enters the labyrinth once again and eventually comes to the center, where he sees a reflection of that world soul (whom the Gnostics named Sophia) whose fall into matter initiated the Creation, and who leads the wandering human soul back home. This occurs during his visit to "The Pines," an old hotel, situated (Edenically) on the southeast side of Mount Ettrick, where summer tourists like an anonymous "Miranda" pencil their names on the balustrade of the look–out tower (the name Miranda, meaning to be admired, or to reflect, links the mirror motif to the incarnation of the Gnostic world soul to appear later in the chapter as Mira). Here on Mount Ettrick a pair of Russian émigrés gather fellow exiles about them on alternate summers for an extended visit which all experience as a kind of surrogate homecoming. Pnin reaches The Pines after turning off the highway into a "maze of doubtful roads" in which he is mislead by a gas station attendant who advises him to bear "north at each crossing" (114). He remains lost in this "maze of forest roads for about an hour" (114), before miraculously arriving at his destination. Bearing left at each crossing is, as Borges tells us, "the common procedure for discovering the central point of certain labyrinths" (22), and indeed, Pnin has now arrived at a central turning point in the middle of his personal maze.

The middle of this maze is signified in several ways: by the "Castle" amidst the forest on the mountainside (castles often being associated with the maze, from the Palace of Knossos on Crete, to Heidelberg Castle, to Kafka's novel); by the interlocked wickets at the center of the croquet court (called the Cage or Mousetrap); and by the forest pool in which Pnin bathes. (Like Mann, Broch, and Borges, Nabokov centers his maze around a mystical water source). Here in the center, Pnin will both find his soul and confront the Minotaur. The bathing scene evokes imagery of baptism, rebirth, and divestiture central to the Gnostic tradition (Jonas 117–18). Pnin sheds cross, wristwatch, rubbers, and bathrobe to purify himself in a "natural swimming pool under the alders and pines," into which a "bubbling and glistening stream" empties itself amidst "the dappled sunlight of the riverside grove" (127–28): it is not the "turbid" and "stagnant" water of death such as the feverish squirrel drank from earlier, it is the "Flowing water, which is of sublime origin and flows in all streams" in Mandaean Gnosticism (Jonas 97). The bathing scene is Elysian, "mythopeic," as Pnin's friend Clements might put it (165), and its symbolism of death and rebirth has been carefully anticipated by Pnin's meditation on Ophelia's drowning earlier in the novel (77–79). Pnin eventually realizes the relevance of this image to Ophelia, who drowns in the river surrounded by flowers and singing snatches of love songs. Her death is balanced by the themes of rebirth in Pnin's discovery of the folk maidens bathing in the river during Green Week, or Whitsuntide (the seventh Sunday after Easter, or Pentecost), a time of the year in both the pagan and the Christian liturgical calendars associated with renewal.

Both aspects of the water symbolism come together in the scene where Pnin sheds his clothing and bathes in the forest pool at The Pines. Although the narrator declares Pnin "agnostic" (129) during this scene, all of its details are indeed mythopoetic, in the sense of evoking mythological associations without delineating specific allegorical allusions. In Gnosticism, for example, the shedding of clothing is associated with death and the return to the spirit (Jonas 122), while in Neoplatonic allegory, clothing represents the body and earthly love, while nakedness represents the spirit of celestial love (Wind 138–39). In the novel, some articles of Pnin's discarded clothing unsettle a "score of small butterflies," revealing "tiny orange–rimmed peacock spots along the hind–wing margins" and "the celestial hue of their upper surface" (128). The scene is indeed Elysian, a brief recovery of Pnin's "celestial" homeland, enriched by those symbols most dear to Nabokov's heart. The "peacock spots" are intriguing, since "In early Christian art the peacock, like the phoenix, was symbolic of the Resurrection," and "In alchemy the technical term 'peacock's tail," *cauda pavonis*, referred to a stage of the process immediately following the *mortificatio* and *ablutio*, when in the vas there appeared, or seemed to appear, 'many colors' (*omnes colores*)" (Campbell, *Creative* 501). Curious, then, that in *Pnin*, the many colors of the butterfly reveal themselves after Pnin has bathed himself (the *ablutio*) in what might be taken as an alchemical cauldron (the *vas alchemicum*). Like the peacock, the butterfly is also an ancient symbol of the soul which, after enduring the torments of the world, sheds its cocoon (i.e., the body) in order to ascend into heaven (Nabokov is said to have died while thinking of butterflies in a mountain meadow). Gnostic iconography represented Psyche as a butterfly tormented by Eros (von Franz, *Golden Ass* 66), while the Greek word Psyche meant both soul and butterfly, "dating from the belief that human souls became butterflies while searching for a new incarnation" (Walker, *Dictionary* 415). A most curious connection exists between the butterfly and the labyrinth, evidenced by a small "Butterfly engraved on a straight–edged double–axe" from Crete, which may signify "death and rebirth" (Johnson 195). Crete, as we know, was the location of the labyrinthine Palace of Knossos, and the word labyrinth refers to the "'House of the Double Axe,'" from *labrys*, the ceremonial axe used to sacrifice bulls to the Cretan Moon–goddess" (Walker, *Encyclopedia* 523). Hence, the symbolism of death and rebirth suggested by Pnin's dip in the forest pool and by the butterflies seems also to link up with the imagery of the labyrinth, which, as Mircea Eliade also argues, is a "destination where rites of initiation as well as funerary rituals would ensue" (75; my trans.).

But Nabokov's labyrinth, alas, has also its sacrificial victims and its Minotaur, its funereal as well as initiatory rituals. In the novel, the Pearl is not represented by the treacherous wife Liza, but by Pnin's first love, Mira, whom he vividly remembers the evening after the bathing scene. The Minotaur at the center of this maze is Nazi Germany. Immediately after Pnin finishes the croquet game, running the ball "With geometrical gusto" through all the hoops around the Mousetrap in the center, one of the guests mentions Mira Belochkin and her "terrible end" (130–31). Like Pnin, Mira went into exile after the Revolution, but she ultimately died in a concentration camp. Pnin remembers Mira's beauty as "immortal" (134), and the thought of her sufferings and death is more than he can bear: it is his most deeply repressed trauma that he begins to recall here in the center of the maze, in the most moving passage in all of Nabokov's oeuvre (135). Mira clearly represents something universal for Nabokov; her suffering is archetypal, much like the torment inflicted upon the Gnostic Sophia after her descent or imprisonment in the realm of matter.

With her exile, her "immortal" beauty, her outrageous suffering, her capacity to undergo innumerable deaths and resurrections, Mira seems a fit incarnation of the *anima mundi* of the Gnostics and the Neoplatonists, who interpreted tales as "Cupid and Psyche" by Apuleius as symbolic of the sadistic torture inflicted upon the soul by God, in his effort to purify and recall the fallen soul to Himself. Hence, intaglio coins and gems from Hellenistic art show Eros "holding a butterfly and sadistically burning it with his torch," or pressing "the butterfly painfully against his chest, representing the idea of the soul being developed and tortured" (von Franz, *Golden Ass* 66–67). That Mira is meant to be seen as an aspect of Pnin himself, a reflection of his own soul (*anima*) as well as the universal soul of mankind, is suggested by her name, which means "mirror," and is related to Miranda (to be admired)—the name inscribed by summer tourists on the balustrade of the watchtower at the beginning of the chapter—and to the word "*mira*cle," one of the last words of the novel, when we see Pnin, "free at last," driving "up the shining road, which one could make out narrowing to a thread of gold in the soft mist where hill after hill made beauty of distance, and where there was simply no saying what *miracle* might happen" (191; my italics). Not merely pedestrian, this passage, with its golden thread, its beautiful hills, its journey upward, and its promise of miracle, evokes the myth of the soul's ascent from the labyrinth of the world, towards the Elysian meadows and mountains of the Homeland. It is by means of Ariadne's thread, of course, that Theseus solved the mystery of the maze in Crete, and here we find Pnin (on his birthday, February 15th) following a "thread of gold" that leads to his freedom. It is possibly also of significance that this "golden thread" is formed by the brightly shining morning sun, since Sir James G. Frazer (among others) associated the "Cretan maze with sun worship" and suggested that "'Ariadne's dance [may] have been an imitation of the sun's course in the sky'" (qtd. in Bord: 61). The narrator, who has betrayed Pnin and stolen his job, is left behind in a maze of his own making, to have a breakfast of "depressing kidney and fish" with his host Cockerell, whose name is coyly significant: C.R. Cockerell was a 19th century explorer of Crete who "wisely took a length of string with" him into the Gortyna caves, where one had "sometimes to choose one of three or four roads" (Bord 35).

Günter Grass

In 1959, Günter Grass presented a unique version of the mythic maze in *The Tin Drum*. The chapter called "Niobe" employs aspects of the same Cretan mythology that fascinated Nabokov and Borges with its portrayal of the great matriarch of the Minoan world. Her symbol was the double–bladed ax, and her rituals involved the sacrifice of a bull, which also represented the husband or consort with whom she was joined in a sacred marriage (di Stasi 105; Campbell, *Occidental* 45–71). The iconography of the Cretan Goddess, then, usually gathers together the symbols of the labyrinth, the ax, the sacrificial bull, and the sacred marriage, and we find all of these in the passages devoted to Herbert Truczinski and his perverse obsession with a bizarre figurehead, "answering to the name of Niobe" (189), installed in the Maritime Museum where Herbert gets a job. What had drawn the dwarfish Oskar to Herbert in the previous chapter had been the elaborate network of scars etched on his "lengthwise and crosswise belabored back" (183): Oskar amuses himself by touching each scar with his drumstick, hence eliciting from Herbert the story of whichever Latvian, Swede, Pole, Finn, or German had carved it upon him in whichever of the many brawls Herbert engaged in as bouncer of a local, polyglot bar. Oskar associates these wounds with "a woman's scarlike parts" (178), and dwells upon them, he tells us, for the "sole purpose" of getting "back to the umbilical cord" (179). In addition, he sees his own fate in this "sensitive labyrinth of scars" (196), thus linking the presence of the Goddess of fate with the Cretan symbolism of the maze and the bull consort. As a bouncer in a Swedish bar, weighing "well over two hundred pounds" (176) and with a large muscular back rounded like a Brahma bull (177), Herbert embodies the image of the bovine consort of the Goddess. The fact that Oskar taps the labyrinth of scars on this rounded back as he later taps on his own drum to tell his own stories provides, then, another curious linkage to the mythology of the Goddess and her ritually slain consort in Ancient Mesopotamia: for the surface of the temple kettledrum was provided by the hide of a "mythic lunar bull, lord of the rhythm of the universe, whose song all mortality is dancing in a round of birth, death, and new birth," and which was evoked by "the sounds of the drum" (Campbell, *Occidental* 56–7).

Like the Minoan Goddess, Niobe becomes a goddess of death (everyone involved with her, from her creator to the museum guards who watch over her, ends up dead), and she holds a double–bladed ax in her hand. The bullish Herbert will play the role of sacrificial victim, impaling himself on one blade of a "double–edged ship's ax" (195), the other blade of which he madly drives into Niobe's greenish wooden body. Museum officials find him "perfectly united" with the figurehead from the top up, but dangling free from the bottom down, "his member still emerged, stiff and perplexed, from his open trousers" (196). The Cretan double ax "points two ways," one towards life and the other towards death (Campbell, *Occidental* 71), and so here one blade impales Herbert while the other points to the immortal green wood of the Goddess. Hence, Herbert plays the role of sacrificial bull, consort of the Goddess, with whom union and annihilation coincide: she is the loving and terrible archetype of the Mother, whose dying and resurrecting husband–sons constituted the stuff of Mediterranean mythology for millennia before the Christian era, Osiris, Adonis, and Tammuz having been the incarnations of central interest to Sir James Frazer and subsequently to Eliot in *The Waste Land*. Edward Diller, in fact, argued that statues of Osiris were painted green in ancient Egypt, just as the Niobe figurehead is painted green on an extraordinary wood "made immune to worms, immortal" (193). In Egyptian myth, the cedar–wood coffin in which Osiris is interred and from which his sister–bride Isis rescued him became a symbol of his immortality (Wilkinson 165), here appropriated by Grass's "Green Kitten" of the Maritime Museum. That Grass gives his "bringer of disaster" (187) a feline nickname also links her to such Ancient Near Eastern avatars of the Goddess of death and rebirth as the lion–throned mothers of Çatal Hüyük, Minoan Crete, and Ephesus, alluded to by Eliot's lady with the leopards in "Ash Wednesday." As Joseph Campbell suggests, the general notion seems to have been of the Goddess as the solar lion which pounces on the moon bull to devour him every month in the lunar cycle ("Goddess" 78).

In *The Tin Drum*, Herbert impales himself on the body of the figurehead at the time of day when the afternoon sun strikes its "amber eye and sets it aflame" (194). The connection between the eye and the sun is also suggestive here, since in the early mythologies of the Mediterranean and Ancient Near East, the eye was associated with the Goddess and the maze: in the Sumerian myth of the descent of Inanna, from about 1750 B.C.E., it is the "eye of death" fastened upon Ereshkigal, Queen of the Underworld, which kills Inanna (Wolkstein and Kramer 60), while numerous other eye–idols from the third millennium in Sumer seem more benevolent—and more labyrinthine.[4] The eye motif gradually evolved into the form of the spiral labyrinth, inscribed on stone entrances to such monuments to the Great Goddess as the ones found in Malta, Minoan Crete, and Newgrange in Ireland, where "they guard both the womb–earth where life begins and the womb–tomb where life ends" (di Stasi 109). What Grass has done then is to bring together the various details of the iconography of the Minoan Goddess (the maze, the lion, the double ax, the sacrifice, the marriage, and the eye symbolism) to create a portrait of the devouring mother, who, in her dark role, dominates the novel from this point onwards, as we move to the chapters dealing with the Second World War. It is not accidental that on the day when Oskar attempts to stab Maria, pregnant with his child, Grass focuses on the radio blaring out news regarding a "landing on the stony soil of Crete" in the background, mentioning Crete three times in two pages (298).

Another motif associated with the Cretan Ladies of the Labyrinth which Grass picks up later in *The Tin Drum* has to do with their connection with bee symbolism: many of the seal ring impressions excavated by Sir Arthur Evans depict the Goddesses with waspish waists and bee–like heads; Minoan burial sites like the tomb at Pylos were in the shape of a large beehive; and one of the famous Linear B tablets from Knossos offers "a jar of honey" to the "Lady of the Labyrinth" (Campbell, *Occidental Myth* 50, 47). From around 3500–1750 B.C. in Asia Minor, the dead were embalmed in honey, and euphemistically said to have fallen into jars (pithoi) of honey. The myths imply the use of bee–balm to restore the dead, a magical ritual presided over by the various Goddesses of the Ancient Mediterranean world: Demeter was called "pure mother bee" and offered honey cakes in the shape of genitalia at the Thesmophoria, while the priestesses of Aphrodite at Eryx were called bees (melissae) and the Goddess herself Melissa, or Queen bee, whose male consort was annually sacrificed (Walker 407). Her symbol was the golden honeycomb which was the last gift of

Daedalus to Aphrodite (Davenport 58). In her *Prolegomena* of 1903, Jane Harrison notes a connection between *poesis* and *thriambos*, the mad song sung by the inspired priestesses of Delphi, bee goddesses who became prophetic when intoxicated by a honey mead (441–42). There is also an archaic connection between the bee goddess and the bull, both symbols of death and rebirth which Porphyry refers to in his commentary on the "Cave of the Nymphs" in Homer (Gimbutas 270). An onyx gem from Knossos depicts a bee–headed nymph with bull horns and a "double–axe shaped butterfly" above her head (Gimbutas 272).

It is therefore curious to find that Oskar's grandmother and Maria both sell honey, that the landlord during his post–war years in Dusseldorf is named Zeidler, which means "beekeeper" (Diller 113), and that Oskar worships one of the other tenants in the house (Sister Dorothea) as a kind of Queen Bee, into whose wardrobe he crawls one night to masturbate, in a scene which recapitulates all of Oskar's earlier encounters with the Goddess as aborted efforts to return his grandmother's skirts on "the first day of Creation" (192). The wardrobe, that is to say, is the womb–tomb into which Oskar descends to be reborn: the next chapter is set on Easter, suggesting the kind of linkage between the maze and the liturgical calendar which we also find in Nabokov.

Gabriel García Márquez

The image of the labyrinth surfaces several times in the great novel by Gabriel García Márquez, *One Hundred Years of Solitude*, first published in 1967. There are labyrinths of love (28), of disappointment (213), of mountains (246), of dead people (347), of kinship (414), and of blood (422). The very flow of the narrative is suggestive of the maze, spiraling back and forth in time and between characters whose lives are neatly interlaced from chapter to chapter, and generation to generation. In this respect, the narrative resembles those "Textual Labyrinths" of the Middle Ages which wind "circuitously back and forth in time" (Doob 205), and hence exploit what Eugene Vinaver described as the "great aesthetic possibilities of digression and recurrence'" (qtd. in Doob: 208).[5] The first explicit image of the labyrinth in *One Hundred Years* evokes the themes of the mother and death. When José Arcadio dies mysteriously of a pistol shot in the bathroom of his home, a trail of blood proceeds out the door and all the way back along the twisting streets of the town of Macondo to the house of Buendia, where it arrives at his mother's feet. Ursula then follows the red thread of blood back along its many windings to the Minotaur lying dead in his lair. The two sentences describing the blood's path leading both to and from the mother are parallel in their details and in the labyrinthine structure of their clauses. The first follows the thread of blood from the dead son to the mother, leaving the living room into the street, and continuing across the terraces, climbing over curbs, passing along the Street of the Turks, turning corners to the right and left, entering the Buendía house under the closed door, crossing the parlor by the walls, curving around the dining room table to the porch, passing under Amaranta's chair to the pantry, and finally arriving in the kitchen, where Ursula is making bread (135). Ursula then follows the thread back along its path to find her dead son lying on the floor of his bathroom.

In addition to the enormous size of José Arcadio (his coffin is seven and a half feet long, four feet wide, and reinforced with iron plates and steel bolts), his bizarre tattooing, and his brutality, several other details in this elaborate description evoke the myth of the maze and the Minotaur (caught here in the maze of politics and assassinations which have embroiled the country for years). When Ursula follows the blood from her home to José Arcadio's body, it is referred to as a "thread of blood" (135), which suggests the Ariadnean thread by which Theseus found egress from the maze after the massacre of the Minotaur. Curiously enough, we found a similar linkage of the ribbon and the maze in Nabokov's *Pale Fire.* The affiliation of the thread and the maze is extremely ancient: as Coomaraswamy has shown, the one thread from which many knots are tied in such elaborate designs as those of Dürer and Leonardo approximate in two dimensions the form of the spiral labyrinth, just as the winding and unwinding of the ribbons which attach the dancers to the Maypole approximate the form of the maze in motion. For Coomaraswamy, the winding and unwinding of the thread and the ribbons of the dancers suggests the "paired motions of evolution and involution, birth and death" (30). As the Daemmrichs have suggested, the inward turning centripetal spiral is often associated with those socio–political forces of death which destroy José Arcadio.

In Márquez, therefore, the "thread" which attaches mother and son at the moment of death is also the thread of the umbilical cord, suggestive of rebirth: in a sense, José Arcadio refuses to stay dead; the smell of gunpowder from his corpse permeates the town irrepressibly. On a political level, then the maze and the thread of blood evoke the mess of Latin American history, with its endless coups, its labyrinthine bureaucracies, and shifting allegiances. But on the mythopoetic level of the novel, the image of the maze and the mother in association with death evokes a long history of symbolism, as we have noted above. Joseph Campbell also noted the connection between the Goddess and the labyrinth: in his lectures on the Classical Mysteries of Eleusis, he often showed a slide of a pig Goddess with the "labyrinth of the underworld" inscribed on her body, and in his commentary on Homer's *Odyssey*, he suggested that "the goddess who in her terrible aspect is the cannibal ogress of the Underworld was in her benign aspect the guide and guardian to that realm and, as such, the giver of immortal life" (*Occidental* 171).

That Márquez should link the image of the maze and the mother with respect to the theme of death suggests the mythopoetic nature of his 'magic realism.' The connection between the labyrinth and funereal imagery is also evident the way Márquez handles the death of the great patriarch of the family, José Arcadio Buendía. In this sequence, the labyrinth is not the town of Macondo through which the red thread of blood passes to link mother and child, but the "dream of the infinite rooms," which the old patriarch penetrates ever more deeply during his dying days. He dreams that he gets out of his bed and walks into an identical room adjacent, and then on "into another that was just the same, the door of which would open into another that was just the same, the door of which would open into another one just the same, and then into another exactly alike, and so on to infinity. He liked to go from room to room, as in a gallery of parallel mirrors" (143). He dies when he gets confused and remains in an intermediate room, which he mistakes for his own. This sequence evokes many of the standard motifs of the mythology of the maze. One of the oldest of these has to do with the idea of death as a passage through a sequence of doorways (there are three doors mentioned in the above passage and an infinity of doorways suggested), which we find in Sumero–Babylonian and Egyptian prototypes like "The Descent of Inanna" (Wolkstein and Kramer 52–60) and the Egyptian Book of Gates (Budge 175–205). The possibility that these early images of the House of Death are rudimentary prototypes of the labyrinth is supported by the fact that the first royal tombs of Egypt were laid out as a maze of corridors and doorways designed to bewilder potential grave robbers, and by the fact that the seals and plaques found in the tombs are frequently inscribed with patterns which suggest "a definite link between the labyrinth and death" (Bord 33–34). A portion of the evocative power of this memorable image of the maze in Márquez must therefore be attributed to the archetypal ramifications of the doorway and chamber motifs.

Another such archetypal image associated with the maze in the death sequence of José Arcadio Buendía is the "gallery of parallel mirrors" radiating out into infinity (143). Henry Corbin discusses the "chamber of mirrors" with reference to Islamic mysticism and to Leonardo's "genial invention" of a labyrinth, the central sanctuary of which is an octagonal chamber of mirrors which multiply to infinity, on all eight sides, the image of the initiate, who has traversed the "interminable paths among the tortuous turnings" to the place of revelation, which, Corbin writes, is neither the place of combat with the monstrous Minotaur, nor the celestial Jerusalem searched for by the Medieval pilgrim traversing the labyrinths figured on the pavements of the Cathedrals (such as Chartres in France, or Ely outside of Cambridge in England): rather, it is the place where the initiate contemplates himself as the "Giver of Forms": "He who knows the giver," Corbin concludes, "is no longer the slave of the givens" (101–02; my trans.).

In Gnostic cosmologies, as we have seen, the maze is the material world in which the soul has fallen, or into which it has stepped like an image into a mirror. Gilles Quispel, for example, suggests that it was not the Soul itself which fell into the material world of darkness, but the image of the Soul, variously referred to as its "Eidolon" (220), reflection "Abbild" (232), or shadow "Schattenbild" (213). It is as if the soul of the world, Sophia or anima mundi, had briefly glimpsed her reflection in a mirror which retains her image as the basis for the creation of the world: "The Light had only thrown a glimpse into the darkness, as into a mirror. Consequently, it was only an image of the Light which came down into the darkness. The darkness had only received a glimpse, an image into its material realm" (232; my trans.). This reflection of Sophia is torn apart, mixed with the forces of the darkness ("Schalengewalten"), and used to "shape a world which is only a likeness" (ein Gleichnes) (232; my trans.), a symbol of the higher realm of Light. The mirror becomes the maze of the material world, shaped by the powers of the complexes of the unconscious, just as our fragile egos are formed largely by the forces from below.

Corbin pursues the image of the mirror in his delineation of the Gnosis of Islam, which we can also see as an image ("ein Gleichnis") of the creation of consciousness and the analytical process of individuation. For Corbin, the Minotaur that we find imprisoned in the middle of the maze of mirrors is essentially the image (Urbild) of ourselves, which we see reflected (Abbilder), in sequences of infinite regressions, upon the surfaces of the octagonal "chamber of mirrors" surrounding the center. Each of these reflections represents "a world of pure imaginal perception, a world in which God has created for each soul a universe to which it corresponds, so well that when the mystic contemplates this universe, it is himself, his proper soul, which he contemplates upon there" (62; my trans). This universe is Hûrqalyâ, "an intermediary world where the spiritual takes body and shape, and where the material spiritualizes itself into autonomous forms and images, which ... consist completely free of any other matter than their own proper light, the way images consist of the intangible reflections of the mirror" (66; my trans). The soul does not actually descend into the world; it simply projects its reflection into the maze of materiality, "the way an image of the human person makes his entry as an apparition into a *mirror*" (70; my trans). The world, that is to say, is the mirror which reflects the archetypal forms by which the Self projects itself into the seven worlds of the *mundus archetypus*. The center of the octagonal chamber of mirrors is "the place of self contemplation" (101; my trans.).

In Márquez, therefore, the "dream of infinite rooms" and passage into "a gallery of mirrors" (143) evokes those ancient images of the metaphysical (often Gnostic) which Jorge Luis Borges was so fond of, and which he saw as a "branch of fantastic literature" (*Labyrinths* 10). Vladimir Nabokov also incorporated Gnostic themes and the mythology of the maze into his work, as in Lucette's death scene in *Ada*. Like José Arcadio Buendía, Ada's sister fades away into "a series of receding Lucettes" created by "a trick crystal regression" (494). And in *Pale Fire*, the "mirror of exile" (267) also represents the world, in which the soul is sometimes shattered into a multiplicity of perplexing shadows, as when Kinbote hilariously imagines himself, John Shade, and his wife Sybil all refracted (with the demons of his "goetic" mirror) into "an endless sequence of green–shorted Kinbotes meeting an anthology of poets and a brocken of their wives" (183). For Márquez, Nabokov, and Borges, the text itself is a labyrinthine hall of mirrors, a library, in which the reader loses him or herself. In "The Garden of Forking Paths," the text was itself the world, a maze of multicursal turnings in which both the writer, his characters, and the reader become inextricably entangled. In *One Hundred Years of Solitude*, the maze is the text written by the mysterious alchemist, Melquíades, which Aureliano finally deciphers during last pages of the novel, when the "final keys were revealed" and the end circles back to the beginning (420). At this point Aureliano is reading the text which tells the story of his family, and fulfilling its final apocalyptic prophecies in the very act of reading. He presents us with an image of a reader trapped within the text, a reflection of ourselves enmeshed in the endless cycles of the hermeneutic process, just as Melquíades presents us with the traditional portrait of the artist as Daedalus, artificer of those mazes in which he himself becomes imprisoned. For Márquez, then, the labyrinth is an image both of poesis and hermeneusis, as well as an image of time and the cycles of world history. The last page of the novel brings all this together in a remarkable fusion of the imagery of the maze, the maelstrom, and the mirror: as scorpions devour the child born to Aureliano and his aunt Amaranta Ursula, he reads about the journey "through the most intricate labyrinths of blood" that has brought them together to "engender the mythological animal that was to bring the line to an end" (422). This animal is their child, both Minotaur and beast of the apocalypse, devoured by scorpions as the "whirlwind of dust and rubble being spun about by the wrath of the biblical hurricane" destroys Macondo (422). In the last seconds before the final apocalypse, Aureliano penetrates the mystery of the maze by deciphering the text, into which he looks "as if he were looking into a speaking mirror" (422). The "city of mirrors" which he finds there is the labyrinthine history of his family and the city of Macondo, and the text which embodies them, the inner shape and significance of which is revealed only as the end circles back to the beginning.

Umberto Eco

The most recent treatment of the maze as a nearly indecipherable text and symbol of the world also conflates the myth of the labyrinth with the apocalypse and the underworld. Umberto Eco's *The Name of the Rose* acknowledges a debt to the Borgesian conception of the maze in "The Library of Babel," and develops the hermeneutic problem associated with it. Eco fuses the mirror and the maze with the apocalypse in a manner similar to Borges and Márquez, but with a stronger focus on the theoretical issues of semiotics and the interpretation of texts. For Eco, the world is a forest of signs and symbols (as Baudelaire puts it), signatures of all things which we are here to read (as Stephen puts it in *Ulysses*), or "an endless array of symbols" (24) written by God in "the great book of nature" (25) which it is our duty to read and interpret (as Eco's William of Baskerville puts it). Eco announces from the beginning of his tale that the key to deciphering the scriptural maze of the world resides within the octagonal Aedificium, the library of the monastery, which the abbot describes as a "spiritual" and "terrestrial" labyrinth of books (37–38). It is toward the apocalyptic revelation of that key which unlocks the mysteries of the murders at the Abbey and deciphers the inscrutable "designs of the Almighty" (29) that the novel moves. Its plot is therefore based on the breaking of the seven seals (with a section of chapters for each day of the apocalypse), a hermeneutic process which proceeds via a sequence of four climactic and revelatory descents into the depths of the labyrinthine library, each one symmetrically positioned as the climax of the chapters in which they occur.

The first entrance into the labyrinth occurs during the climactic chapter of the "Second Day," in which Eco fuses the mythologies of the apocalypse, the underworld, and the maze with an elaborate range of geometrical symbols. Like Borges, Eco takes considerable pains to portray the exact geometrical configuration of the sequence of rooms, which will not be fully understood until after William's second penetration of the maze in the penultimate chapter of the "Fourth Day." During this first visit, William and Adso become lost in a bewildering succession of "quadrangular or vaguely trapezoidal rooms, each with one window, arranged around a windowless heptagonal room to which the stairway leads" (170). This "elementary" arrangement is then complicated by varying numbers of false doors, false windows, and mirrors. Each room has a scroll above one of the arched doorways inscribed with a verse from Revelation, the letters of which will ultimately be decisive in the final penetration of the mysteries of the maze. In addition to the apocalyptic keys discovered during this first visit, the maze is also inhabited by a Minotaur, one created by mirrors and intoxicating herbal fumes. When Adso stumbles upon the first mirror, he sees "A giant of threatening dimensions" which he suspects is a "ghost" or a "devil," but which turns out to be his own image, "enlarged and distorted" and "grotesquely misshapen" by the "powers of mirrors" (172). Like Leonardo's ingenious plan for an octagonal chamber of mirrors with the Minotaur of the Self in the center, Eco's labyrinth is Arabic in its inspired use of mirrors and in the bestiaries and Mozarabic apocalypses which Adso next stumbles upon.

He does so in a chamber where he finds an "uncovered thurible" flickering on a table, as a light ash burns with "some substances capable of inducing visions" (174–75). Here the Minotaur is not a reflected image of the Self, but the beast of the Apocalypse painted in a "brightly colored book" lying open beside the hallucinogenic thurible which intensifies Adso's perceptions: he sees "a great dragon with ten heads, dragging after him the stars of the sky and with his tail making them fall to earth" (174). After the scales of the dragon multiply and disintegrate into a "forest of glittering shards" which encircles Adso's head, he then hears the seductive hiss of a thousand serpents and sees a woman "bathed in light," who later turns out to be the "mulier amicta sole" illuminated on the page of a "beautiful Mozarabic apocalypse" (175). I suspect that Eco's fusion of sensual and intellectual temptations in "this place of forbidden knowledge" (176) owes something to Gide's *Thesée*, with its portrait of the lair of the Minotaur, in the middle of the maze, as a garden of "intoxicating vapors" which befuddle all but Theseus, who protects himself with a "piece of rag drenched with a powerful specific against the gases" (86). But Eco's maze is also the underworld, and the Minotaur is the ghost or devil who presides there: William and Adso exit the library through "the corridor of the ossarium" that leads to the tombstones (upon which they sit down happily) outside the north door of the Church (178); and while lost within the maze, William suggests that the herbal lamp, the sounds of the wind created by the ventilation slits, and the mirror were all "set here to convince the monks that the library is inhabited by the souls of the dead" (174). Indeed, as they roam through the doorways, chambers, stairways, and corridors (shades of Cocteau!), Adso feels "an invisible hand stroke [his] cheek, while a groan, not human and not animal, echoed in both that room and the next, as if a ghost were wandering from one to the other" (177). Eco's Minotaur is, as convention dictates, a chimaeric hybrid, half human and half animal; but it is also part devil and part ghost, and his maze both apocalyptic and infernal.

It is also textual, and hence hermeneutic. During his second, solitary visit to the labyrinth, Adso passes once again through the "magic of mirrors" (239), in order to arrive at a room where he opens a "richly illuminated volume that, by its style, seemed to me to come from the monasteries of Ultima Thule" (240). Adso's description of the lion representing the apostle Mark and the man representing Matthew clearly evoke the intricate interlacings of the Book of Kells, from 800 A.D., in which the interlacings of the serpent represent the phenomenal maze of space and time, while the lion emerging from its mouth represents the Redeemer who effects our escape from the maze (Campbell, *Occidental Myth* 467f.). Adso describes a man and an animal emerging from "a pattern of interlocking labyrinths" very much like "the tangle of rooms and corridors" in which he himself is wandering" (241). It is as if two mirrors were held up face to face with each other in this scene, to produce that series of infinite regressions of which Corbin writes in his discussion of Islamic mysticism. Here, Adso sees the labyrinth of his life reflected by the labyrinth of the text, so that the lion and man who emerge from the serpentine interlockings of the Celtic maze come to represent not only the murderer running rampant in the Abbey, but also Adso himself: all are entangled in the labyrinth of the world, which is the text we must decipher, for the purpose of liberation from the maze, and hence of salvation. Eco presents his protagonist here as a reader within the text, whose hermeneutic dilemma reflects our own, for in observing Adso observing the man entangled in the maze of the illuminated manuscript, we are also observing a mirror image of ourselves in the intricate process of treading the maze of the text.

After pondering these hermeneutic mysteries, however, Adso prepares himself, unwittingly, for entrance into a maze of a different color: he picks up an Hispanic apocalypse and "happened upon the page of the mulier amicta sole," whose face, bosom, and "curving thighs" he then proceeds to dwell upon, before turning to another page depicting the "whore of Babylon" (241). These images lead directly to Adso's encounter with the peasant girl in the refectory, and the rather lovely scene in which he falls back on the Song of Songs to describe her beauty and his own sexual ecstasy (245–49). She is the Ariadne anticipated by the "threads" and "ribbons" Adso had seen on the pages of the illuminated Irish apocalypse, but they lead him more deeply into the labyrinth, rather than out of it. Like Racine and like Thomas Mann, Eco here suggests that love is a labyrinth, one in which sin and virtue, and disease and health, become inextricable.

The connections between the apocalypse, the underworld, love, and the labyrinth are evoked again during Adso's third and William's second "journey into the bowels of the labyrinth" (309) in the penultimate chapter of the "Fourth Day," when the secret plan of the maze is made plain, though its final mysteries remain mute. Before the chapter begins, William announces that he has figured out the plan of the labyrinthine library by observing it from the outside, rather than by treading the maze from within, a fact which startles Adso. Each room, William reasons, is marked by the initial letter of the verses cited from Revelation, and taken all together "make up some text," much "Like a figured poem," which they must discover together (218). Eco here literalizes the notion of the textual maze, creating a figure by scrambling the letters of scripture in a way that resembles the word labyrinths of the 18th century, in which biblical verses were written out in bilingual citations shaped into the twisting patterns of the maze (Bord Pl. 173, 174). As in Borges, the text mimics the maze of the world, and the world mimics the text, both waiting to be read and deciphered before liberation or understanding may occur.

In response to Adso's question about how William was "able to solve the mystery of the library looking at it from the outside, and you were unable to solve it when you were inside?" (218), Eco brings up another traditional problem linked to the idea of the labyrinth in the Middle Ages: its convertibility from an image of inextricable disorder, to an image of the divine, if impenetrable mystery, of God's orderly Creation. Doob suggests that "Classical labyrinth texts reveal the labyrinth's duality: embodying both superb design and unfathomable chaos" (52). As Eco's William puts it, in response to Adso's query, the labyrinth of the library represents "The maximum of confusion achieved with the maximum of order" (217), but it is an order revealed only by reaching a divine point of view. To decipher the textual clues which reveal the secret plan of the maze, William must see the library as God sees the world, from the outside: "Thus God knows the world," he says, "because He conceived it in His mind, as if from the outside, before it was created, and we do not know its rule, because we live inside it, having found it already made" (218). Like the protagonist of a novel, lost in the maze of the plot, we cannot see the rule according to which life has been planned, unless, like the narrator of the novel, looking down at the events like God from on high, we can achieve that elevated perspective from which the entire plan of the labyrinth is made plain.

Prepared with this kind of perception and point of view, William and Adso are ready to enter the library a second time together. By writing down the first letters of the scriptural verses inscribed on the scrolls above the arched doorways of each of the sixteen rooms of the bifurcated octagonal wings of the central axis of the library, and of the seven rooms which surround the central heptagonal chambers of each of the four towers of the library, they discover that "the library was truly laid out and arranged according to the image of the terraqueous orb," with the appropriate letters naming the regions to the north, west, south an east inscribed at the entrance (320). The only mystery left after the revelation of this ingenious plan, which reduces the world to its fundamental elements (the letters of the alphabet), is the inaccessibility of the central heptagonal room of the south tower, which has apparently been walled up. Noticing a mirror on the blind wall, and referring back to the original cryptogramatic text which initiated their journey into the maze, William and Adso realize the importance of the mirror and the scrolled verse above it: "'eidolon' is image as well as ghost, and the mirror reflects our own image, distorted," William exclaims, and then concludes that "this mirror is a door" that leads into the inaccessible heptagonal chamber of the south tower (319). The room is called the "finis Africae," but the key to that door will remain a secret until the end of the novel, when the two sleuths finally discover the ultimate plan of the maze during their third visit together.

This third visit—the climax of the novel—occurs during the apocalyptic closing section, the "Seventh Day," after the last of the murders has taken place and the monastery is rapidly burning to the ground. It is during these last chapters that all of the murder mysteries are solved, and that the final secrets of the maze are disclosed. After rushing into the "mirror room," the secret of which William has finally discovered, he reaches up to the inscription and presses the first and seventh letters (alpha and omega) of the word "quatuor," at which point

"The whole frame of the mirror seemed to shudder, and the glass surface snapped back" (460). As in the films of Cocteau, the entrance to the otherworld, where all mysteries revealed and the plan of the world disclosed, is a mirror and a door. It leads, in Eco's novel, into the last unexplored chamber of the labyrinth, where the Minotaur awaits the detectives: "Two hours after compline, at the end of the sixth day, in the heart of the night that was giving birth to the seventh day, we entered the finis Africae" (460), says Adso. The entry occurs at the hour conventionally associated with the depths of the underworld, and at the apocalyptic end of the novel.

Inside the room, William and Adso find Jorge, the blind librarian who has dominated the life of the Abbey for forty years, and who is responsible for the murders of the previous six days. He is the Minotaur seated in his lair, "the master of this abbey," as William calls him (464), and the mastermind of the murders. He is holding the lost second book of Aristotle's *Poetics*, which the victims died in pursuit of, poisoned while turning its pages with wet thumbs to read. Though Jorge sees himself as an instrument of God, protecting the Word of God from the destructive doctrines of comedy espoused in the Philosopher's pages, William sees him as the Minotaur in the middle of a maze rendered infernal by his tyranny: "You are the Devil," William says to Jorge, "and like the Devil you live in darkness" (477). After Jorge performs a parody of Revelation by eating Aristotle's poisoned book, he appears even more chimerical, one fourth human, one fourth animal, one fourth demon, and one fourth ghost: "His face, in the reddish glow of the lamp, now seemed horrible to us: the features were distorted, a malignant sweat streaked his brow and cheeks, his eyes, usually deathly white, were bloodshot, from his mouth came scraps of parchment, and he looked like a ravening beast who had stuffed himself and could no longer swallow his food" (483). Like the Minotaur, devouring the sacrificial tribute of Athenian youths, "the old man now seemed disgusting and grotesque" (483), monstrous in his arrogance and murderous in his zeal.

Eco ends his novel with a meditation on the ideas of order conventionally expressed by the mysteries of the maze. William's job had been to read the signatures of all things inscribed in the events at the Abbey, and to interpret them by discovering the pattern that gave them shape and significance. But his realization that he had "conceived a false pattern to interpret the moves of the guilty man, and the guilty man fell in with it" (470), leads William to the conclusion that the "apocalyptic pattern that seemed to underlie all the crimes" was purely "accidental" (492). Where a former time would have seen the maze as a masterly expression of the divine order of the world, William condemns himself for "pursuing a semblance of order, when I should have known well that there is no order in the universe" (492). Adso, the narrator of the tale, is left with the task of reconstructing the destroyed manuscript which tells the story of the library and the doomed Abbey: he must do so from the splintered remains of the original maze, the "fragments, quotations, unfinished sentences, amputated stumps of books" left by the apocalyptic incineration of the library. Originally a reader of the signs and letters inscribed on the arched doorways of the maze, he is now a writer reconstructing the maze in a new text, modeled on a lost original. The end of the novel takes us back to the beginning, where we were first introduced to

Adso and the manuscript which he was simultaneously reconstructing and interpreting. The world, that is to say, has become a text, a labyrinth for the reader to penetrate; but the reader then becomes a dedalian craftsman in his own right, reconstructing the maze by an act of interpretation or poesis.

James Merrill

The maze has long served as a flexible symbol for various aspects of poesis, human and divine—the poet builds poems the way God shapes the universe. The intricacies of its construction may represent either the artistry of the writer (poesis), or the ingenuity of the reader (hermeneusis), and both writer and reader may become imprisoned in the maze of the work or art. But when the soul, or the mind, sprouts wings upon which to rise above the maze, the labyrinth is converted from an image of demonic complexity into a radiant manifestation of divine coherence. Hence, from antiquity to the present, the maze has served as a metaphor for the world and the text, both in their creation and in their interpretation. James Merrill frequently alludes to the myth of the maze in his great poem, *The Changing Light at Sandover*, which consistently incorporates the archetypal iconography associated both with it and the descent to the underworld (spirals, mirrors, doorways, and eyes).

Initially, the maze is a self–referential image of the text, which has much in common with *A Vision*, "That maze of inner logic, dogma, dates" (14). Like Yeats, Merrill uses the figure to explore the cycles of history (genesis, the three Edens, the myths of Atlantis and Thebes, the evolution of the human species, and the restoration of the lost paradise). Unlike Yeats, Merrill incorporates the "maze / of meanings" in contemporary science, from the microscopic (protons, polypeptides, polarities, tendencies, spectral lines, ions, organelles, neutrons, mitochondria, cells, formulas, and elements) to the astronomic (galaxies, UFO's, radio wave signals from deepest space, black holes, cosmic dust). We move from the vast to the minuscule with a simple reversal of the lenses of the spyglass (perception itself represented by the maze). Like Borges, Merrill portrays the vastness of time itself as "THAT MAZE" from which mankind struggles "TO ESCAPE" (146). We are compared to "red–eyed mice" upon whom a "maze / Is printed" (209) by the bat–winged souls in the research lab of the underworld, a metaphor that links Mirabell and his kind with the Minotaur, and with the "mental maze of the fallen mind" (Doob 157). When the archangels take over the lessons, however, the infernal labyrinth of the laboratory is transfigured into the paradisal maze in the garden outside the classroom at Sandover (320). It is a transformation entirely consistent with the traditional symbolism of the maze, which seen from one perspective represents chaos, but from another, "the complex order" of the cosmos (Doob 24).

One icon of this complex order—one frequently found in postmodernism (Borges, Marquez, Cocteau, Eco, Nabokov)—is the hall of mirrors and the perceptual confusion it creates. Merrill uses the mirror maze to express the bewildering repetition of those basic forms and formulae which give matter shape and significance, from the microscopic to the astronomic levels: in "Mirabell" he notes that "the 12:88 / Ratio is tuned to resonate / Like mirrors seen in mirrors down the whole length of the gallery" (238), an image which recalls Cocteau's Beauty floating down the corridor leading to her room in the Beast's chateau. As in *Orphée*, it is "mirror in the facing chair," and then the large Victorian mirror DJ brings home, that inaugurate the seances in "Ephraim" (6). In "Mirabell," the mirror enables the poets to "Look *beyond*" (249) themselves into the world of the dead, who "swarm out of the black / Into our mirror's lit space, joyously / Greeting one another" (313). Although some of the more powerful souls of the underworld (the immortal five) are excluded by "A STYX OF QUICKSILVER" (359), DJ and JM enter the mirror for hours on end (358), and the main members of the seminar hover perpetually in its twilight room, residual images multiplied into infinity. A world of mirrors within mirrors (rather like the halls José Arcadio Buendia enters when he dies in *One Hundred Years of Solitude*) is suggested when Mirabell confides that a "BENIGN POLICE FORCE" (shades of Cocteau's *Orphée*) keeps its eye on the proceedings of the seminars: "AS WE WATCH U THRU YR MIRROR ARE WE OURSELVES WATCHD THUS?" he wonders (187). Finally, we learn in "Scripts for the Pageant" that the communications with the world of the dead will be ended by "the shattering of a glass" which the "poem's logic" requires (364). As this comes to pass, Maria recalls a similar episode "OUR SILLY EPHRAIM / PARTICIPATED IN," when "THE ENFANT OF FRANCE WAS CARRIED BAWLING INTO / THE HALL OF MIRRORS" at Versailles (516).

Merrill composes innumerable variations on the theme of the mirror maze, incorporating a wide range of reflective surfaces and lenses into the imagery of his grand trilogy. Most of these have to do with the problems of perception and poesis conventionally associated with the labyrinth. In "Ephraim," the "figure in the mirror" reverses the letters beginning a sequence of phrases, since words held up to mirrors are spelled backwards, "'Contrary to appearances'" (69). Hence, we read "grums of class" instead of 'crumbs of glass'; "You clothe my mowing as I don your flask," instead of 'You clothe my flowing as I don your mask'; "One wand hashes the other" instead of 'One hand washes the other'; and "You clam down" instead of 'You calm down' (69). A more perceptual kind of "Reversibility" is the subject of a marvelous sonnet on a "toy spyglass" in "Mirabell," which focuses on the "vastness and impersonality" of "Time and Space" seen through one end of the spyglass, and on the "selves reduced to specks" through the other (174). This sonnet cleverly announces that the imagery of "lenses" are "Central to this bOOk," and develops the kind of perceptual dichotomy characteristic of the mirror maze (the peacock seen both as "subatomic x" and "great glaring bugaboo"). A similar reversibility between the vast and the minute, the "holy" and the "homely," the cosmic ("Galactic pollen") and the domestic ("brick and thatch"), results from the "Two lenses" inscribed within the great stone–circle maze of Avebury, the subject of another marvelous sonnet in "Mirabell" (112). Like the "twin zeros" of the lenses of the "bOOk" and "toy spyglass" (174), the "Two lenses" of the "Two lesser, not quite tangent O's / Plotted monolith by monolith" within the "'greater circle'" of Avebury's standing stones bring into focus the immensity of time and the minute particulars of the quotidian moment—"As Earth revolves, or a sheepdog barks" (112). Indeed, it is a polarity of perception celebrated throughout the poem, which constantly juxtaposes lower and uppercase letters, the cells beneath the microscope, and the stars brought into view by the "MAGNIFYING LENSES" of the telescope, and of "THE IMAGINATION" (174).

Merrill's mastery of the sonnet form cannot pass unmentioned here: for if the "rooms" of the poem's settings slowly turn to "stanzas" (430), and if, "Minding the thread, losing the maze, we curse / Language's misleading apparatus," getting lost in its "ins and outs" (453), then the sonnet itself can be seen as a miniature maze, full of the syntactical turnings and twistings enclosed by the smaller rooms of quatrain, sestet, octave, tercet, and couplet which compose the labyrinth. Both of these sonnets focuses on the perceptual maze created by lenses. The spyglass sonnet is a gracefully classical Petrarchan piece, an octave broken into two quatrains rhymed abba abba, and a sestet broken into two tercets rhymed cde cde. The Avebury sonnet is incorporated into the preceding verses by parentheses at the beginning and the end, and by an unrhymed tercet which introduces the subject of the 14 lines to follow. These lines compose a variation on the Petrarchan form, the octave broken into two quatrains (the first enclosing two unrhymed lines (abca), and the second off–rhymed with the first quatrain ("stone" and "stand") (dbde)); and a sestet (linked to the previous quatrain by a couplet ("site" and "white") and a slant rhyme "track" and "barks"), and composed of two additional couplets. This rhyme scheme is itself a labyrinthine linkage of stanzas and lines, and the maze like impression is reinforced by the three sets of parentheses enclosed within the larger parenthesis of the 17 lines (three introducing the sonnet). These enclosed parentheses form a chiasmus of turnings and reversals, thus (()()()), which figure the enclosure of the "Two lesser" stone circles within the "greater circle" of monoliths demarcating Avebury's perimeter (lenses within lenses of a primordial telescope). The slippage in the rhyme scheme, furthermore, parallel the enclosed circles of the henge, which are, as the poet astutely observes, "not quite tangent O's" (there is, appropriately, no rhyme for "O's" to make it strictly tangent with the other lines).

Nothing is wasted or unprepared for in this long masterpiece of a poem, which obeys Mirabell's "NO ACCIDENT" clause: the configuration joining lenses, prosody, reversibility, ocular symbolism, and telescopic visions of the cosmos in the Avebury and toy spyglass sonnets had been established way back in "The Book of Ephraim," when Merrill complained that "In neither / The world's poem nor the poem's world have I / Learned to think for myself" (85). The result is that the chaotic "twinklings of / Insight" have "no / Metrical lens to focus them, no kismet / Veiled as a stern rhyme sound, to obey whose wink / Floods with rapture its galaxy of sisters" (85). This passage suggests an equation between prosody and the lenses which shape our perception order in the chaos of the cosmos. The equation is consistent: Merrill concludes the marvelous terza rime section of "Ephraim" with the triadic theme (composed of metrics, lenses, and reversibility) when he writes "for near turns far, and former latter /—Syntax reversing her binoculars" (82). Terza rime itself forms a labyrinthine figure combining forward movement with turns and twists, incorporating one rhyme from the previous stanza, and preparing the linking rhyme with the next. The binocular reversibility of syntax Merrill alludes to characterizes the poem as a whole, in the rest of which we find a wide range of reflective lenses and surfaces, which can illuminate or bewilder—from the cameras (75), window pane's (26), garden globe (41) and X–rays (83) of "Ephraim;" to the 'MAGNIFYING LENSES" and telescopes of "Mirabell" (174). All these lenses figure "THE IMAGINATION" and the powers of poesis, which shape the chaotic labyrinth of perception into the divine honeycomb of the cosmos.

The garden globe in "The Book of Ephraim" is a particularly interesting reflective surface, since it serves as a kind of mirror held up to nature. It also combines geometrical symbolism with the motif of lenses. When the mirror flouts "its flat convention," it surfaces "as a solid," as a "whole small globe" over which stars crawl "like bees" (42). Like the Victorian mirror inside the house in Stonington, the globe is "Rinsed with mercury," and its mottled cracks enable the poet to see "through that craze / Of its own creation / Into another life" (42). Four lovely sestets register the globe's replication of reality. Hence, like the toy spyglass and the enmeshed circular mazes of Avebury, the small garden globe reflects the quotidian world of the birds and the bees, as well as the cosmic realms of the stars and the afterlife.

The geometric figure most naturally aligned with the labyrinth, however, is not the globe but the spiral, which forms another recurrent motif in *The Changing Light at Sandover*. It can serve as a metaphor for the maze of time, as in the lines "Another decade wound itself in slow / Glinting coils about the status quo" (98), or it can represent the "whole adventure" of the poem, evoked as a "spiral forever widening" in an "outward / curve to insight" (111): rather like the Yeatsian gyres, this centrifugal spiral represents that movement from the human to the divine noted by the Daemmrichs in their study. But Merrill's spiral can also turn inward to the minutiae of the microscope. The DNA molecule JM studies in the Boston Museum of science is a spiraling double helix, like a necklace, and the "froth of electrons" which spin around the nucleus of the atom do so in a spiral pattern. Merrill evokes both the globe, the atom, and the spiral in a dazzling Petrarchan sonnet devoted to Sarah Bernhardt in "Mirabell." In the octave, she stands at the "still center" of a staircase, which she allows to "unwind / Her profiles" as she descends, while small bronze "Globes" along the banister light up with "Counterspiraling ascents" (203). The sestet compares this movement to the swirling electrons of a "pale purple atom (phosphorus) / Periodic among satellites" (203), so that, once again, our maze of reflection (globes on banister) moves from the vast spiral forms of the galaxies, to the minute particles of atoms encoded in the DNA's helix. Furthermore, the staircase embraces the complete cycle of the soul's journey, its descent into the maze of the material world, followed by its return to the spiraling majesty of the empyrean. The same metaphor of incarnation recurs in the "Coda" to the trilogy, when Robert Morse evokes his imminent rebirth with the words "ALAS / DOWN TO EARTH I SPIRAL LIKE A LEAF / WHO'D GLADLY STAY" (531), and when the archangel Michael echoes Shakespeare by comparing incarnation to entering "THE MORTAL COIL" (553) which Hamlet imagines shuffling off at the moment of death. Characteristically, variations on the spiral motif recur throughout the poem, linking the mundane with the sublime, as in the sonnet sequence in "Scripts for the Pageant," in which we move from a "Hose coiled" in the garden, to the "unblinking / Coil of hieratic coldness" seated at the base of the "reptilian / Inmost brain" (332). These passages echo both Dante and Milton: *The Divine Comedy* records a centripetal descent into the hermetically sealed spiral labyrinth of the *Inferno*, followed by the winding ascent of the purgatorial mountain; while, in *Paradise Lost*, the serpent is consistently associated with the maze, as a symbol of rhetoric and forbidden knowledge.

In "Scripts for the Pageant," that knowledge is most frequently scientific, and the spiral remains a central motif, with a variegated clutter of associations. During the archangel Gabriel's lessons, George Cotzias concentrates on the "ATTRACTION AND REPULSION" which keep the froth of electrons spiraling around the nucleus within the atom, and he suggests that "IN THAT WHIRL IS A REVERSE WHIRL / MAKING, AS IN THE BEATEN WHITE OF EGG, / FOR THICKENING, FOR DENSITY, FOR MATTER" (396). This passage exemplifies the consistent virtue of Merrill's poem to translate the complexities of quantum physics into the homely language of daily life: for as surely as beaten egg white thickens when spun, the electron's tendencies to spin, simultaneously, in opposite directions, creates density (Capra 83–84). The opposing directions of electron spirals recall the Daemmrichs' distinction between the centrifugal and centripetal spirals of life and death. They become, for Merrill, a metaphor of the interplay between the positive and negative forces within the atom, the tendency of "antiparticles" towards "oblivion" countered by "powerful chains / of molecules" sent by the "Lord of Light" to "annihilate" the death wish of the "Monitor" (398). This is another instance of the poem's theme of reversibility, as an aspect of the labyrinth of time, a dynamo also driven by counterspiraling particles. In a dazzling pair of quatrains, devoted to the "Grand Design" of the universe "outspiraling past all detail," Merrill correlates the coils of "history's great worm," turning and turning like Yeatsian gyres, "because of twin / Forces balanced and alert within / Any least atom" (478). This version of the spiral motif combines the influence of both Yeats and Wagner, evident elsewhere in "Scripts" in the "SPINNING GYRES" the ghost of Yeats evokes during the pageant (486), in the "shuddering iron spiral" of the staircase in Athens (reminiscent of "the winding ancient stair" in "A Dialogue of Self and Soul"), and in the Wagnerian image of dinosaurs as "Fafners of those green aeons, coil by coil / Concentrated to deep coal, to oil" (452).

Coiling hose, double helix, spiraling electrons, winding staircases, gyrating aeons and decades of the Great Design—all these motifs are unified by the image of Mirabell's miraculous maze. The entire poem may be compared to a maze, itself composed of the numerous miniature labyrinths of the sonnet, canzone, villanelle and ballade, octave and septet, masque and operetta. Indeed, Merrill encourages us to see the maze as a metaphor of the poem by choosing a "stark / Twinbladed axe" as its heraldic hieroglyph, the double X inscribed upon the board by Gabriel in Lesson 8 (475), and by the hand of God himself in the climactic tenth lesson (493). By pointing out that the double X has a "MINOAN WAIST" (475), Gabriel evokes the Cretan prototype of his hieroglyph, since the word labyrinth means "House of the Double Ax" (Walker 523), a consistent motif in Mycenaean and Minoan iconography, in which the twin–bladed axe is consistently associated with the wings of the butterfly as a symbol of resurrection

(Gimbutas 471–75). Perhaps that is why Merrill saves his tale of the prank played by the dead Nabokov (releasing "EXQUISITE HORDES OF NYMPHALIS 10" in Luca's chapel (545)) to the end of the poem, after the ceremonies associated with Robert's rebirth. But, alas, Merrill's maze may also have a monster in its core, hidden deep within the "spinning ball" of the globe (484). Merrill calls it the "Monitor," a haunting icon of Gabriel, the archangel of death, whose "relation to the Monitor" is the same as that of "MAZE TO MINOTAUR" (399). It is a kind of Fenris wolf locked up in the burning core beneath the earth's crust, waiting to be released during the cataclysm of the last day.

Chapter 2
Our Lady of the Honeycomb

The foundations for the imagery of the Great Goddess in the literature written after the Second World War are in the archaeological digs in Crete by Sir Arthur Evans, in Mesopotamia by Sir Leonard Wooley and others, and in the writings of the pre–War modernists. In one sense, the image of the Goddess represents "the archetypal realm" as a whole, "the realm of the primordial images" ('der Ort der Urbilder') (Quispel 220). Much work was done to recover the primacy of Goddess oriented imagery both before and during the great periods of modernism: Bachofen's *Das Mutterrecht* (*Mother Right,* first published in 1861, but reprinted in 1897 at the beginning of the modernist movement) uncovered a stratum of Roman myth concerned with the symbolism of the feminine, which the mythographic aspects of Jung's work expanded on, particularly his *Wandlungen und Symbole der Libido* of 1911–12, eventually revised and translated as *Symbols of Transformation*, the central theme of which is the descent into the matrix of the collective unconscious. Both Bachofen and Jung influenced those German speaking modernists (Mann, Hesse, Broch, and Grass) in whose work the imagery of the Great Goddess is found. Thomas Mann read *Das Mutterrecht* while working on *Joseph and His Brothers*, and was also influenced (as was Hermann Broch, and, I suspect, many others) by the articles he found collected in the *Eranos–Jahrbuch* of 1938, *Gestalt und Kult der "Großen Mutter*" (especially Heinrich Zimmer's "Die indische Weltmutter") (Mann *Diaries* 182, 385).[6]

In England, interest in the symbolism of the Great Goddess was generated by two powerful books, both with an enormous impact on the literature of modernism. Sir James George Frazer's *The Golden Bough* (first published in 1890 and then in the massive twelve volumes released between 1907 and 1915, climactic years in the emergence of modernism) documented the mythological imagery and ritual practices associated with the dying and resurrecting consorts of the Great Goddess of the Ancient Mediterranean world (Attis, Adonis, and Osiris). Jane Ellen Harrison's *Prolegomena to a Study of Greek Religion* of 1903 discerned the central importance of the matrifocal imagery of the pre–Homeric period, a thesis which seemed more or less confirmed by the archaeological findings of Sir Arthur Evans on Crete during the 1920's, which revealed the prominence of the Great Goddess and her son–consort Poseidon in the pre–Hellenic world (Campbell, *Mother Right*: liv.–lv.). Virtually all of the anthropological lore associated with the Goddess was gathered together by Robert Briffault, whose three volume *The Mothers: A Study of the Origins and Sentiments and Institutions*, of 1927, epitomized "the concerns of the American and English 1920s" (Hagstrum 24). Since that time, the presence of the Great Goddess become increasingly prominent in the culture of postmodernism, as the result of such influential literary studies as *The White Goddess* by Robert Graves, such archaeological studies as *The Language of the Goddess*, by Marija Gimbutas, comparative studies like *The Masks of God* by Joseph Campbell, and such psychological tomes as *The Great Mother*, by Erich Neumann (upon all of which feminism has recently built in works by Marilyn French, Adrienne Rich, Merlin Stone, Norma Goodrich, Barbara Walker, and many others).

The great literary sources of Goddess imagery in the Ancient World begin with the Sumerian accounts of Inanna, the Goddess who descends through seven gateways into the underworld, shedding an article of royal clothing at each, until she stands naked in the presence of her sister Ereshkigal, Queen of the Kur (the Sumerian word for both mountain and underworld), who kills her with the eye of death. This myth, to which we will return again and again in our discussion, first became known in 1896, and its gradual elaboration has punctuated the Modernist period, from the work of Langdon in 1914, to Samuel Noah Kramer in 1951 (Burkert, *Structure* n.12–13, 188). Later literary sources of Goddess imagery include the "Homeric Hymn to Demeter," the *Odyssey*, and later *The Golden Ass* of Apuleius.[7] The mythologies of the Great Goddess serve naturally as an image of the processes of creation and destruction throughout the literature of postmodernism. For all things return to the tomb, where the bodily organs disintegrate into those elements (earth, air, fire, and water) from which new creation emerges. The elements, that is to say, become the embryonic seeds of renewal, as the tomb yields mysteriously to the womb. But the classical manifestations of the Goddess in modernism gradually yield to extreme forms, verging on the grotesque, in works by Carrington, Pynchon, Lessing, and Grass. Although the anthropological and psychological sacralizaton of the Goddess continues in the poetry of H.D. and David Jones, a strongly ludic element enlivens many of the works of postmodernism. While the modernist might generally be classified under the genus of Homo faber, forgers of supreme fictions in myth and literature, the postmodernist more typically represents Homo ludens, in the tendency towards playful, self–reflexive portraits of the Great Goddess.

Günter Grass

One of the greatest recent novels informed by the imagery of the Great Goddess, as developed in the modernist mode, is *The Tin Drum*, by Günter Grass. The book begins and ends with an epiphany of the Goddess as the womb from which the life of the novel emerges in the first chapter, and the tomb which prepares to devour that same life in the last, while in between we are presented with a fascinating procession of Her various incarnations (as Susie, Luzie, Niobe, Lux, etc.). Grass tells us that The "Black Witch" who haunts the thirty year old Oskar in a station of the Metro in the last pages of the novel is the "exact opposite" of his "grandmother Anna Koljaiczek standing there like a mountain" ready to give birth in the first pages (586), and the recapitulatory hymn that Oskar sings on the last page suggests that all the female characters in his life have been avatars of the Great Goddess, whether as the Mothers (Anna and Agnes), or as the "Witch who blackens every confessional with her shadow" and who pursues Oskar on the last page.

Edward Diller's fine book on *The Tin Drum* approaches Oskar as an epic hero of the classical tradition whose adventures constitute a unique version of the monomyth, but one which is closer to Joycean and Eliotic modernism than to the solar symbolism of the nineteenth century. Diller argues that Oskar represents a chthonic earthbound hero who is constantly associated with images of the womb (under the table, in the cellar, under the Rostrum, in the boxcar, beneath his grandmother's skirts, in the nurse's wardrobe). Oskar's grandmother, Anna Bronski, is the first avatar of the Great Mother in the text: she sits like a mountain in the winter fields cooking potatoes, and she wears four skirts, under which the fugitive Joseph Koljaiczek takes refuge from the police. She is a kind of axis mundi or omphalos, the mother of the four elements of the creation (her four skirts), whose union with Joseph unites heaven and earth and initiates a new cycle of life (Diller 24). She tends the fire like Hestia, and is rooted in the earth like the mountain Goddesses of Crete and Çatal Hüyük, both of whom will continue to play a central role in the novel.[8] Diller argues that Anna is a kind of Kashubian Potato Goddess, citing Frazer's discussion in *The Golden Bough* of the "Old Potato Woman" as a northern form of Demeter, who was also worshipped in rituals of sacred marriage performed in mysteries hidden underground during late autumn. Grass evokes the all–embracing powers of the Goddess as both womb and tomb when he writes that "all was still as on the first day of Creation or the last," when Joseph takes refuge beneath Anna's skirts (21–2).

Furthermore, this grand, quirky first chapter also establishes the elemental symbolism of fire and water and the syncretism of Christian and pagan motifs associated with postmodernism's Great Goddess: Anna is the name of the mother of the Virgin Mary, while the name Bronski suggests both the German words for fountain (Brunnen) and burning (brinnen). Joseph Koljaiczek reinforces these connotations by his names (one Christian, one pagan) and his actions: he is a firebug wanted for arson, yet he ultimately disappears under the water of the river, to emerge later reborn as an American millionaire! Bring fire and water together and you have new life, as well as death and rebirth in association with Joseph as the consort of the Goddess. The Celtic associations of the name Bronski may be relevant here as well: the Welsh Bran the Blessed lives in the Land under the Waves, and is also called Bron, the "Rich Fisher," a lord of sea and fish enthroned in a whirling castle below the waves (Campbell, *Creative* 418, 549). These details connect the notions of fire, water, wealth, and rebirth with Joseph as consort of Anna, the Great Goddess in the first chapter, but also look forward to the important role that fish will play in the portrait of Agnes in subsequent chapters.

Before moving to Agnes, however, we should note that her son Oskar's size and his drum both serve to link him to the realm of the Goddess. After falling into the basement as a child, Oskar stops growing, and remains dwarfish for many years, until the burial of his legal father Matzerath (like all heroic consorts of the Goddess, Oskar's paternity is uncertain). In Greek mythology, dwarves and smiths (variously called dactyloi or kabeiroi) were servants of the Great Goddess who, working the forges in the womb of Her subterranean caves, mimicked the creative processes of the feminine in their mystical crafts (like Mime in Wagner's *Ring* or Hephaistos in Greek myth). Hephaistos, for example, the crippled deformed smith born of Hera and married to Aphrodite, sired the Cabeiroi, little trolls toiling in the mines and caves beneath the mountains. Günter Grass was himself a sculptor, and in *The Tin Drum* portrays Oskar as a divinely inspired drummer who frequently associates with practitioners of the plastic arts, and who is consistently linked with subterranean enclosures (basement, boxcar, pillbox, wardrobe) and at one point pictured seated on the lap of the Virgin Mary. The allusions to Minoan myths which permeate the novel (as we will see with reference to Niobe below) may also be relevant to Oskar's dwarfish stature: Rhea gave birth to Zeus on Crete, in a cave on Mt. Ida, with the help of the dactyloi, little midwives who emerge from the dirt which Rhea's fingers dig into during labor, and who protect the infant Zeus from the wrath of his father Chronos by drumming on their shields to drown out the sound of the baby crying. Diller notes that these dwarfish beings all have the status of demi–gods in the service of the Goddess and are at odds with both men and the Gods: the Korybantes, Kuretes, Daktyls, and Telchines are "enthusiastic and Bacchic types, who in the guise of acolytes, by dances in arms with tumult, noise, cymbals, tympana and weapons ... arouse the passions in the course of religious ceremonies" (Diller 99).

Classical myth, that is to say, provided Grass with a precedent for the linkage of the Goddess, artistry, drumming, and dwarfishness. Mickey Hart has noted that the possession cults of the Great Mother in the ancient Mediterranean world were all drum driven, and cites a passage in *The Bacchae* of Euripides which attributes the invention of the Phrygian drums to "'Rhea, the Great Mother'" (207). Marija Gimbutas has traced the "intimate relation between the drum and the Goddess" back to at least 4500 B.C.E. in Bulgaria (71–73). Hart found that the first images of the drum from 2200 B.C.E. are associated with female drummers, and that the first named drummer was a Sumerian woman of Ur, who played in a temple of the moon in 2280 B.C.E. (75). Oskar's choice of instrument seems then, particularly apt, given his intimate relationship with the Goddess throughout the novel. In fact, there may even be a mythological source for the metaphor Grass gives us later in the novel, when Oskar experiences intercourse as the discovery of the drumstick which Maria brings into action between his legs (265). He spends the rest of the night drumming! We find a similar linkage between the female body and the drum in a wonderfully crude tale about the Raven, who flies up to Universe to see why it is raining so hard, and finds Universe striking a drum made from wife Rain Woman's vulva (Hart 39).

Oskar's mother Agnes enacts the role of Aphrodite for most of the novel, until, on Good Friday, a terrible sight at the seashore unleashes the dark side of the Terrible Mother. Strolling with Jan, Matzerath, and Oskar along a breakwater, Agnes comes upon a fisherman, who pulls a hideous horse head out of the water with eels slithering through its eye and nose sockets. This is an image of the devouring Goddess, on a level of intensity that surpasses even Mann's portrayals, though it may in fact have been derived from the same source: in the article on Persephone which so influenced the *Joseph* novels, Karl Kerényi speaks of the "Black Demeter in Phigalia" (125) who withdrew into a cave to escape the advances of Poseidon (Lord of the Sea) while in search of her abducted daughter Persephone. During the Phigalian festival, she appeared in a long robe and wearing a horse head, to which legend added details to be found in *The Tin Drum*: "Her image in the Phigalian cave," Kerényi writes, "was distinguished not only by a horse's head with 'snakes and other animals growing out of it,' but by a dolphin and a bird as well" (123). It is also curious to find that the Argive sacrifice of a horse to Poseidon (the bull from the sea) may have been motivated by the "rich supply of fish" expected in reward, and that in Argive pottery "we find constantly the horse associated with fish," a fact which Walter Burkert brings to bear in his reading of the myth of Hippolytus and Aphrodite (114). Burkert includes in his discussion an illustration of a sculpted horse head, from Anatolia, and first published in Berlin in 1942, with a naked goddess on the top (Fig. 10). These amplifications provide a rich mythological background to the scene in *The Tin Drum* (made famous by the movie version) when Agnes walks away from the eels slithering out of the horse's head on the breakwater. Hordes of screaming gulls swirl above the carcass and descend to feed, while Agnes vomits against the rocks. The old symbolism of the Goddess in the form of the bird, then, also surfaces in this terrifying epiphany of her darker side. Agnes subsequently turns from erotic creatrix (the loving mother) to the devouring Goddess of death. She develops an unappeasable appetite for fish which eventually kills her, and which foreshadows the carnage of the War that follows as much as it suggests such blood–drinking Goddesses as Kali, whose insatiable appetite for corpses symbolizes the bottomless pit of the earth which swallows every life.

Grass presents another face of the Death Goddess in the chapter called "Niobe," which employs aspects of Minoan mythology in its portrayal of the great matriarch of the Cretan world, and the maze, ax, and lunar bull which were her symbols. Details associated with the Cretan Goddess and the maze get picked up again after Oskar's departure to the war zone, constellating around the pillbox called Dora 7, which has a labyrinthine pretzel inscribed above its entrance, and where, later in the novel, the sculptor Lankes rapes a nun named Agneta, who later drowns herself in response to the trauma. Diller's commentary on this scene directs us towards the abduction of Persephone (131–33), and towards Persephone's mother Demeter in a later scene (in which Oskar ascends an elevator in the Paris Metro two steps above an old woman wearing fruit on her hat and a pair of lovers), which he argues reenacts the processions of the Eleusinian mysteries (155). I would like, however, to conclude with a motif far more central to Grass's conception of the Goddess: i.e., the devouring mother, or "wicked black Witch" whom Oskar juxtaposes with Sister Dorothea in the wardrobe scene (494), from whom he flees in the Paris Metro, and with whom the book closes.

After the scene in the wardrobe, when Oskar becomes a famous entertainer, he drums the tune of "The Wicked Black Witch" to a group of hardened old miners, who are so terrified by the song that they let forth "bloodcurdling screams" which demolish the windows in the theatre (555). Shortly thereafter, Oskar is led to a ring finger lying in a rye field by a black dog named Lux (561), and the finger turns out to be the dismembered digit of the recently murdered Sister Dorothea. Oskar is accused of the murder, partly because he puts the finger in a jar of formaldehyde and worships it as a sort of relic, one that he associates with his drumstick and the scars on Herbert Truczinski's back (568). As Diller suggests, "Oskar is praying to an impressionistic pattern of elements characterizing all of the women who have ever contributed some maternal significance to his life" (144), and doing so in a way which evokes the archetypal fantasy of the Great Goddess: the "cornflowers" which Sister Dorothea was said to have been picking when "the murderer arrived" (Grass 569) link her to Persephone, abducted by Hades while picking flowers in the plains of Nyssa; while the finger itself evokes the Idaen dwarfs, called daktyloi, 'little fingers' who helped the Goddess Rhea give birth to Zeus in the Cretan cave of Mt. Ida. The finger, then, sums up the imagery of drumstick, labyrinth, and Goddess which permeates the entire novel, which ends, however, with an evocation of the peculiarly Germanic form of the devouring Goddess as the "Wicked Black Witch" whom Oskar flees at its close.

Oskar flees his accusers in Dusseldorf by taking a train to Paris, and he hears the rails singing "Where's the Witch, black as pitch? Here's the black, wicked Witch" as he rides the train in terror on his getaway journey (580). It is the "Witch, black as pitch" (581) who dominates the last pages of the novel: she is the "Black Witch" whom Oskar says he has never before feared in all his life, and yet in whom he now recognizes the "number of forms" which she has assumed in his life (581): she was the one who frightened Oskar on the cellar stairs, who darkened the air when his mother devoured and was devoured by the black eels, who compelled Herbert to assault Niobe in the Maritime Museum, who "blackens every confessional with her shadow," whose song the neighborhood brats sang when they cooked their "brick meal soup" flavored with urine, who inhabited Sister Dorothea's wardrobe and "every clothes cupboard" Oskar ever sat in, who "borrowed Lucy Rennwand's triangular fox face, ate sausages skins and all and sent the Dusters up on the diving tower," the old woman with the hat decorated with fruit two steps down whom Oskar sees behind him on the escalator in the Paris Metro, and finally the "black wicked Witch" he also fears awaits him at the top of the moving staircase (588). This recapitulatory catalogue reminds us that the fantasy of the Great Goddess, in her various aspects and manifestations, has been the archetypal configuration shaping the major episodes of the entire novel, its entelechy, so to speak. Oskar realizes as much when he says that his ascent up the escalator of the Paris Metro is like Goethe returning from a "visit to the Mothers" (583), only to encounter the "terribly placid countenance of the Black Witch among the passers–by on the avenue" above (587): she is above and below, the end and the beginning, the Alpha and the Omega of all life.

The German phrase translated by "Black Witch" in these passages shows that the specific costume worn by the Goddess in the novel is that of the "Schwarze Köchin" (734), or 'hell cook,' a popular image of the devouring divinity of the tomb which we find in such diverse sources as the

"Teufelsköchin" or 'Hell Cook' in Hieronymous Bosch's "Gluttony" series in Vienna, to the wicked witch in "Hansel and Gretel." Bosch's painting shows a bizarre ape–faced female putting the lid down onto a pot and stirring the contents; while a desperate hand waves from inside the lid, a hideous broth of blood pours from a spout in the lower belly of the cauldron. The cauldron is, as Jung notes, a maternal symbol (*Four Archetypes* 16). In "Hansel and Gretel" the oven is an image of the tomb, but also of the womb of the Goddess: the Witch must feel Hansel's 'finger' each day to see if it is 'fat enough' to put in her 'oven' (popular parlance says the pregnant mother has "one in the oven"), so that the sexual imagery of the child, the finger, and the oven of the Witch, is brought together by the tale in a way quite similar to *The Tin Drum*. Of the previous female characters in the novel whom Oskar associates with the "Schwarze Köchin" confronting him at its close, three are concerned with cooking and eating: Susi Kater spices the soup she forces Oskar to drink with urine; Lucy Rennwand's triangular face and sausages evoke the vagina dendata (a popular image of the devouring jaws of hell in Medieval iconography); and Agnes, of course, is unforgettably memorable for the eels she sees devouring the horse head, and for which she subsequently develops an insatiable appetite. The repetition of the motif of the devouring Goddess is incremental, moving relentlessly to the awaited epiphany of the "Black Cook" in the last chapter, in which the word "Schwarze Köchin" occurs fourteen times as a sort of leit–motiv (Wagner having been alluded to earlier in "The Rostrum" chapter). In the first line of the little 'Märchen' jingle with which the novel closes, she is referred to simply as "Die Köchin" (734).

Hence the English translation deprives the reader of an extremely interesting set of mythological associations revolving around eating, the Goddess, and the cauldron, in which a special, often sacrificial meal, is prepared. In addition to the Nordic images found in Bosch and the Grimms, one thinks of Medea and other Goddesses of the Ancient Mediterranean world, as well as of the Egyptian sky Goddess Nut, or the Oriental Goddess of the burning ground, Kali. Medea illustrates both the creative and destructive poles of the archetype: she rejuvenates an old ram (and some versions say, her old father) by dismembering and boiling, but kills Pelias by the same method, so that the cauldron becomes both the womb and the tomb. An Attic vase reproduced by Kerényi shows a child in a cauldron surrounded by Goddesses: is he being cooked or emerging reborn from having been boiled? In the iconography of the Chinese, sacrificial vessels were inscribed with the fangs and jaws of the tiger, a "feline symbol of the consuming power of Mother Earth" (Campbell, *Mythic Image* 127), and the term for the vessels, *t'ao–t'ieh*, means Glutton, linking them to Bosch's "Teufelsköchin" in the "Gluttony" series. Furthermore, our own word 'sarcophagus' is derived "from the Greek *sarx*, *sarkos*, 'flesh,' plus *phagein*, 'to eat'" (Campbell, *Mythic Image* 126), yielding flesh–eating stone. More generally, with respect to the imagery of the devouring Goddess, we have the Hindu Goddess Kali devouring the entrails of a corpse named ignorance lying at her feet, but offering the breast with her left hand (Campbell, *Mythic Image* 351); and we find the sky Goddess Nut in Ancient Egypt swallowing the sun each night, which then travels through the digestive underworld of her bowels to be reborn from her womb the next morning (Campbell, *Mythic Image* 180).

In *The Tin Drum*, Grass encloses the pages of the novel with two contrary images of the divine feminine: Anna Koljaiczek at the beginning and the "exact opposite of the Black Witch" at the end, standing there like a mountain waiting to receive Oskar beneath her skirts at the top of the escalator of the Maison Blanche metro stop in Paris (586). The loving mother and the terrible goddess of death merge in this last archetypal fantasy: she gives birth at the beginning of the novel and waits to devour Oskar at its close. The effect is very like the one achieved by Hans Jürgens Syberberg's production of Wagner's *Parsifal*, in which we see the daemonic Kundry enclosing a globe in the first and the last shots of the film. The Goddess, then, embraces the world, and, along with her ovens and sacrificial cauldrons, is both the womb and the tomb, the beginning and the end.

Thomas Pynchon

Since the publication of *The Tin Drum*, two other rather extraordinary epiphanies of the Goddess in postmodernist literature have occurred, in Thomas Pynchon's *Gravity's Rainbow*, and in Doris Lessing's *Briefing for a Descent into Hell*. Pynchon's novel adapts the same characters from the Eleusinian mysteries which influenced his earlier precursors: Hades, Demeter, and Persephone appear in *Gravity's Rainbow* as Thanatz, Gretta, and Bianca, a trinity Slothrop encounters during a phantasmagoric trip down the Rhine on a boat named after the Egyptian patron of mummification: the *Anubis*. In addition to his name, Thanatz is endowed with features that identify him as a Hellenistic Lord of the Underworld: we first see him with "eyebrows feathering out like trailing edges of hawk's wings, drinking absinthe out of a souvenir stein on which, in colors made ghastly by the carnival lights on deck, bony and giggling Death is about to surprise two lovers in bed" (464). The "hawk's wings" suggest the Egyptian Horus, a hawk–headed deity, while the marriage to Greta suggests the complex family tree of Persephone, at once daughter and wife to the man who abducted and fathered her, Hades–Zeus chthonious (Kerényi, *Gods* 252). Both women in the affair become images of the Great Goddess, who presides over the realms of death and life. When the daughter Bianca drowns in the river, Slothrop is reminded that he had dreamt of her mother Greta drowning earlier in the novel in images which evoke the unity of the womb and the tomb: "at the bottom of the river. She has drowned. But all forms of life fill her womb .... From out of her body streams a flood now of different creatures, octopuses, reindeer, kangaroos. 'Who can say all the life / That left her womb that day?'" (447).

Later in the novel, Greta is clearly seen as a "destroying goddess" (494) when she becomes a psychopathic child murderer whom Ensign Morituri discovers one day drowning a boy in a pool of mud outside the German spa Pynchon shamelessly calls Bad Karma. Morituri, a Japanese naval officer, follows Greta one night out to "the edge of the black mud pool: that underground presence, old as Earth, partly enclosed back at the Spa," where she will try to smother a boy with hair like "cold snow" (477). During this scene, Greta has the burning eyes of Ereshkigal, Pudding's dark Queen of the Night, and she identifies herself with Shekhinah, the female side of God in cabbalah (Fowler 196): "'You know who I am too,'" she intones to her snow haired victim,

> 'My home is the form of Light .... I wander all the Diaspora looking for my strayed children, I am Israel. I am the Shekhinah, queen, daughter, bride, and mother of God. And I will take you back, you fragment of smashed vessel, even if I must pull you by your nasty little circumcised penis.' (483)

Shekhinah, Ereshkigal, Inanna, Demeter, Persephone, Gretel: as Greta herself acknowledges., she has more "identities than she knew what to do with" (482). Here she plays the Gnostic role of the angel of death who recalls those children who have strayed from their Father's Kingdom into the material realm, from which they must be delivered by death. The reference to the child as a "smashed vessel" alludes to the cabalistic notion of the shevirah, the shattering of the colored vessels of the Sefiroth when the light of the creative power of God (the En–Sof) poured through the eyes of Adam Kadmon, and the "light which composed the vessels themselves shattered into sparks and fell into the realm of the demonic kelippoth or shells, the evil powers" (Poncé 81). The reformation of the vessels is called tikkun, and Greta here imagines herself as the female counterpart of God's grace, playing an active (if destructive) role in the redemption of the world. As always in Pynchon, there are apocalyptic overtones, for the revelation of that "form of Light" which Greta represents comes only with annihilation. The Goddess of Death is here associated with the revelation of the ultimate secret (the "*form* of Light") that gives shape and significance to life. In an allusion to the stripping of Inanna, Pynchon adds another "one of the veils she had shed" to this complex of death and revelation: "an insomniac sleepwalker who found a corpse at night in Berlin which she took in her arms to hear the secrets of the dead. "We live very far beneath the black mud," it tells her, "Days of traveling .... It's so dark that things glow. We have flight. There's no sex. But there are fantasies" (483). The description recalls the bird–souls in the unappetizing dust of the underworld in *The Epic of Gilgamesh*, and keeps Greta tied to the chthonic cycles of the earth, our universal womb and tomb.

Doris Lessing

The overall affiliation of the devouring Goddess both with the disaster of the second World War (seen also in Hesse and Thomas Mann) and with the revelation of those archetypal forms governing life is also suggested by Doris Lessing's evocation of the dark feminine face of God in a scene from *Briefing for a Descent into Hell,* which would appear to owe much to Mann's witches in *The Magic Mountain*. During a psychotic breakdown, Lessing's protagonist, Charles Watkins, hallucinates a journey across the water to an otherworldly island, where he comes upon a city inhabited by violent and lustful rat–dogs and apes. In an effort to escape, Watkins goes into the woods outside the city, where, however, he is confronted with vision of horror much like Hans Castorp's dream in the "Snow" chapter. Watkins sees three women feasting on a slaughtered cow and dancing wildly around a fire, with blood smeared around their mouths and trickling down their chins. Three "bloody drunk" boys join in and a dead newborn is thrown on a heap of meat on the fire around which they dance (62–65). The psychological context suggests that Watkins is being devoured by the matrix of his own unconscious, into which his psychotic breakdown has pitched him. The breakdown, however, will ultimately lead to both to the revelation of the archetypes and to rebirth: after Watkins clears the square at the center of the city, "the inner pattern of light" which forms the blueprint of the Creation is revealed to him, and at the end of the novel he is preparing to be reborn as a kind of missionary from the realm of light.

Pynchon's "form of Light" and Lessing's "inner pattern of light" both evoke that sense of the elemental structures of life, which are revealed by the encounter with the loving and terrible Goddess as the basis of Creation. The return to the womb of the Goddess (ricorso) catalyzes the revelation of those forms which make creative reformation possible. The revelation has basically to do with the recognition of what Hermann Broch called "the unity of all existence" 'die Erkenntniseinheit des Seins' (*Virgil* 91; 86). This revelation always attends the return to the origins in postmodernism, though it need not always involve the wildly demonic experience of the devouring Goddess.

Robert Frost, for example, though no stranger to the terrors of life, summed up the imagery of the Goddess as the universal mother of all living things in the very tender sonnet called "The Silken Tent." Frost compares a woman standing in a field at "midday" with the wind gently blowing her skirts to silk tent flapping loosely in the breeze, yet held steady by numerous guy lines attaching it to the ground. The "supporting central cedar pole" of the tent is analogous to the spine, because both "point heavenward" and "signify the sureness of the soul." Frost's image is an archetypal vision of the feminine as the axis mundi, that "still point of the turning world" evoked by Eliot in *Four Quartets*. On the vertical axis she unites the earth with the heavens by simply standing still, and on the horizontal axis she binds all living things together within herself by the power of love: though "strictly held by none" she remains "loosely bound / By countless silken ties of love and thought / To everything on earth the compass round." In addition, she embodies the moral oppositions of freedom and free will, of "capriciousness" and "bondage," which the poem itself embodies by its playful syntax and strict form: it is composed of a single sentence stretched across the fourteen lines of an exact Shakespearean sonnet which in itself reconciles the opposites implied by the words "Strictly" and "loosely." She is the glass of fashion and the mold of form, that life which gives shape and being to the world.

Leonora Carrington

Like Grass and Lessing, Leonora Carrington's imagery of the Goddess revolves around cauldrons and cooking, but expands to embrace such motifs as the planet Venus, geese, bees and honey. Carrington's work, like the poetry of H.D., can be seen as a quest for the recovery of a Goddess purified of patriarchal values who may serve as a muse and as an instrument of cultural and personal metamorphosis for women. In fact, Carrington implies that without the recovery of the Goddess, the modern world faces extinction and apocalypse.

The plot of *The Hearing Trumpet* begins with the protagonist, Leonora, being taken to a home for the aged, where a sequence of mysteries begins, revolving around the need to find a sacred cup and return it to the Great Goddess. The Goddess first materializes in the form of a portrait of a "leering abbess," hanging in the dining room (43), whom Leonora calls "the winking Nun," because she seems "blind in one eye" (41). Leonora imagines her as an abbess of a convent called "El Convento de Santa Barbara de Tartarus, the bearded patroness of Limbo said to play with unbaptized children in this nether region" (43). She is "superbly blackly depressing," dressed in "the colour of Limbo," with a ruffled frill "luminous as the full moon" surrounding her face (43). She is obviously a Goddess of Hades: the focus on her eyes recalls Ereshkigal from the Sumerian descent of Innana, as does her mountainous retreat, but the full moon suggests Isis or the Lady of the Apocalypse in Revelation. She also tends to appear when "Venus sparkled over the trees" (40), the planet which the Sumerians associated with the Goddess Inanna.

Soon the related motifs of bees, cups, and cauldrons emerge as one of Leonora's friends writes to her of a persistent dream of the "winking nun" in which she finds "a silver chalice brimming over with golden honey" at the base of a "marble statue of Diana and her dogs" (58). After licking the honey off the "rim of the chalice," she returns it "nearly full of honey to the Goddess," and then makes her way (like the Inanna of Sumerian myth) through a sequence of doorways in a mossy wall which leads to a luxurious bedroom where the "leering abbess" sits "winking" at her (58). A cachet of secret letters given Leonora later in the novel reveals how prophetic this dream is, and keeps our attention focused on the cup, honey, and Goddess, "Santa Barbara of Tartarus," around whom the plot revolves (72). Once again, Venus "sparkled over the tower" on the night when Leonora reads the old Latin and Hebrew parchments (72), which tell the story of Mary Magdalen, "a high initiate of the mysteries of the Goddess" who had been executed for selling "certain secrets of her cult to Jesus of Nazareth" (75). The essential secret has to do with an "elixir" or "the precious ointment" buried in Nineveh in the tomb of Mary Magdalen (75). The Abbess, who has "extensive knowledge of herbs" and is "well versed in witchcraft" (76), discovers the secret formula of the elixir, which she shares with a consort she addresses as her "Fat Wildboar" or her "Rampant Wildpig" (75–76), since the boar is an immemorial symbol of the Great Goddess. I focus on the details of this legendary portrait of Mary Magdalen as a devotee of the Great Goddess of the ancient Mediterranean world because she will show up in a similar and also profoundly original guise in H.D.'s *Trilogy*, in which the magical jar contains the myrrh associated with both the birth and death to Jesus.[9]

As Leonora continues to read the letters, we learn that the symbolism of honey is connected to the symbolism of the horse, the pig, and the cup, which turns out to be the Holy Grail. The Abbess learns from her consort, the "Fat Wildboar," that the Grail has been stolen from the Goddess Venus, its original owner, by a group of Templar Knights, who retain the Grail in the vault of an Irish keep called the Rath of Conor. Carrington's revisioning of the Grail legend is a powerful attempt to restore the Goddess to her rightful position in the Arthurian corpus: in her version of the myth, the "original chalice held the elixir of life," which Venus drinks from while pregnant with Cupid. During the birth of the god, the cup falls to earth into a deep cavern sacred to "Epona the Horse Goddess" (91), who is also called Barbarus, a bearded, hermaphroditic, "subterranean Goddess" who is worshipped as "the life giver" (91). We have seen the connection between the mare and the Goddess already in Grass, where Black Demeter appeared in the form of a horse head with snakes, but Carrington seems rather to draw on Celtic matrifocal iconography linking the Goddess and the white mare evident at in such mythological figures as the Irish Macha (Green 139; Stone 53), and in such sites as the White Horse carved in the chalk of the Berkshire downs (Michell Fig. 31). This image of the Goddess threatened by patriarchy also occurs in Carrington's dream of the death of "a small white horse" recorded in her novella *Down Below* (38).

When the Abbess learns that this "Cup of Pneuma" or "Holy Vessel" must be replenished with honey, restored to the Triple Goddess "Epona, Barbarus, Hekate," and returned to "Her Most Rightful Realm in the Caverns of Her Most Secret Mysteries" (94), she sets off from the convent on her black stallion Homunculus, and journeys to Rath Conor, the keep of the Templar Knights. Disguised as a male, she attempts to steal the Grail with the help of the Bard Taliessin. She gets the Grail, but the Templars retrieve it, and the Abbess returns to her Abbey, pregnant with Taliessin's child, who is born after her belly turns enormously black and bursts (99).

These mysteries provide the background for the sequence of secret rituals which now takes place on the grounds of the home for the aged, which houses the lost mysteries of the Great Goddess and her sacred chalice. A coven of senile conspirators assembles by a pond with some bees "still buzzing over the still dark water of the fountain" to perform their secret rituals (115). These rituals are comprised of Carrington's splendidly surrealistic version of the rites of the great goddess. First, the old ladies perform a version of what Starhawk calls the Spiral Dance, circling "round and around the pond" (117) in a manner which recalls Thomas Mann's portrayal of the labyrinth dance during the marriage of Joseph and Asenath in the last volume of the *Joseph* tetralogy. The Daemmrichs would note that this inner circle gradually revolves centrifugally, spiraling outwards in an apocalyptic rhythm of social reform. The spiral dance is accompanied by incantations and riddles which invoke the Goddess Hecate as "Queen of Tartarus" and "the Queen of all Bees" (117). The Goddess then appears as "The monstrous Queen Bee" revolving slowly above the water of the pond and "beating her crystalline wings so rapidly that they emitted a pale light" (117). She looks like the "winking Abbess," with one eye closed and the air perfumed with "A delicious scent of wild honey" (118).

As we have seen in our discussion of *The Tine Drum*, the connection between the Great Goddess and bees is archaic, primordial in fact. We mentioned there that Aphrodite was called Melissa, or Queen Bee, that honey was involved in burial rituals, and that one of the surviving Minoan fragments offers a jar of honey to the "Lady of the Labyrinth" (Campbell, *Occidental* 47). Several of the dancing priestesses and goddesses of the Cretan–Mycenaean rings excavated by Sir Arthur Evans look like wasps or butterflies, and the especially elaborate "Ring of Nestor" was discovered in "a large beehive tomb at Pylos" (Campbell, *Occidental* 50). Marija Gimbutas notes that the symbolism linking bees, honey, and resurrection survives in Plutarch's "On the Cave of the Nymphs" (270), and reproduces images of bees on Middle Minoan seals and of a bee goddess flanked by dogs on an onyx gemstone from Knossos (272–73). In her *Prolegomena*, Jane Harrison evokes the "honey–priestesses" alluded to in the "Homeric Hymn to Hermes" as "inspired by a honey intoxicant; they are bees, their heads white with pollen" (442). Even the Delphic priestess herself may have been a Bee (442), like the beauty Harrison reproduces embossed on a gold plaque found at Camiros (Fig. 135). Along the same lines, Karl Kerényi suggests that the Sirens of the *Odyssey* were bee creatures whose song (offering knowledge of all things) was inspired by a honey intoxicant. These notions add a crucial dimension to our understanding of the symbolism of the bee Goddesses in Carrington's work: they are symbols of poetry, of the muse, of prophecy, symbols of female power recovered from the detritus of patriarchy.

In the initiatory ritual in the old folks home, the old ladies sip ambrosia from a cup before proposing a series of three riddles for Leonora to answer. Their solution coincides with the Apocalypse and Leonora's final initiation into the mysteries of the Great Goddess, whose return marks the coming of the end (another inversion of patriarchal values, since in *The Hearing Trumpet* we have a once and future goddess, rather than king, and a second coming of a female, rather than a male, savior). During these last rites, the symbolism of the cup shifts to the symbolism of the cauldron. After a cataclysmic explosion of the tower building releases a kind of apocalyptic angel, Christabel takes Leonora into the ruined building, where one flight of crumbled steps leads upwards, and one downwards. Leonora decides for the descent, walking down the "stone stairs" into a "great round chamber" with a fire burning in the middle, and then down a "final flight of steps" into another round chamber, in the middle of which sits "a woman stirring a great iron cauldron" (136). The woman has Leonora's own face, and she explains that her domain is called hell, but that "Really this is the Womb of the World whence all things come" (137).

It also appears to be Leonora's tomb, for the ancient crone, who may yet be an eternal youth, instructs her to leap into the soup boiling in the cauldron. From the pot, Leonora looks into an obsidian mirror "hanging in its usual corner near the bat's nest," and sees three faces reflected therein: first, "the face of the Abbess of Santa Barbara de Tartarus," then the face of the Queen Bee winking its huge eyes at her, and then her own face: "Holding the mirror at arm's length I seemed to see a three–faced female whose eyes winked alternatively. One of the faces was black, one red, one white, and they belonged to the Abbess, the Queen Bee and myself" (138). (The colors represent the three gunas—creation, preservation, and destruction—in Tantric philosophy). Leonora then emerges "refreshed after the hot broth," and returns to the group dancing around the bee pond, who say "'All of us have been down into the underworld'" (140), and ask her if she saw the Abbess, the Queen Bee, and herself (141). Carrington's cauldron seems rather more regenerative than Grass's soup kettle!

The initiatory descent into Hades for the purposes of renewal and the pursuit of wisdom has, as we know, been an aspect of religious mysteries of the Great Goddess since the times of Inanna, Isis, and Demeter. The iconography of the triple–headed Goddess, the mirror, and the cauldron all have their Classical prototypes, in the triune Hecate, the mirror Isis holds during her rites, and the many cups and cauldrons of the archaic period of Greek myth—such as the cauldron Medea cooks an old ram in to renew its life, as she was also said to have cooked Jason himself in as well! (Matthews 46). The image was widespread, with many variations on the theme, as we know from another black–figured Attic vase of a child in a cauldron (Kerényi 23). It survived into the Hellenistic era of the mystery cults of the 2end and 3rd centuries A.D., as we know from an alabaster serpent cup (to which attention was drawn during the 1930's) which contains not one, but sixteen people (Leisegang 194f.). The Pietrosa Bowl of approximately the same period illustrates the entire cycle mystery of death and rebirth, using a syncretic group of mythological figures thought to be Orphic (Campbell, *Mythic Image* 388).

But Leonora Carrington had a Celtic prototype in mind, I believe. That she wants us to associate the cauldron of boiling broth into which she descends with the Holy Grail seems clear from her evocation of the Templar Knights and the bard Taliessin earlier in the novel. For the story of Taliessin brings the Celtic Goddess Ceridwen to mind. Ceridwen tended a large cauldron heated by a fire stoked by the breath of nine virgins blowing steadily for nine months, until the moment for tasting should arrive. When it does, her apprentice Taliessin, rather than her own son, sneaks a fingertip taste, and is immediately inspired with the power of prophetic song and the knowledge of all things. Enraged, Ceridwen pursues, taking as many shapes as Taliessin, until she swallows him after he assumes the form of a grain of corn. He then transforms himself into an embryo, thus turning the Goddess from the tomb into the womb, and is reborn nine months later as the prophetic bard of Celtic world. This specific story is told by Robert Graves in *The White Goddess*, and cauldrons of rejuvenation and poetic inspiration are also to be found throughout Irish and Welsh legendry. The Irish King Matholwch, for example, possessed a magic cauldron into which he cast his dead warriors and cooked them, so that they could rise and fight again the next day (Green 58). Another scene on the famous Gundestrup cauldron (a large silver vessel of the 1st or 2end century B.C. found in a bog in Denmark) shows the Dagda dipping a warrior into the pot, either to partake of its healing brew, or to be cooked (Cunliffe 108).[10]

Carrington returns to the image of the cauldron of regeneration in *The Stone Door*, but there a male giant tends the brew, cooking a goat and humidifying the skin of a dead king to create a magic boat and sail to take the hero into the underworld. This whole network of motifs surrounding the cauldron and the cup is reminiscent of Mann's bitch's brew in Chapter 7 of *Joseph in Egypt*, and of Grass's "Schwarze Köchin" in *The Tin Drum*, which shares with Carrington's work a wild sense of surrealistic humor in its handling of the images of the Goddess. Both works are also apocalyptic. Carrington's *Healing Trumpet* ends, in fact, with the shifting of the polar fields and the end of the world, which can only be redeemed after the second coming of the Goddess, and the restoration of her Holy Grail. In H.D.'s apocalyptic *Trilogy*, the cauldron is domesticated: it becomes a jar filled with myrrh, the ointment of death and resurrection brought to Jesus by Mary Magdalen.

Hilda Doolittle

H.D.'s *Trilogy* is also much concerned with the recovery of "the primal Goddess from which all subsequent religions evolved" for the purposes of poesis (Friedman 228). To this end, the poem employs many of the motifs associated with her worship: the symbolism of birds, bees, butterflies, trees, and sacred vessels, and the iconographic tradition associated with the Goddess lineage, stretching from Lilith and Isis, to Mary Magdalen and the Virgin. The return to origins for H.D. required a revelation of the mythological imagery of the Great Mother, which then led to a personal and poetic process of renewal and re–creation. As Susan Friedman has noted, "Isis and the female processes of pregnancy and childbirth serve as the poet's prototype of artistic creation and liberation," helping a female writer find her place in a patriarchal world (151). Through the mysteries of the great goddess, H.D. explores various images of poesis.

Trilogy is studded with a wide range of allusions to the avatars of the Great Goddess in the Ancient World explored in the work of Bachofen, Frazer, Harrison, Freud, Jung, Neumann, Graves, Campbell, and Gimbutas. H.D. evokes the Goddess by the many names recovered by the scholarship of her day—Lilith, Eve, Astarte, Astoroth, Isis, Serquet, Demeter, Aphrodite, Santa Sophia, Psyche, Mary Magdalen, Cybele (the Mother of Mutilations), and the Virgin Mary, with her many epithets (Lady of the Goldfinch, Candelabra, Pomegranate, Snow, and Chair). H.D.'s reconstitution of the divine "matrilineage" was a kind of ricorso, a "journey to beginnings which makes the rebirth of Psyche possible," for behind every Christian shrine lies an "'earlier altar'" sacred to the Great Goddess (Friedman 146). The process of recovery was much facilitated by H.D.'s sessions with Freud, who helped her rediscover her own mother as a source of personal and artistic power. Freud, therefore, like the other important men in H.D.'s life (her father, Pound, Aldington, D.H. Lawrence, Sir John Ellerman), gradually crystallized into the kind of patriarchal symbol of creative power represented in *Trilogy* by Amen, Christos, Osiris, and Kaspar. It seems H.D. felt comfortable with male as well as female avatars of the divine: *Trilogy* in fact is a finely balanced poem, with the dream epiphanies of the "world father" in "The Walls Do Not Fall," and of the Lady in "Tribute to Angels" leading naturally to the mystical union of Kaspar and Mary Magdalen (and subsequent birth of the Christ child) in "The Flowering of the Rod." Creative power emerges here not just from a ricorso to an archetypal mother or father, but to their union in what Freud would call the "primal scene." As an aside, it is intriguing to note that this structure is exactly the one D.H. Lawrence used to organize his great trilogy, completed around the time of his involvement with H.D.: we have the male protagonist of *Sons and Lovers* replaced by the female protagonist of *The Rainbow*, and the union of male and female at the conclusion of *Women in Love*. Janice Robinson pursues such allusions to Lawrence in H.D.'s work, but rather reductively, while Susan Friedman is primarily interested in H.D.'s involvement with Freud and hermeticism. I would like therefore to focus on the mythological allusions in the poem, with an emphasis here on the feminine and geometrical symbols of divine creativity.

H.D. weaves an extremely intricate and subtle tapestry of such allusions into her *Trilogy*, with many deft touches establishing a fine fabric of repeated motifs linking together the individual poems internally and to each other. Many of these leit–motifs are derived from the long lineage of Goddess iconography explored in this chapter: birds, bees, butterflies, trees, seed kernels, and sacred vessels among them. H.D. evokes the honeycomb of remembrance (532), the city of Venice dusted with pollen shaken from the belfries by enormous bees (556), and she imagines resurrection as a return to the honeycomb (583). As with Leonora Carrington and Günter Grass, bees and honey are associated with the Goddess as images of death and rebirth, and as mythological images of wisdom and inspiration: in Norse myth, for example, Odin drinks honey mixed with the blood of the sage Kvasir, which enables its imbibers to speak "magic words known only to those who have drunk divine mead" (Crossley–Holland 32). Likewise, the butterflies which H.D. repeatedly evokes can represent both personal and poetic rebirth from periods of fallow crisis: the cycle leading from chrysalis to butterfly is a lovely image of the resurrection of the soul, the creation of a poem, and the revelation of the Goddess, for the head–dress of Isis can approximate either an erect cobra or the antennae of the butterfly (515–516). Indeed, the Lady of the dream vision in "Tribute to Angels" is ultimately identified as Psyche, whose symbol is the butterfly released from the cocoon (570). She is the primal Goddess, more ancient than the Vestal of Numa, Bona Dea, or the Virgin Mary. She gives birth both to poet and poem, for words are like little boxes hatching butterflies (540).

Throughout *Trilogy*, motifs like birds, bees, butterflies, and the boxes of the previous citation merge to create a complex metaphor of re–creation which H.D. liked to call a "hieroglyph." Like the hieroglyph, these image clusters gather separate motifs together into a single richly suggestive icon. The birds which H.D. most frequently associates with this process of ontogenesis and poesis are herons and geese, both birds with a long matrilineage. H.D. associates the esoteric wisdom which the poem hopes to recover with the signature of the heron's plume (517), since the heron nests along the Nile (528). The heron is analogous to the ibis, symbol of Thoth and Hermes, the divine patrons of poetry for H.D. But it has a more specific affiliation with the phoenix,[11] the benu bird of "The Walls Do Not Fall," which long ago mysteriously dropped a burning seed into the poet's heart, which only now germinates, shattering the vessel which received it, and blossoming as an archetypal dream of Amen Ra (528). The benu bird was an Egyptian symbol of the first emergence of life and light out of the primeval darkness, an embodiment of the "original logos" (Clark 246), since it was often seen standing alone on high ground after the yearly inundation of the Nile (Wilkinson 91). It was also a "manifestation of the resurrected Osiris" (Wilkinson 91), and a symbol of the planet Venus (Clark 246) which H.D.

evokes later in the poem. Herodotus tells a fairy tale in which the Benu–Phoenix carries its dead parent, encased in myrrh, to an "Isle of Fire," where it will be reborn (myrrh becomes an important symbol of death and rebirth in "The Flowering of the Rod"). It is also said that the benu bird returns from this island of fire (to which the gods also retreat for rebirth) carrying the "seed corn of every god" (Clark 248). Hence, the flaming seed dropped by H.D.'s phoenix ultimately contains the energies of the entire Creation, and of every prayer, invocation, or poem which evokes the gods (529).

Curiously enough, from the perspective of the poet's interest in the divine matrilineage, the other birds evoked in *Trilogy* are wild geese, primordial symbols of the Great Goddess as far back as the burial sites of Malta near Lake Baikal of about 20,000 B.C.E. The migration of the ivory geese found buried there, in a shrine of the Paleolithic Goddess, can be traced all the way through the fascinating ceramics of archaic Greece (which often show the Goddess flanked by geese) to Leonardo's portrait of Leda embraced by Zeus in the form of a swan. In "The Wild Swans at Coole," Yeats associated the sacred birds with the spiraling movement of their flight. As the Daemmrichs might note, their centrifugal spiral suggests liberation and the movement from the human to the divine, rather than the reverse descent towards death of the centripetal spiral. The affiliation between the bird, the Goddess, and the spiral maze also has its roots in the Siberian burial site at Malta, which included an ivory buckle stippled on the back with a spiral labyrinth. Hence, in "The Flowering of the Rod," we find the wild geese flying at the apex of a spiral above the Islands of the Hesperides (581), which themselves form a spiral maze of islands circling about the lost Atlantis (601). We know, furthermore, that the Hesperides were sacred to the Goddesses who lived there, tending the golden apples, which hung from a tree with serpent coiling up its stem and a duck waddling around its roots (Campbell, *Mythic Image* Fig. 174). For H.D., as for the pre–literate priestesses of the Paleolithic, the geese symbolized resurrection (579) and the return to the blessed Islands (583), to which the soul intuitively takes flight at the moment of death, like the wild snow–geese of the Arctic (579). Indeed, H.D. goes so far as to call Jesus the first goose to fly from Tree of the Crucifixion to the Tree of Life, and from thence to return to its gaggle with the gift of resurrection (586).

Along with these ornithological motifs, H.D.'s hieroglyph of the Goddess includes, perhaps most centrally, the symbolism of the sacred vessel of myrrh, with which Mary Magdalen anoints the body of Jesus before his burial. Little jars and boxes punctuate the iconography of the poem throughout, and, as H.D. must have known from her work with Freud, jars and suchlike sacred vessels are symbols of the feminine.[12] In "The Flowering of the Rod," Mary Magdalen goes to Kaspar, one of the Magi, for a jar of myrrh; and in "The Walls Do Not Fall," she invokes the Magi awaiting her behind a half–open door holding a Genii of myrrh in his jar (515). Later in "The Walls," H.D. draws on the astrological lore traditionally associated with the Magi, comparing stars to small jewelled jars and boxes containing healing herbs (529). And in "Tribute to the Angels," the second poem of the *Trilogy*, H.D. looks forward to the Kaspar's jar of myrrh in the last poem by comparing the unwritten tale on the blank pages of the book carried by the Lady of her dream to a jar containing the story of a Fisherman to be told in "The Flowering of the Rod" (571). Here, in the last poem of the *Trilogy*, Mary Magdalen steps through the half–open door (another element in H.D.'s hieroglyph) into Kaspar's room, in search of the alabaster containing the sacred distillate of myrrh, the fragrance of which escapes the seal (587–88). The jars containing the healing unguent are compared to the alabaster boxes of the Hyksos Princesses, which were sealed with hieroglyphic spells (589). In the manner of apocalyptic thinking, H.D. associates the two jars of this Chaldean Magician, who knows the beginning and the end (592), both with the myrrh of the Nativity and the ointment of the Entombment, which seem to occur simultaneously, in the single moment during which the last poem takes place (608). For as Kaspar places his jar on the ox–stall floor (609), he notes the symbolism linking the unbroken seal of the jar with the Virgin Mary (612).

H.D.'s union of the three Marys of the Gospels, and of the two sacred vessels, is consistent both with the triple Goddess of Robert Graves and with the legendry surrounding Mary Magdalen, the Virgin, and the mysterious Mary who attends the tomb of the resurrection. The early Christians called Mary "Myrrh of the Sea," a name looking back to a temple maiden Myrrha, mother of Adonis, given birth in the cave of Bethlehem where Jesus was too was born. She was an emblem of Mara, mother of Death, hence linking the dual powers of the Goddess, symbolized in the Gospels by the myrrh brought to Jesus at the Nativity, and at the Entombment, when Mary anointed his body with a fragrant oil of myrrh (Walker, *Encyclopedia* 614, 702). One Gnostic poem even has Mary Magdalen say "I am first and last, whore and holy one" (Walker 614). Like Pandora, Mary Magdalen's jar contains *all* of life, its blessings and its curses, a duality embraced by the wholeness of the Goddess in H.D.'s poem as well. For Mary is diversely identified as Mara, Cybele, Isis, Astarte, Cyprus, Demeter, and (590–96). The Goddess, that is to say, is a mother of "meter," of poetry, as well as the divine mother of life and death. When H.D. links Mary Magdalen with the blessedness of myrrh and the bitterness of death (590), she is drawing on a perennial view of the Goddess as both the womb and the tomb, and invoking Her by using the primordial hieroglyph of the sacred vessel.

The hieroglyph of the sacred vessel has a long and complex lineage. The Egyptian canopic jars or libation vessels were associated with Isis and Osiris, which H.D. may have seen on the temple walls of Abydos, or on an offering table in the British Museum, showing two water jars beside a tree sacred to the Goddess (Wilkinson 177, 205). Pandora', of course, had a famous jar, and the Farnese Isis holds a mirror in one hand, and a jar lowered in the left (Bonnefoy 253). In Apuleius' *Golden Ass*, Osiris holds "a small round shining golden jar, covered with hieroglyphs" (173), and Psyche must retrieve the beauty box of Persephone from the underworld. In Medieval paintings of Mary, the Virgin holds christening vases of holy oil (Walker, *Encyclopedia* 614). The Eleusinian and Bacchic mysteries of such interest to Jane Ellen Harrison (whose work H.D. surely knew) are replete with sacred vessels, such as the Kernos, with eight cups surrounding a central bowl, or the bowls extended to Persephone by Bacchus or Hades (Harrison Figs. 15, 101). Other instances of the vessel motif include the archaic funerary vessels in which, Frobenius reports, the secretions of the corpse were gathered, prototypes, perhaps, of the Grails and crucibles of the Middle

Ages (von Franz, *Golden Ass* 173). Earliest of all sacred vessels are King Gudea of Lagash's libation cup (which H.D. must surely have seen in the Louvre), or the overflowing vessels of the Sumerian Enki, or the serpent feeding from Hygeia's cup (Campbell, *Mythic Image* Figs. 251, 262, 413) which H.D. evokes in her poem *Hermetic Definition* (33).

Kathleen Raine suggests that the sacred vessel in the form of the urn entered English poetry not with the "Ode" of Keats, but with Blake's engravings for Erasmus Darwin's discussion of the Portland Vase, thought to be inscribed with figures depicting the immortality of the soul from the Eleusinian mysteries (34). But the urn and sacred vessel have actually a much longer history in English literature, taking us back beyond the *Urn Burial* of Sir Thomas Browne to the Grails of Arthurian romance. H.D. drew on this long tradition, adapting it to her own unique sensibility as a poetess by giving us jars, crucibles, and alabaster boxes as symbols not only of death and resurrection, but of the mysterious and sacred processes of gestation and birth, and thereby of poesis itself. A variety of sacred vessels occur in her other works. She kept her horoscope book in a box decorated with vases (Friedman 166), and, in her autobiographical novel, *The Gift*, she links the chalice of her Moravian heritage with the Calixenes, "'a Greek word that has something to do with a cup, like calix is the part of a flower that is shaped like a cup'" (qtd. in Robinson 84). Elsewhere she notes that the Moravians were called Calixenes, meaning "'cult of the cup or chalice'" (qtd. Robinson 85). In her poem called "Hymn," H.D. speaks also of an alabaster unguent jar of myrrh, and in *Helen in Egypt* an onyx jar holds a candle. Several of the dreams and hallucinatory visions H.D. experienced after the First World War involve sacred vessels as well: in *Tribute to Freud*, she records a vision of being suspended in bell jar (176), a dream of a beautiful jewelry box given to her by her mother (165), and a powerful hallucination in Corfu involving a soldier, a sun disk, a tripod, the Niké of Samothrace, and a chalice (56).

At the beginning of her analysis with Freud, when H.D. attempted to come to grips with these dreams and visions, she was much taken by the "exquisite Greek tear–jars and iridescent glass bowls and vases" which she could see gleaming in the dusky cabinets of Freud's apartments (*Tribute* 14). Using the cabalistic metaphor (which runs throughout the *Trilogy)* of the shevirah, or breaking of vessels, H.D. compared the famous interpreter of dreams to an archaeologist assembling the fragments of an ancient vase. The notion of the broken vessel came up again in an odd visionary fantasy about a man named Peter Rodeck, whom H.D. met during a boat trip to Greece in 1920. Rodeck was an architect who helped Sir Arthur Evans restore Cretan vases at the Palace of Knossos (Friedman 159). There is no doubt that Freud would have seen these vessels, whole or broken, as signs and symbols of female genitalia: H.D. herself concludes *Trilogy* with an analogy between the Virgin Mary and a jar with an unbroken seal (612). It is true that in *Trilogy*, Freudian sexual innuendo is not irrelevant: H.D. associates the vessel with the heart, broken by the scalding grain dropped by the benu bird (532), or by the flooding of the soul into a cup too small and porous to contain its power (534). Both images suggest traumatic insemination sublimated into spiritual ecstasy (seed and soul flowing abundantly into vessels too weak to hold them). But H.D. is more concerned with the heart's carnelian urn, into which the seed falls (531). Even more significantly for H.D. as a poet, the jars and little boxes become symbols of the gestation of the poem, itself a mystic container of the energies of life, distilled by years of suffering into the short pungent lines for which H.D. is famous. The poet is a Magi, well versed in signs and symbols (600), mistress of the alchemy of distillation (589), creatress of exquisite little short–lined stanzas, containers covered like Freud's little tear–jars with hieroglyphs (589). H.D. makes the analogy between poems and sacred vessels explicit when she suggests that words cryptically contain the butterflies hatched by the poem (540). The analogy recalls the moment in *Advent* when a butterfly escapes a box and lands on her father's skull (qtd. Robinson 298), and links all of the elements of the hieroglyph together: death and resurrection, the search for the father, and the box which is tomb, womb, and poem.

As beautiful as these matrifocal metaphors of poesis are (bird, bee, box, and butterfly), H.D. reserves her utmost eloquence for the climax of *Trilogy* in "The Flowering of the Rod," in which the feminine symbols of the lily and the grain of seed combine with the imagery of the doorway and divestiture to create a powerful hieroglyph of the Goddess. Unlike any of the male revelations of archetypal form which we have examined in these pages, in association with the myths of the Goddess, the underworld, alchemy, and the apocalypse, H.D.'s ultimate vision is stimulated by a ray of light striking a lovely woman's hair. As the Magi Kaspar stoops to pick Mary Magdalen's scarf up from the floor, he glances at her hair, illuminated from behind by light coming through the half–open doorway, and notices her eyes becoming large and dark (590). This imagery of the eye, divestiture, and the doorway itself (in which the entire action of the "Flowering" proceeds) had been affiliated with the Goddess as far back as Sumerian times, during which Inanna was represented in cylinder seals by enlarged eyes, a doorpost, and one of the gateways at which she shed an article of clothing during her descent (Wolkstein and Kramer 184). As the door closes, after Kaspar's vision of the grain of light in Mary Magdalen's hair, she refastens her scarf, smoothes the pleats of her robe, and lifts the latch on the door, which is completely covered with hieroglyphic scratches (607). Like the doorways through which the soul passes in the Books of the Dead, which H.D. evokes at the beginning of the *Trilogy* (509), this doorway is inscribed the "words of power, and prayers, and incantations" that procure ingress and egress through the chambers of the underworld (Budge 174). Furthermore, the linkage of doorways, clothing, and revelation would remain a standard feature of the Goddess hieroglyph all the way up to such Annunciations of the Middle Ages and the Renaissance as the "Christ in the Virgin's Womb" of 1400 in Germany, in which a rather bewildered Joseph peaks in through a narrow window frame on the left at the splendidly robed Virgin, whose left hand points up towards a bobbin at the top of a fully open portal on the right, from which a thread passes down to the embryo of the Christ Child in her womb (Campbell, *The Mythic Image* Fig. 52).

Like the door and the box, the egg is indeed a natural symbol of the powers of the Great Goddess, for she contains within herself the energies of the entire Creation. It is an important symbol in Leonora Carrington's work, and, in *Trilogy*, the embryo takes the form of the spectral seed which emanates from the light in Mary Magdalen's hair, as she pauses in the half–open doorway to put her scarf back on. Like the Aleph of Borges (revealed, by the way, on the underside of the doorway leading down into a basement), this seed bears within itself all the potential forms of the world, like Blake's "grain of sand." It slowly opens (601) into the lily evoked earlier in the poem, each petal unfolding into the aeon of a kingdom (585). The petals are held by the circular centre, which widens into the islands of the Hesperides spiralling around the lost Atlantis (601). In a fine instance of hermetic syncretism, H.D. identifies this labyrinthine network of islands in the centre of the lily as the promised land, where Kaspar is made to see the entire plan of the earth and its civilization in all its scope and mystery (601–02). Like the narrator of Borges' "Aleph," Kaspar sees the minute particulars of all Creation and Civilization, only here in the speck emanating from the Magdalen's hair (602).

It is an apocalyptic revelation, a return to the first and last syllable of recorded time, to the Logos which initiates the Creation, as it does in the revelations of Borges, Broch, Kazantzakis, and Mann. H.D. evokes the sound of waters flowing through Kaspar's vision at the center of the maze (602), and allusions to John's Apocalypse are sprinkled throughout the *Trilogy*, especially in "Tribute to Angels," a poem written when H.D. "'really DID feel that a new heaven and a new earth were about to materialize'" (qtd. in Robinson 316). At the end of "The Flowering of the Rod," H.D. uses the image of the well or fountain found also in the apocalyptic ricorsos of Mann, Borges, Broch, and David Jones. Like Mann, she speaks of a descent down the well into prehistoric times (608), with the important difference being that the voices in the well are female, rather than male. The revelation is ultimately, for H.D. of the Goddess, as mother of life and death, and as muse, mother of meter (596). For after the cosmic lily flowers from its tiny grain or seed, Kaspar hears the spirals of the shell echo with the enchanted syllables of an unknown tongue from the distant past (602–03). Here, H.D. links the mythologies of the maze, the apocalypse, and the Goddess into a powerful hieroglyph of ricorso and revelation. And what the echoed syllables conform to is the single word, at the beginning and end of time, which contains within itself the triune energies of the Great Goddess, and hence of all creation (603).

Chapter 3
Squaring the Circle

Several of the fundamental metaphors of medieval alchemy survive in the scholarship and literature of postmodernism, including the notion of the breakdown of molecular compounds to the four elements from which all creation (cosmogonic, ontogenetic, poetic) derives. This occurs in a variety of symbolic crucibles, and precipitates postmodernist variants of such hermetic symbols of the completed opus as the conjunction of Sol and Luna, the Child, the philosopher's stone, and an extremely diverse array of geometrical figures (of particular importance is the hermetic problem of the squaring the circle with the use of a triangle). Informing the whole process is the notion of transfiguration, an alchemical allegory of poesis which we find in modernism all the way from Strindberg to H.D., and on into postmodernism.

In 1893, Arthur Waite published his *Hermetic Museum Restored and Enlarged*, first published as *Musaeum hermeticum* in Frankfort in 1678. The publication of Walter Scott's edition of the *Hermetica* in 1924 coincided with the first great flowering of modernism and sustained the interest in alchemical motifs evident in the work of such continental scholars as Silberer, Reitzenstein, Preisendanz, Ruska, Sudhoff, and others.[13] Thomas Mann's interest in alchemical Freemasonry in *The Magic Mountain* of 1924 evokes the long historical process by which the hermeticism of the Renaissance magus passed into the Rosicrucian manifestoes of the early 17th century, into the scientific societies of the Enlightenment, and on into the Masonic brotherhoods which influenced the work of Mozart and Goethe (who wrote an allegory based on the *Chemical Wedding*). A new edition of the *Chymische Hochzeit Christiani Rosencreutz* of 1616 was published by Ferdinand Maack in Berlin in 1913, just when Mann began work on *The Magic Mountain*.[14] Jung's alchemical studies, beginning in 1929, are part of this German branch of hermeticism, and coincide with key Modernist works.[15] A poet like H.D., however, preferred to take her "alchemists straight," relying instead on French studies of mysticism and hermeticism.[16] Alchemical themes in the work of such French speaking surrealists as André Breton and Leonora Carrington have received some attention, but the importance of alchemy from mainstream modernism into postmodernism has been largely neglected.[17]

The postmodernists use the same hermetic myths which we find in the major works of modernism.[18] But postmodernism employs Eliot's "mythical method" in the elaborate, ornate, ludic, and self–reflexive manner that we find in works by Carrington, Merrill, Márquez, Borges, or Pynchon.[19] Their work achieves a reconciliation of science, poetry, and spirituality, an 'updating' and "refurbishing" of the Biblical and hermetic paradigms, in an effort to redeem religion from "fundamentalist clichés."[20] It is the kind of reconciliation Tennyson achieved in *In Memoriam*, by revisioning the myth of the apocalypse to unite evolutionary theory with Scripture. In his classic study, *Natural Supernaturalism*, M.H. Abrams described this process of secularization, whereby the biblical paradigm was translated into the intellectual terminology current during the 19th century. The term today might well be sacralization, to indicate that process of re–mythologizing, whereby the languages of history (private and public) and science are transfigured by the power of the poetic imagination, so that their facts become truths.

This union of science and spirituality, through the operations of the Great Art, with the intention of effecting a general reformation of the world, has always been a key element of the Hermetic program, from its first flowering in the Renaissance, to the Rosicrucian revival of the early 17th century. It is my view, in fact, that postmodern hermeticism stands in approximately the same relation to the modernist use of alchemical myth (early in our century), as the Rosicrucian Baroque stands in relation to the Hermetic Renaissance: the Work of the Rosicrucians, like that of the postmodernists, employed the basic motifs of alchemical tradition, but developed those motifs into the elaborate, ornately wrought forms we think of as Baroque.[21]

Jorge Luis Borges

While it is more or less impossible for most of us to determine the ontological validity of religious visions and the theological systems derived from them, it is certain that the imaginative faculties of the human mind play a central role in the form those systems of belief ultimately take: in the absence of absolute knowledge, we have the ecstatic imaginings of the mystics, which can be approached as literature of the fantastic. This is in fact the approach suggested by Jorge Luis Borges, when he argued that the true message of the Book of Job is that God's inscrutable nature can only be represented by symbols of the enigmatic ("monstrous, uncanny, or fantastic"), like the golem or puzzle game of letters in the cabala (Aizenberg 79). According to Borges, these "uncanny symbols" are "the heart of the fantastic" (Aizenberg 80), which explains his "frequent coupling of religious works and the fantastic" (Aizenberg 81). For Borges, "metaphysics is a branch of fantastic literature" (*Obras Completas* 23), so that the creation of the golem becomes a metaphor of poesis.

The notion that the creation of the world and of the human body and mind resulted from the emanations of a mystical alphabet is a metaphysical fantasy which we find in the cabala and in a variety of other hermetic systems, as well as in the postmodernist fictions of such writers as Borges. In the Tantric and Kundalini yoga systems, for example, the world and the body are created and destroyed through the medium of a sacred language. The creation and destruction of the golem through the manipulation of mystical letters, and the creation and destruction of mankind by Hindu Goddess Kali (through the manipulation of the Sacred Letters of the Sanskrit alphabet) are fantasies symbolic of divine and human creativity. The analogous power of the writer to create worlds through the medium of lettered fantasy suggests that the golem and Kali's Garland of Letters can be seen as metaphors for *poesis*. This notion is exemplified by epiphanies of the golem in the works of Jorge Luis Borges.

In the cabalistic *Sefer Yezirah* (Book of Creation), the alphabet is the divine instrument of God's Creation (Poncé 39): "Twenty two letter elements: He outlined them, hewed them out, weighed them, combined them and exchanged them, and through them created the soul of all creation and everything else that was ever to be created" (Maclagan 30). "He combined, weighed and changed the Aleph with all the other letters in succession, and all the others again with the Aleph .... and so with the whole series of letters. Hence it follows that there are two hundred and thirty–one formations and that every creature and every word emanated from one name" (Maclagan 30). There are twenty two letters: three Mothers (Aleph, Mem, Shin) associated with the three basic elements of creation, three seasons, and three basic parts of the body (Aleph–Air–Head, Shin–Fire–Body, Mem–Water–Stomach); seven double letters linked to the seven coordinates of space (four corners, above and below, center), seven planets, seven days of the week, and the seven gates of the Merkabah mystics (Poncé 42); and finally there are the twelve simple letters which incorporate the entire range of sensual experience and the twelve signs of zodiac (Poncé 44). Further correspondences link the letters symbolizing the four worlds of the sephirotic tree to the body of Adam (brain, heart, breath, genitals) (Poncé 53). The golem (an early form of Adam) is created by inscribing the word *Emet* on the forehead, which brings it to life, while erasing the first letter of that word yields *Met*, the word for death, and results in its destruction (a ritual analogous to the Tantric symbolism associated with Kali).[22]

Other mythic fantasies in which a sacred alphabet serves as a medium of creation include the Egyptian, the Hermetic, the Islamic, the Aztec, the Dogon, the Native American, and the Nordic cosmogonies. In Egyptian theology, "The real creator was the Word—the primeval speech which came from God wherein all things got their name" (Clark 63). In some texts Atum was the deity who "delivered the creative Word," "the intermediary between God's thought and the multitude of created things" (Clark 63), while in other texts it is Ptah who creates the gods and the world simultaneously with the creation of "'every Divine Word'" (Clark 65). In the Coffin Texts of the Herakleopolitan Period the creative Word was understood as the 'Command' which establishes the order of the Creation (Clark 63). Clark summarizes as follows: "The Egyptian theologians were convinced that the world was governed by ideas, the 'words' of the gods," and they conceived of "God as the mythical first being, as the Divine Word and Creator" (267).[23] This notion corresponds to the role played by Nous, the Divine Word, as the archetype and demi–urge of the Creation, in the *Poimandres* of Hermes Trismegistus (Jonas 149–50). In the Koran, God looks at a tablet 360 times a day, each time creating and destroying a world. In the *Popul Vuh,* the Aztec creation myth, the first men are created by sole power of word, "by means of incantation" (Maclagan 30). In the Navajo creation myth, each of the womb chambers of the underworlds from which our world emerges are called a "speech–action"; while among the Hopi, Spider Woman creates all life forms, which she animates by singing the Creation Song (Maclagan 30). This is echoed in the story of the Buffalo maiden, who gets a vertebra of her dead father, puts it under a blanket, and then sings a certain song which reassembles the scattered pieces of her father into a whole and brings him to life (Campbell "Myths and Mysteries"). Among the Dogon of Africa, various creative activities (dancing, weaving, agriculture, sex) are all forms of "speech which reproduce the original words of creation" (Maclagan 31). In the Norse poem called the *Havamal* (Utterance of the High One), the runes that Wotan wins by hanging from Yggdrasil nine days and nights have the power to bring the dead to life (as in the legend of the Golem brought to life by the esoteric rituals and naming and incantation) (Cavendish 69).

Some of the most sophisticated of these mythological fantasies occurs in Oriental philosophies. According to the Markandeya Purana, the creator god Brahma first manifests himself as "a golden embryo of sound," a vowel vibrating in the "formless realm of pure ideas" (Eliot 62). The vibration creates an interference pattern of waves which criss–cross to become the wind and water which form the womb of the world (Eliot 62). In another Hindu myth, Prajapati, hatched from cosmic egg, speaks three words (Bhuh, Bhuvah, Svar) which create Earth, Aether, and Sky; while in Tantrism, the Creator, Preserver, and Destroyer of all things is the Goddess Kali, "so called because she devours Kala (Time)" (Woodroffe 235). From Kali "issue all letters and words (*Sabda*) and the world of things (*Artha*) which they denote. Into Her as Kali they are dissolved" (Woodroffe 236). A necklace of freshly severed heads which hangs from her neck represents the Garland of Letters, the fifty–one letters of the Sanskrit Alphabet from which the universe of names and forms is derived. As Sir John Woodroffe notes, "She wears the Letters which She, as Creatrix, bore. She wears the Letters which She, as the Dissolving Power, takes to Herself again" (238). The letters, that is to say, are the means of the Creation and Dissolution—like those placed on the forehead of the Golem to bring him to life, and erased to destroy him. In this sense the Hebrew ritual reenacts the Creation and Destruction of all mankind, and represents a form of ritual worship which, like the worship of Kali, is meant to shift our center of consciousness from the mortal ego to the immortal Self. This "lettered sound" (Sabda) "is in its causal state (*Parasabda*) known as 'Supreme Speech (*Para–Vak*). It is the Logos, "that aspect of Reality or Consciousness (Cit)" which is "the immediate cause of creation" (Woodroffe 239), i.e., the letters, as in cabbalah, are the medium of the Creation. As *Madhyama–Sabda*, or "Inner Naming," the spoken letters of the gross plane of actual speech are called the "Little Mothers," i.e., those lettered–sounds (as in the three mothers of the Hebrew mystical alphabet) which give birth to the Creation. Related to these notions is the tradition of the lost letters and names of a universal speech, of which the entire Universe is composed. When Kali destroys the world, she does so (again as in the cabalistic legend of the golem) by withdrawing (devouring) the "names and forms which the Letters signify" (Woodroffe 240). This is what is signified by the severed heads on her garland.

In the Kundalini Yoga system, the seed syllable Om is "source of all mantras and a key to realization. It is made up of three sounds, a, u, m, which symbolically represent ... creation, preservation, dissolution—and encompass all the knowledge of the different planes of the universe" (Mookerjee 133). Joseph Campbell shows how the three letters correspond to the three levels of consciousness (waking, dream, and deep dreamless sleep). These three letters, as the seed of all material and spiritual forms of Creation, correspond to the mother letters of the Hebrew alphabet (Aleph, Mem, Shin), which are also the source of all things, and to the three words spoken by Prajapati in the Hindu creation myth (Maclagan 30). Various deities have sequences of syllables to be repeated in meditation and correlated with the breath in order to invoke the deity and to create in the meditator that state of higher consciousness symbolized by the deity (Mookerjee 134). Each of the psychic centers of the body in kundalini yoga has a seed syllable in the center of a lotus, the petals of which are inscribed with other letters, which all taken together represent the subtle energies of the spiritual body, of which the physical body itself is a gross manifestation.[24] This notion corresponds to the cabalistic conception of the body of Adam having been created by divine speech, a conception illustrated in pictures which show the body with different letters associated with different parts, lined up to correspond to the Tree of the Sephirot (Poncé 150–54).

If we turn now to postmodern literature in which cabalistic imagery occurs, we find that the secret names of God and the creation of the golem are seen as metaphors of poetic creation. Poesis means to make, so a poem is an utterance which recreates the world, and then by reading it we return to the original world of the lost paradise. The notion of the making (and unmaking) of the world through the power of the letter and of the word is closely related to the Apocalypse, in which Christ appears with the sword of the Logos to annihilate the old world and replace it with a new. Borges had a profound interest in Jewish mysticism, and, during the apocalyptic years of the Second World War, he created works in which the golem appears.

Borges adapts the Kabbalistic idea of the secret creative powers of the letters and words of the Hebrew Scripture in "The Aleph" and "Death and the Compass;" he has meditated upon "the golem in poems and narratives—"El golem," "Las ruinas circulares"—pondering the mysteries of creation" (Aizenberg 89); and he discusses the cabbalah and golem making in his lectures on "El misticismo judio y las leyendes de la cábala" (Aizenberg 126, n.9) and "Vindication of the Kabbalah." The central appeal of the creative power of the letters and names of god in the creation of the golem was, for Borges, metaphorical, since for him "the work of art is to its maker, the writer, as the golem is to his creator, the Kabbalist or rabbi" (Borges interview paraphrased by Aizenberg 126, n.9). The creation of the golem, that is to say, is an image of *poesis*, and the writer mimics God in his "inventions," since for the cabalists "the Divinity was the archetypal writer, who chose to express His will through a scripture" (Aizenberg 92). In fact, Borges creates what Aizenberg calls a "golem–writer," i.e., fictitious narrators of non–existent works, in stories like "The Circular Ruins" and "Seis problemas para don Isidro Parodi" (101). Borges may have seen himself as a rabbi mimicking God in his efforts to create living texts.

In "The Circular Ruins," first published in 1940, a "silent man" from the South spends his last days in the middle of a ruined temple in an Oriental jungle where he attempts to "dream a man" and "insert him into reality" (46). His first successful attempt comes one night after he had "uttered the lawful syllables of a powerful name" and "dreamt of a "beating heart" (47). The next night, he "invoked the name of a planet and set about to envision another of the principle organs" and then he continues during the course of the year all the way to "the skeleton, the eyelids" until he had "dreamt a complete man" (48). But here his work fails, as the youth created "could not rise nor did he speak" (48): he has created a golem, envisaged in "Gnostic cosmogonies" as a "red Adam who cannot stand alone; as unskillful and crude and elementary as this Adam of dust" (48). Scholem describes this "clump of earth" (287) as the "original form of Adam" (288), the "cosmic, gigantic Golem" before he was "shrunken down to customary size" (287; my trans.).

The magician of "The Circular Ruins" creates a human being with the aid of sacred syllables, each one associated with one of the principle organs, and like Rabbi Loew's golem, this being is unable to speak. This means of creation by letters clearly implies links between God the golem maker and man the creator of *ficciones*. In cabalistic speculation, the golem (like every character in every literary work) is created, organ by organ, by the recitation of letters. As Scholem notes, "each member is presided over by one of the letters" (248), but the result is either "soulless," lacking "either reason or libido," or "speechless" (278–89; my trans.). In the Borges story, the magician succeeds in creating a fully live being only with the help of the Fire god of the ruined temple, but his success coincides with a conflagration which consumes him. During his last moments, the man realizes that he too is a golem, the creature of some other being's dream (50). The metaphysical suggestion is that we are all golems, created by the sacred syllables of God, and the aesthetic suggestion is that the artist mimics God (and the cabalistic rabbi) by inventing living beings through the power of the written word.

Similar notions are suggested by Borges in his poem titled "El Golem," which begins with a meditation on the Platonic idea that every thing has an archetypal name, and that hence there should exist some combination of syllables and letters which figure the deity (110–111). As a result of sin, however, that Name has long been forgotten; but the cabalists pursued the Name until Rabbi Loew properly arranged the Hebrew letters in the complicated variations needed to form the name of God, and hence to bring a "dummy" to life (110). Although the rabbi struggles to teach the golem the secrets of the letters, it remains ignorant and incapable of speech (like the dream man in "The Circular Ruins"). Borges then focuses on the uncanny (cats disappear when the golem comes), and on the pathos of a being (much like ourselves) who can only ape prayer with hollow shows of piety (113). The poem ends with the Rabbi's terrified and tender meditation on the being he has created, and with the poet's recognition that both the rabbi and the writer are golems created by God, ignorant of their origins, two more 'integers' in an infinite and futile 'series' of pain and 'cause and effect' (115). The final effect is Escher–like: "El Golem" is a poem written by a man who himself has been mysteriously created by a God whom he cannot comprehend, and who then creates a poem about a being created by a man whom he cannot comprehend. As Patricia Merivale puts it, Borges contemplates a world in which the poet "too is dreamed, a book in which he too is written" (220). While "Poetry can dream into existence only tigers stuffed or flimsy like the Golem," Merivale continues, Borges must persist in the adventure of writing, "since Artifice, the realest thing we can know, is the only thing that can make reality endurable" (223).

Leonora Carrington

In Leonora Carrington's *Down Below*, the descent to the underworld similarly catalyzes the revelation of alchemical archetypes and geometrical symbols. This little surrealist gem of 1940 has much in common with such late works of modernism produced during the years Second World War as *Four Quartets* by Eliot, *The Death of Virgil* by Broch, *Joseph and His Brothers* and *Doctor Faustus* by Thomas Mann, *Under the Volcano* by Malcolm Lowry, or *Trilogy* by H. D. In all of these works, the descent to the underworld leads to the revelation of those archetypal forms of the imagination which give them shape and significance. For Carrington, the forms revealed by the psychotic breakdown recorded in the novel are alchemical as well as mythical. Allusions to the nekyia begin when Leonora leaves Saint–Martin de l'Ardèche with two friends to escape a German occupied France in May, 1940. She packs all of her clothing into a suitcase marked with the word "REVELATION" (8), and then drives all night long to get to Peripignan on the Spanish border. The symbolism of clothing will subsequently become central in the novel, and is, like the notion of revelation, rooted in a mythology of Hades which can be traced as far back as the Sumerian of the Goddess Inanna, who prepares for her descent by putting on royal clothing which she subsequently sheds while passing through a series of seven gateways into the underworld (Wolkstein and Kramer 157–60). She then stands naked before Ereshkigal, who fastens the "eye of death" upon Inanna, then hangs her up to rot on a peg for three days and three nights (Wolkstein and Kramer 60).

The iconography of the journey, divestiture, doorways, and eyes all surface during Carrington's alchemical nekyia. During the night trip southwards to Peripignan, Leonora hallucinates arms and legs dangling out of a truck in front of the car in which she travels with her two friends, and she sees the sides of the road "lined with rows of coffins" (9). She remarks that "*it all stank of death*," and later discovers that "there was a huge military cemetery in Peripignan" (9). These details suggest that her journey is infernal, as do the problems which impede her efforts to "cross the border" into Spain (10). The necessary permission of "higher authorities" takes some time to acquire, delaying the journey by several days, during which Leonora struggles to relieve her nerves, exasperated by "the noise of a river which flowed tirelessly over some rocks" (10), by establishing an "entente" with the mountains and horses outside of Andorra (11). She does this by lying face down against the hillside, "completely absorbed by the earth" (11). As realistic and bizarre as these details are, they suggest the traditional iconography of the journey into Hades, which typically involves a river or mountain crossing (as in Dante, or the *Epic of Gilgamesh*). When Leonora and her friends finally manage the crossing into Spain, the dead throng round her as they do around Odysseus among the Kimmerian shades: "it was my kingdom," Leonora announces (as if she were Persephone); "the red earth was the dried blood of the Revolution. I was choked by the dead, by their thick presence in that lacerated countryside" (12).

After arriving in Madrid, the imagery of rape, divestiture, and the evil eye mark Leonora's passage into the underworld. At the Hotel Roma, she meets a "Nazi agent" named Van Ghent, whose "gaze," she says, "was as painful to me as if he had thrust pins into my eyes" (13). Leonora's paranoia perceives Madrid as an underworld of "zombies" and "slaves," all "made of wood" and hypnotized by the "gaze of that man" (13). It is curious that the emphasis on the evil eye is juxtaposed here with the motif of divestiture, just as it is in the Sumerian "Descent of Inanna": saying she feels compelled to "despoil myself of everything," Leonora attempts to distribute everything she has among the "zombies" gathered at the hotel café, only to be abducted by two officers who, after "tearing off" her "clothes," try unsuccessfully to "rape" her (13). While the notion of the descent as a stripping down derives ultimately from Sumerian myth, the related metaphor of abduction is to be found in the Classical myth of Persephone, who is raped by Hades while playing in a field of poppies. After the abduction, Leonora spends the rest of her time in her Madrid hotel room "taking cold baths," putting on green and pink silk chemises (14), manufacturing "various ceremonial garments out of bath towels" (16), or simply sitting around "naked" (17), much to the chagrin of her friends.

Leonora's mental health continues to degenerate during her time in Madrid: she tries to convince the British consulate that the war is being "waged hypnotically" by Hitler and Van Ghent (16), and that only by belief in a "metaphysical force" can Europe avoid "wandering aimlessly in political and economic labyrinths" (16). The image of the labyrinth, of course, has an archaic association with alchemy, the goddess, and the underworld: it is "at one and the same time the theatre of initiatory rites and the place where the dead are interred" (Eliade "Terre Mère" 75; my trans.), and it is also one of several "poetic images of the alchemical citadel" in the surrealist theater (Orenstein 12). For Fulcanelli, whose works influenced Breton and other surrealists, "The image of the labyrinth is offered to us as emblematic of the entire work of the *Oeuvre*" (qtd. in Orenstein 89). Other images of the nekyia surface in the songs which appeal to Leonora during her last days in Madrid: one called "'Ojos verdes' (Green Eyes)" and another "'El barco velero,' the sail boat which was to take me into the unknown" (19). This journey into the unknown comes when Leonora's condition becomes so bad that she is taken off by car to a mental institution in Santander: she arrives in this deeper circle of hell "like a cadaver," knocked out by an injection of "systemic anesthesia" (17).

When Leonora awakens from the anesthesia, she experiences the sanitarium in terms of the otherworld: it is "some unknown and hostile country" (22) from "another world, another epoch, another civilization, perhaps on another planet which contained the past and the future and, simultaneously, the present" (23).

The eerie timelessness of Hades evoked here recalls the convergence of time past, present, and future in Eliot's *Four Quartets*, in which the myths of the underworld and the apocalypse converge. But Carrington abandons an abstract for a very real and brutal portrait of the inferno, in which the iconography of rape, the evil eye, and divestiture again play a central role. The son of the head doctor, who arrives at the sanitarium in a Mercedes followed by a Faustian "black dog," has "eyes" that are "still more terrifying" than Van Ghent's in Madrid (24). This man's name is Don Luis Morales, and he watches as two of the hospital attendants drag Leonora off to her room, where they tear her "clothes off brutally" and strap her "naked to the bed," where she wallows for several days and nights in her own waste, "bound and naked" and stung relentlessly by mosquitoes which she sees as the "spirits of all the crushed Spaniards" (24–26).

During the nadir of her incarceration, Leonora adds a symbol of the underworld dear to the heart of Thomas Mann in *Joseph and His Brothers*: the well, which Mann describes as "the entrance to the underworld" ('dem Eingang zum Unterwelt') (390; 431). Mann uses the Babylonian term "*'Bôr*,'" a translation of the Sumerian word *kur*, to denote this descent into the underworld, which, furthermore, he calls the "primeval prototype" ('Urvorbild') of all those descents in the novel (390; 431) which ultimately originated in the Sumerian myth of Inanna (Babylonian Ishtar), to which Mann continually alludes. Carrington's surrealistic nekyia powerfully evokes the same symbols when she describes an injection of Cardiazol: "I saw the center of all eyes fixed upon me in a GHASTLY, GHASTLY stare. Don Luis' were tearing my brain apart and I sank, I sank down into a well ... very far .... The bottom of that well was the stopping of my mind for all eternity in the midst of utter anguish" (36). When she rushes "up to the surface with vertiginous speed," Leonora encounters once again "the staring ghastly eyes," which leave her "lying naked on the floor" desperately defeated "without any hope of liberation" (36). When Leonora awakens after a twenty–four hour sleep, she sees a little old man whom she recognizes as "*master* because the tiny pupils of his light–colored eyes were the terminals for the russet rays by which I had already been hypnotized through the stare of Van Ghent and don Luis" (37).

It is very curious to find, throughout Leonora Carrington's psychotic nekyia, the symbolism of divestiture and the "eye of death" found in the Sumerian prototype. Curious also that this Ur–nekyia, as it were, concerns the descent of a woman, not of a man, and is therefore all the more precious, given its scarcity.[25] In postmodernist literature, the descent yields eventually to the revelation of those archetypal forms of the mind (eidola) which provide the basis for a reconstruction of the identity and of the work of art. For Carrington, these elementary forms of the imagination are derived largely from the realm of alchemy (a rich source of imagery for surrealism and its precursors, as for postmodernist writers like Cortázar and Márquez). Along with the revelation of alchemical symbols, however, Carrington's nekyia catalyzed a fascinating network of matrifocal imagery derived from the Goddess traditions of the Ancient Mediterranean mystery rites.

The alchemical revelations begin in Madrid, when Leonora's imperfect command of Spanish makes it possible for her to "invest the most ordinary phrases with a hermetic significance" (12), and continue in the form of "hermetic answers" to her inquiries. She then misreads the corporate logos for the "Amazon Company" and "Imperial Chemicals" as a "secret telegram" bearing the words "Chemistry and Alchemy" (18). The language of the alchemists was notoriously arcane, and one of the signs of progress made by the adept was the ability to interpret the "hermetic significance" of secret tongues, such as the languages of the animals, of colors and vibrations, of sensations and forms which Leonora begins to apprehend in Madrid (18). The imagery of bathing, of the cosmic egg, of the union of the sun and the moon, and the processes of transmutation and the distillation of the elixir vitae so important to alchemy enter Leonora's mind at this time in Madrid. She constantly takes "cold baths" in her hotel room (14, 16), imagines the "past and future of the Universe" represented by the "egg idea," a symbol of the macrocosm and the microcosm" (18), and fantasizes the transformation of her menstrual blood "into comprehensive energy—masculine and feminine, microcosmic and macrocosmic—and also into a wine which was drunk by the moon and the sun" (19).

These are wonderful feminine symbols catalyzed by Leonora's descent (egg, bathing, menstrual blood, the union of sun and moon) which are typical features of alchemical thinking. In 1951, the emerald and the egg appear in Leonora Carrington's play *Une Chemise de Nuit de Flanelle* as a green egg laid by a black swan (Orenstein 139). As Orenstein points out, the egg is "often the name given the athanor, or the alchemistic oven" (12); it is a symbol also of the philosopher's stone frequently found in Carrington's visual and literary work (127–144). Emblem number eight from Michael Maier's *Atalanta Fugiens* of 1617, for example, shows the alchemist about to slice an egg with a sword in front of a furnace and long corridor (Fabricius 129), while the entire sequence from the *Rosarium Philosophorum* of 1550 (which Jung reproduces in *The Psychology of the Transference*) shows a King and a Queen descending into a bath which represents the alchemical crucible. This sequence ends with the completion of the opus symbolized by the androgynous union of the solar King and lunar Queen, a representation of the *mysterium coniunctionus* to be seen in innumerable alchemical plates. Perhaps the most beautiful of these is from the *Aurora Consurgens* of the late 14th century, which shows the alchemical androgyne standing in a pile of dead eagles, but embraced by the wings of the phoenix (De Rola Pl.5).[26]

The union of the sun and the moon becomes a kind of obsession for Leonora in *Down Below*. While basking and dancing in the Sun Room of the sanitarium, she feels herself transformed, "through the agency of the Sun" into "an androgyne, the Moon, the Holy Ghost" as "the third person of the Trinity" (40) which Jung associates with Hermes. As she dances, the sins of the world are transmuted "into Knowledge, the union of Man and Woman with God and the Cosmos;" the lump on her left thigh is transformed into "a sun on the left side of the moon;" and her left hand becomes Eve and her right Adam (40). Later in the little novel, when Leonora improves and is transferred to the building called "Down Below," she sees her room as "the room of the Moon," and the room to the right as the "Sun's, my Androgyne" (47). And when she is taken out of the sanitarium for her first excursion to a German lady's home, she again imagines herself as the "Holy Ghost" in a limbo "where the sun and moon met at dawn and twilight" (50). Now the so–called "Meeting of the Sun and the Moon" has a long mythological heritage, from Homer, where the meeting of Penelope and Odysseus represents the union of time and eternity (Campbell, *Occidental* 163); to the imagery of Kundalini yoga, in which the two nerves coiling up from the base of the spine, solar–masculine (Pingala) and lunar–feminine (Ida), meet at the crown chakra of illumination and liberation (Campbell, *Inner Reaches* 65, 72); to such Christian variations on the theme as Albrecht Dürer's "Great Crucifixion" of 1498, in which the sun and moon appear at opposing upper corners (*Inner Reaches* Fig.4).[27]

These revelations follow Leonora's darkest days of descent in *Down Below*, and allow her to imbue the objects surrounding her with "an alchemistic life" (41). Two jars of face cream, for example, become symbols of "Night, the Left Side, the Moon, Woman, Destruction" on the one hand, and "Man, the Brother, Green Eyes the Sun, Construction" on the other (41). The jars, like Pandora's box, contain the essence of the world, all of its joys, as well as all of its sorrows, in equilibrium. Alchemy, of course, is much concerned with various vessels which contain the world in microcosm—beakers, crucibles, and baths among them. It is there that the opus proceeds, an opus which Jung compares to the individuation process, during which the conscious ego encounters the archetypal elements of the unconscious from which it has emerged, and with which it must achieve a kind of reconciliation in which the opposites (male and female, sun and moon) are balanced. This occurs through the agency of the Self, symbolized in alchemy by the philosopher's stone, and, in Leonora's descent into the depths of her own unconscious, by the sun and the moon.

The climactic revelations of the nekyia occur in the rooms of the building called "Down Below," where objects are imbued with alchemical and biblical meanings to complete the opus. The entrance into this room evokes the passage through a complex sequence of doorways characteristic of the iconography of both the labyrinth and the underworld (as in the seven gateways of the *kur* in Sumerian myth, and in the descent through the twelve chambers of the *tuat* in Egyptian myth), and a typical feature of postmodernist nekyias as well (See Chapter 4). Leonora calls the building her "paradise," and it seems to be guarded by "invisible powers" analogous to the angels against which she must struggle to gain access (42). There are three storeys with a doorway open in each. Leonora climbs the third storey to a "small ogival door" which she opens to find a "spiral staircase" leading up to the "center of the world" (42). In the tower at the top, she finds "a circular room lighted by five bull's eye windows" (42) suggestive of the Minotaur in the center of the Cretan maze, and of those mazes with spiral eyes at the center or at the entrance scattered over the ancient Mediterranean world, such as Hal Tarxien or Hagar Qim from the third millennium B.C. on Malta (Gimbutas 60), or the spiral cemetery from "Val Camonica in Italy, containing at its center not a bull but a pair of eyes" (Di Stasi 104). One of these windows represents the Moon, the other the Sun, and all revolve around a column serving as an axis which passes through a pentagonal table in the center of the room (43). It is interesting to note the archaic symbolism of the axis mundi in the passage, the still point at which Eliot arrives in *Four Quartets*, here represented by the room itself and by the column, for Gimbutas has shown that the column is a symbol associated with the Great Goddess of Neolithic Europe (221f.).

Many of the objects Leonora finds on the table in the center of this room are, in fact, derivative of a profoundly archaic mysticism of the Goddess which was passed on into the alchemical lore of the Middle Ages, along with the symbolism of the Hellenistic mystery cults of the Mediterranean world, after the Theodosian Code banned all forms of pagan worship in 438 A.D. (Campbell, *Creative Myth* 406). Among the objects scattered on the pentagonal table are some laboratory saucers, "some crescent shaped, others half–moon shaped, the remainder perfectly round (43). These suggest the three phases of the moon, virgin, crescent, and full, which Robert Graves associated with the triune manifestations of the Triple Goddess, all of which taken together would represent a special experience of wholeness within the Self, a wholeness in which past, present, and future are united into a vision of totality outside of time. The pentagonal shape of this room at the center of the world, along with the five windows, creates a geometrical configuration which Jung called the mandala, and reinforces the sense of wholeness conveyed by the ritual Leonora performs with the objects on the table. She takes two pieces of wood, which she says represent the opposites of male and female, and sprinkles gold dust (suggestive of alchemical symbolism) on them. Also alchemical is the "triangle" formed by three "rectangular" tanks attached to the "circular" walls of the room, another geometrical figure of wholeness: squaring a circle by inscribing a triangle around a man and a woman is an old alchemical conundrum, one found in Michael Maier's *Scrutinium Chymicum* of 1687 (Jaffé 106). The circle, the square, and the triangle are among the most archetypal of forms, and their revelation here in *Down Below* recalls works by Borges, Mann, Yeats, and Cortázar in which geometrical figures represent the climax of the nekyia. A preoccupation with number symbolism follows this episode, as Leonora becomes obsessed with "lengthy calculations" based on the numbers 6, 8, and 20, which eventually yield the number 1600, which Leonora associates with Queen Elizabeth. This is interesting in an alchemical context, since, as Dame Frances Yates has shown, Elizabeth patronized such Renaissance philosophers interested in hermetic lore as John Dee and Giordano Bruno.

The manipulation of the objects on the table and the numerical calculations which follow bring Leonora's opus to a close: "Having concluded the Work," she says, "I walked down the stairs and returned to 'Egypt'" (44). The alchemists often capitalized the word "Work" to suggest the special nature of their opus, the completion of which was sometimes compared to the entry into the Holy City in *Revelation* (Jung, *Mysterium* 52). It is interesting, therefore, to find Leonora compare the special room in "Down Below" to Jerusalem, and her other room as "Egypt" (42). This suggests an allegory of exile and homecoming as prevalent in alchemical lore as in postmodernist versions of the descent into Hades. After Leonora completes her opus, and the archetypal forms of the human imagination have revealed themselves, she begins to get well. Her return to "lucidity" follows her awakening from one final "cataleptic" seizure, during which she thought she "was dead" (52). With the descent complete, she has come full circle, and one suspects it is to the revelation of the fundamental forms of the imagination that Leonora owes the recreation of her world, and the creation of the text recording her nekyia.

Hilda Doolittle

One of the most explicit analogies between alchemy and poesis occurs in *Trilogy,* a masterpiece written almost exactly the same time Leonora Carrington was at work on *Down Below* (1942–1944). As Susan Stanford Friedman has pointed out, H.D.'s "poetic" or "etymological alchemy" of the "Word" serves as a metaphor for "cultural metamorphosis," for the recovery of personal authenticity for women, and for the "linguistic restoration" of the Goddess (221, 249, 253). It also serves as a metaphor of personal and poetic transubstantiation (560), as H.D. puts it in the poem, for *Trilogy* marks a pivotal point in her life and work. Personally, she at last comes to terms with the traumatic events of her life during the First World War. Friedman compares H.D.'s personal development during the years between the two wars to "a descent to the underworld from which she had to emerge in a process of spiritual rebirth that was decades in the making" (9). Poetically, *Trilogy* marks the transformation of her work from the short lyric image of her early years to the expansive hieroglyph of the later. H.D. saw Hermes Trismegistus as the patron of this process of personal and poetic metamorphosis, and drew upon such hermetic motifs as the crucible, the breaking of vessels (shevirah), geometrical symbols, and the philosopher's stone to create the "spiritual realism" of her later poetry.

H.D. begins the *Trilogy* by comparing the pen dipped in corrosive to the caduceus carried by Hermes, which has the power to heal, to evoke the dead, and to animate the living (512). The pen is ultimately more powerful than the sword, for the Word existed before it, in the beginning (519). H.D. notes that the Hermetic pen and brush survive, even though books were burned during the War to make cartridge boxes (518). Something of the magic of poetry, painting, and music (all inventions of Hermes) transcends death, and remains indelibly recorded upon the spirit (519). The original pen and papyrus were hermetic, and their recovery promises a new kind of spiritually realistic poetry, sacred to the alchemical magic of Hermes Trismegistus (537). Ricorso leads to recreation, as the poet recovers the sacred script originally invented by Hermes, thereby transforming the pen into the caduceus of Hermes or the ankh of the Egyptian Thoth, a symbol of power and life, which became, in Coptic times, a cross with an eye handle (Wilkinson 177).

A variant form of the ankh was the Isis knot, in which the transverse arms of the cross are doubled and curved downwards, sometimes to form the pleating in the robe worn by the Goddess (Wilkinson 201). It too represented the power of resurrection and life, a theme central to H.D.'s poem. In "The Tribute to Angels," the hermetic syncretism expands to embrace Thoth, Hermes, and the Archangel Michael (ruler of Mercury) into a single hieroglyph representing the powers of guidance, prayer, and knowledge (567). H.D. combines apocalyptic and alchemical motifs here in her reversion to the Egyptian and Greek prototypes of Michael: the spear with which the archangel defeats Satanic power during Armageddon was originally the ankh and the caduceus of Thoth and Hermes, and it is now the pen of the poetess, who, like the alchemist of the Middle Ages, struggles to transmute the Dragon's darkness into the radiant life–renewing power of verse. The dragon, of course, is an extremely complex alchemical figure, often depicted in stunning plates biting its tail, a symbol of "the beginning and end of the work," of the prima materia and the philosopher's stone. It is, in fact, a symbol of Hermes, of Mercury: "as dragon he devours himself and as dragon he dies, to rise again as the *lapis*" (Jung, *Psychology and Alchemy* 293).

Like Jung, H.D. saw Hermes as a patron of psychoanalysis, as well as of poesis and resurrection. She described Freud in her *Tribute* as the "alchemist si remarkable" (116), and in "The Walls Do Not Fall" suggested an equation between hermeticism and the interpretation of dreams, which she compares to the Holy Ghost, the inspiration of which is commonly available to all humanity. The Holy Ghost represents the agency by which the symbols are interpreted, the power which brings the past and the future together in the dream itself, and the insight which reveals the deepest secrets of the alchemist (526). Like the Dragon, the Holy Ghost could stand as a synonym for Hermes–Mercurius (Jung, *Psychology and Alchemy* 432), especially in his capacity to mediate between heaven and earth, delivering messages from the gods in the same way the dream does. And like the Dragon, the Holy Ghost is apocalyptic, linking the beginning and the end, just as the dream links the far–distant future to the remotest antiquity.

The poet does the same, finding contemporary parallels for such alchemical symbols as the crucible and the stone, which give shape and significance to the present (539). Poetry is the alchemical process by which current events are melted down to those archetypes of the past and the future which give them meaning, and the poem is therefore analogous to the philosopher's stone. The poet's stylus unlocks alchemical doors and distills life into the philosopher's stone (533). The opus proceeds in a *vas hermeticum;* for H.D., it is the crucible, in which important names are broken down to syllables for the poetic purpose of recovering their hidden meaning. Poesis is a process of melting down, a cabalistic collecting together of the fragments of a shattered vessel (shevirah) in order to reconstruct them (tikkun). Hence, "Tribute to the Angels" begins with an invocation to Hermes Trismegistus, the alchemical patron of poetry, who must melt and fuse the fragments of a few essential symbols to create the philosopher's stone. H.D. enjoins her fellow poets to recover the fragments of antiquity, buried in Mithraic tombs, preserved but shattered by the rituals of the modern Church. From the splinters of glass, H.D. urges them to forge new vessels, using the fire and breath of verse (547). For the cabalists, the vessels created by God to contain the outflowing of his divine energy (through the eyes of Adam Kadmon, the first human form) shattered, sending a shower of sparks downwards to mix with the dark realm of matter in which they became imprisoned. Restoration of the soul–sparks to their original home in the realm of light then constitutes the work of redemption known as tikkun (Poncé 80–83). H.D. would most likely have encountered this magnificent myth later, in her reading of Robert Ambelain's *Le kabbale practique*, and may have known it earlier, since her reading covered a wide range of hermetic topics from *Trilogy* onwards. In this beautiful invocation of Hermes Trismegistus at the beginning of the "Tribute to the Angels," the shattered fragments of ancient symbols are distilled in the crucible to create various forms of the stone (onyx, obsidian, and opal). The purpose is both Poundian and apocalyptic: to make things new (549).

Spiritually, the alchemical rhythm has to do with the power of resurrection (552), a process which H.D. experienced psychologically during her work with Freud. Poetically, it is a process of what Friedman calls "etymological alchemy" (247), by which the bitter words for death and brine are melted down to their root syllables, in a crucible on a burner, so that the original meanings of Mother and Mary may be recovered (552). The poet must combine the two poles of the Goddess (her womb and her tomb) into a single hieroglyph, which embraces and transcends the opposites, without negating them. The purpose is to break words down to their fundamental and original roots (ricorso) (554), in order to transmute the syllables of such names as Osiris (540), Mary, (552), and Venus (553). Out of the flames rises the essence of new names and attributes, recovered by the alchemy of poetry. It is often a process of "cultural metamorphosis," of the recovery of the archetypal power of the Goddess purified of patriarchal denigration, and hence a process of "linguistic restoration" analogous to Pound's efforts to purify the dialect of the tribe (Friedman 249). The symbol of this restoration, and of the poem itself, is a jewel which combines the colors green, white, opal, blue, rose, agate, and violet (554)—a rainbow of colors and variety of gems symbolic of the philosopher's stone. The jewel is later melted down in the crucible (557), a spiritual vessel, to form a face like a rose (574) which prefigures of the Christ Child of the Nativity at the end of the poem (612)

The stone is hence the homunculus, the child in the beaker, but also the poem created by H.D.'s etymological alchemy. The alchemical motifs of stone, seed, and syllable as symbols of the union of Time and Eternity merge in the great climax of "The Flowering of the Rod." When Kaspar stoops to recover Mary Magdalen's scarf from the floor, a flicker of light from her hair becomes both a flaw in the circle of square gemstones crowning her head (599), and the grain of seed which opens petal by petal into a lily which I discussed in detail in the chapter on the Goddess. Here I want to focus on the magnificent epiphany of the stone, the beauty of which completely surpasses the magian Kaspar's previous experience of jewels, stones, and sapphires (598). The ecstasy produced by the sight of this stone is likewise more exalted than the ecstasy of pearl or opal (599). For this stone radiates from a circle of blue, purple, and violet gems cut in squares. The whole figure combines the circle and the square, so crucial to alchemical geometry, with the symbol of the mirror and the maze, for the crown of gems creates a dazzling array of reflective facets (599). The crown of stones is a hologlyph: it contains the entire Creation in minute particularity, from the ships in the harbor to the islands of the Hesperides (601–02). But the stone also echoes the syllables of the Logos, but they are spoken by a female, not a male Creator (603). The stone is what the Orient called the jewel in the lotus, the seed syllable from which the entire creation emerges, a symbol sometimes literally depicted as a letter in a crucible formed by lotus flowers and supported by the vajra thunderbolt representing Enlightenment (Matthews 95). The symbolism is essentially the same as the image of Jesus—the Logos, or seed syllable of the beginning—sitting in the Grail in Malory.

H.D.'s grand passage combines such notions with a lovely hermetic use of colors and geometry. The stone is nearly every symbolic color associated with the stages of the alchemical opus, and it assumes the forms of the circle and the square. H.D. describes the crown on Mary Magdalen's head as a circle of square stones, alluding to the alchemical problem of squaring the circle found in Mann's *Magic Mountain* and best illustrated in Michael Maier's plate from *Atalanta Fugiens* of an alchemist squaring a circle containing a man and a woman, a "Figure conteyning all the secrets of the Treatise both great and small" (Fabricius Fig. 382). Again, this alchemical geometry has an apocalyptic dimension, alluded to earlier in *Trilogy* by the focus on the four square walls and twelve foundation slabs of John's heavenly Jerusalem, which H.D. replaces with an octagon of jasper (548). Like the Aleph, wheel, or hexagonal labyrinth in Borges; like the many geometrical figurations in Cortázar's work; or like the meditations upon the line, the circle, and the sphere in Mann's *Joseph* novels, the stone contains within itself all possible forms, seen from all angles (599), and its revelation is hence an alchemical archetype of poesis.

Gabriel García Márquez

In the great Latin American novel, *One Hundred Years of Solitude*, Gabriel García Márquez uses alchemy as a symbol both of writing and reading. For, at the end of the novel, we learn that the text has been composed by the alchemist Melquíades, and that all subsequent attempts in later generations of the Buendía family to decipher the text have taken place in "the laboratory of an alchemist" which he gave to its patriarch, José Arcadio Buendía (5). The old wizard Melquíades is the portrait of an alchemist infused with the energy of the philosopher's stone: prodigiously resilient and nearly immortal, he has survived "pellagra in Persia, scurvy in the Malayan archipelago, leprosy in Alexandria, beriberi in Japan, bubonic plague in Madagascar, an earthquake in Sicily, and a disastrous shipwreck in the Strait of Magellan" (6). He has an "Asiatic look that seemed to know what was on the other side of things" and he wears a "large black hat that looked like a raven with widespread wings" (6), a chapeau which suggests he is a descendant of the Norse God Wotan. The "rudimentary laboratory" which he gives José Arcadio Buendía is delightfully delineated: it consists of a water pipe, a glass reproduction of the athanor, a still, and a three–armed alembic (7). Along with these vessels, the alchemist Melquíades has left samples of the metals, the formulas of Moses and Zosimos, and notes on the transmutation of philosopher' stone (7). José Arcadio Buendía then takes his wife's gold coins and "In risky and desperate processes of distillation, melted with the seven planetary metals, mixed with hermetic mercury and vitriol of Cyprus, and put back to cook in hog fat for lack of any radish oil, Ursula's precious inheritance was reduced to a large piece of hog cracklings that was firmly stuck to the bottom of the pot" (8).

His mistake is the typical one, made many years ago by Chaucer's alchemical patrons in "The Canon Yeoman's Tale," of taking the process literally. José and his son Aureliano make the same mistake later when they announce they have "succeeded in penetrating the metallic debris and had separated Ursula's gold" (29). When they show the "dry and yellowish mass" in the crucible to Aureliano's brother, José Arcadio, he answers the question of what it looks like sincerely, "Dog shit"! (29). The point is the old alchemical maxim, that the philosopher's gold is not the banker's gold, but rather a spiritual, aesthetic, or psychological symbol. Aureliano inherits the obsession with the alchemical work in the second generation of the family, spending "interminable hours in the abandoned laboratory, learning the art of silverwork by his own experimentation" (40) until he develops mystical powers of prophecy. He becomes an "expert silversmith" in the "mad laboratory," while Melquíades and his father "interpreted the predictions of Nostradamus amidst a noise of flasks and trays, and the disaster of spilled acids and silver bromide that was lost in the twists and turns it gave at every instant" (52).

Melquíades eventually comes to prefer Aureliano's workshop to the old laboratory, and in his last years spends all his time their amid "flaky stacks of paper covered with indecipherable signs .... scribbling his enigmatic literature on the parchments he had brought with him" from his world wanderings (73). One day Aureliano's brother Arcadio wanders into the room, and "Melquíades made him listen to several pages of his impenetrable writing" which Arcadio cannot understand but which sound like the "encyclicals" that he remembers years later at the moment of his death (74, 123). The old alchemist drowns shortly thereafter, washing up "on a bright bend in the river and with a solitary vulture sitting on his stomach" (75). José Arcadio Buendía refuses to bury Melquíades; proclaiming him "immortal," José Arcadio Buendía performs the "formula of his resurrection" by bringing out the water pipe and putting "a kettle of mercury to boil next to the body" (75). But when the "mercurial incense" burns for seventy–two hours, and the body begins to "burst with a livid fluorescence, the soft whistles of which impregnated the house with a pestilential vapor," the burial proceeds (75). Once again, the old patriarch has taken the alchemical formula literally, leaving us to discover many pages later the continued existence of Melquíades in the realm of the spirit.

This occurs when Aureliano Segundo, at twelve years old begins reading the books and sets upon the task of "deciphering the manuscripts" of Melquíades, and the old dead alchemist appears to him, one hot noontime, sitting against the light of the window with his hands on his knees and wearing the same vest and hat with "raven's wings" that he had worn when he was under forty (189). Around this time Colonel Aureliano Buendía retires from the endless revolutionary wars, from which he retreats by making little golden fishes in the workshop of his youth. Here he performs the operation which the alchemists call circulatio, an endless repetition of the same procedure which ultimately leads to the revelation of the secret stone (Edinger 142–44). The Colonel makes the little fishes from the same golden coins which he receives in payment for them, "with the result that he had to work all the harder with the more he sold in order to satisfy an exasperating vicious circle" (204). Bad business, "but the implacable concentration awarded him with a peace of the spirit" (204). This image of the relentless circulation in alchemical work, is actually a metaphorical representation of the theme of repetition in the novel, as each generation circles back to its beginnings and re–enacts the biblical paradigm of paradise, paradise lost, and paradise regained (which is discussed in detail in the chapter on apocalypse). It is also an image of what Freud would have called the "repetition compulsion," an important concept in Jungian theory as well, which postulates that "One must make the circuit of one's complexes again and again in the course of their transformation" (Edinger 144). What lies in the center of this labyrinthine procedure, demon or Self?

However that may be, the novel turns from this point on to the hermeneutic problems implied by the alchemical circulatio: in order to decipher the texts left behind by Melquíades, they must be read and re–read within and between generations. After the death of Colonel Aureliano Buendía, this task falls to José Arcadio Segundo, who takes refuge in the alchemical rooms after fleeing from the police during the Banana Massacre. Here he locks himself up for the rest of his life, dedicated to the perusal of "the manuscripts of Melquíades many times" (318), "reading and rereading the unintelligible parchments" until he is "illuminated by a seraphic glow" (319). José Arcadio Segundo also communes with the dead Melquíades, who appears to him as an "atavistic vision of an old man, his back to the window, wearing a hat with a brim like the wings of a crow," with whose help he manages to "classify the cryptic letters of the parchments" into an alphabet of "fifty–three characters" which look like "pieces of clothing put out to dry on a line" (355).

Aureliano, the last of the Buendía line, takes up the task of his fathers and grandfathers, "reading and rereading the parchments" (370). It is Aureliano, that "hermetic man" (388), who discovers that the letters are Sanskrit (362), finds the "last keys," and deciphers the hermetic predictions (397). He also does so with the help of the spirit of Melquíades, whom he sees "One burning noon ... against the light of the window ... with his crow's–wing hat like the materialization of a memory that had been in his head since long before he was born" (362). The hat and raven's wings suggest the Norse Wotan, world wanderer who wrested the runes of wisdom from the underworld during his nine day long vigil hanging from Yggdrasil, the World Tree. His is the hermeneutic mystery of the hieroglyph, of writing and of reading. The iconography of the text he composes employs the standard alchemical representation of the Great Work, focusing on the marriage of male and female, King and Queen, Golden Sun and Silver Moon. As in the *Rosarium Philosophorum*, we witness the marriage, in each generation of the family, from its joyful beginning, to the hard work of breakdown through the various operations (coniunctio, fermentatio, putrefactio, impregnatio, ablutio, and sublimatio), that then leads towards the glorious restoration of the couple as the alchemical hermaphrodite, symbol of the stone (Jung, *Transference* Figs.1–10). It is enacted and reenacted over the course of the generations, until the final revelation brings the opus to a close. On that day, however, the sun and moon are darkened by the apocalyptic hurricane that destroys the family.

James Merrill

James Merrill has recently been hailed as "the poet of our moment, a great artist," whose magnificent trilogy, *The Changing Light at Sandover*, is replete with "picturesque poetic ruins, where one can wander almost endlessly, beholding giant splendors simply not available elsewhere" (Bloom 7)[28] High praise for a poem composed with the assistance of the Ouija Board, and taking its diligent (and delighted) readers through a sequence of spiritual lessons, presided over first by a familiar named Ephraim, then by a creature from "B4" time called Mirabell, and finally by the Archangels themselves. Merrill's work has generated a growing body of admiring criticism, all of it acknowledging the technical mastery and power of vision which redeems *The Changing Light* from the banalities of pop–spiritualism. Keeping in mind Charles Berger's crucial point that Merrill achieves a re–sacralization by liberating "mythology from its grounding in any particular culture," Merrill's work can indeed be seen as incorporating the conventional motifs of hermetic myth into a "religious rhetoric" that revives a "lost hieratic discourse" (183), in order to shape what Helen Vendler calls an "expository theology" (91). As such, *The Changing Light at Sandover* is indeed admirable for its "bearing upon our contemporary search for self–transcendence in a world demonstrably without absolutes" (Galassi 181). The poem incorporates many motifs of the hermetic tradition, including the Magus, conjuration, cabala, the four elements, geometric figures, the peacock's tail, the laboratory, and the philosopher's stone—all of which play a central role in Merrill's sacralization of the languages of history and contemporary science.

Merrill specifically invokes four Magi of hermetic tradition—Hermes, Gandalf, Faust, and Prospero. Dame Frances Yates has shown how closely the latter two were linked to the hermetic traditions in Elizabethan England (particularly with John Dee and Edward Kelly). Hermes, the patron of the various philosophies associated with the alchemical tradition, appears in "Ephraim" as "Mrs. Smith" (58) and in "Mirabell" as the "Mercury!" lining the mirror, which enables JM and DJ to "Look *beyond*" themselves, into the twilight world of the spirit, over which Hermes traditionally presides (249). He appears (coyly) in "Scripts for the Pageant" as the "distant guide" in the classroom at Sandover, evoked as the "two floating poles / Of color" that "Undulate and intertwine like snakes" (like the caduceus), "hermetically" sealing the two mediums inside (336). Finally, after appearing with the Buddha and Jesus as the representative of Greek religion, Mercury inscribes the alphabet on the board in the form of a rainbow (446). The rainbow is an appropriate symbol of the messenger of the gods, whose gift—the alphabet—is the one hermetic tradition assigned to Hermes, who, like his Egyptian ancestor Thoth, was traditionally reckoned as the "scribe of the gods" and the 'lord of writing" (Drucker 58).[29]

The opus as a whole, however, is a Faustian endeavor. As in Thomas Mann's great novel, Faust represents the poet, and the alchemical opus represents the mysteries of poesis associated with the descent to the underworld. Faust first makes his presence felt in the poem when a doorbell rings in Athens as JM and DJ sit communing with the dead at the Ouija board. There's no one at the door other than "an unfamiliar / Black dog, leg lifted at our iron gate" (107). The epiphany occurs at twilight (the evening star rippling in the heat above distant pines), provoking the suspicion that the spirit messengers of the Ouija board are "fallen angels," and that the "black poodle" is "A kind of feeler Mephistopheles / Sends out before appearing," as in Goethe's "*Faust*" (144). Nevertheless, a humorous sense of metaphor allows the poet to strike a bargain, since after all "Faust got his youth back—or was it life / Eternal?" (129). In response to the question of whether there ever was a "real Faust," Mirabell, the conjured spirit, tells the boys at the board that the legend is "AN OLD ONE BASED UPON FACT": Faust was Pope Innocent VI, who asked for immortality and was given the power to dispel the plague by boiling water (129–30). Faust, of course, is intimate with the papacy in Marlowe, but in Merrill, he is more poet–scientist than Anti–Christ: Merrill replaces the devils of the "fierce original" bargain with those "Ministers of eternal tedium" who will lead them through "ten thousand" lessons in the mysteries of the universe (266). These lessons—punctuated throughout with poems, some dictated and transcribed, others composed in reflection—eventually lead to the transfiguration of Merrill and David Jackson, until their souls are sufficiently refined to communicate with the angels "Scripts for the Pageant." It is therefore appropriate that, shortly before the epiphany of the angel Michael (which concludes "Mirabell"), Mephisto's black dog appears briefly again, this time as "THE WOUNDED BLACK HOUND OF HEAVEN" the poet runs over en route to a dinner party (270). After this point, the demon yields to the angel, Mephisto to Michael.

From Marlowe to Mann, Faust has been associated with the occult arts of the hermetic tradition, part scientist, part poet. Those arts are predicated on the reduction of molecular compounds to the base elements, for the purpose of re–creation. This occurs throughout *The Changing Light* as a metaphor for science, as the Angels preside over the experiments of the bat–winged souls in the research lab, where souls are recycled and given those higher densities necessary to restore the lost paradise on earth, and to confer immortality upon our species. To achieve this ultimate goal of the opus, the alchemical spirits manipulate the base elements of the creation, which take various forms in the poem: letters, numbers, formulas, geometric figures, cells, and atoms. In fact, the entire poem results from the manipulation of letters, as the hands rove through the alphabet on the Ouija board. In the Kabbalistic tradition, the letters are given numerical equivalencies, and recombined to produce spiritually efficacious names of the deity and his messengers. Hence, Merrill gives his bat–messengers, angels, and human beings numerical equivalents: in fact, the whole creation is the result of a "formula made flesh" (225). Like Borges and H.D., Merrill uses the Kabbalistic image of God manipulating the letters of the Hebrew alphabet to create the universe, a metaphor which links genesis to poesis.[30] But Merrill characteristically combines the holy with the homely to establish this metaphor, giving us a glimpse of God and his twin sister sitting together in "poor lamplight, / Her deft hands full of mending, His roughened ones / Forming letters which the flame, tipped blue / As if with cold, breathes fitful life into" (494). This marvelous image of God forming fiery letters and breathing life into them hearkens way back to the Kabbalistic creation myths, according to which the twenty–two letters of the Hebrew alphabet are "the very elements by which God brings the world into being. For the Kabbalist, God's writing is the world" (Drucker 129). There is also a Greek basis for this hermetic tradition: since the Greek word for the alphabet, *stoicheia*, also means elements, "the letters had an atomistic and elemental character" (Drucker 56).

Hence, the numbers and letters of the formula correspond to the base elements of the creation, not only earth, air, fire, and water, but also the cells and atoms which compose the building blocks of the physical world. Hermetic metaphors of creation (of world, and of poem) proceed by a reduction of material compounds to base elements, followed by a sequence of transfigurations, as numerical formula becomes word becomes flesh. Thus, the emphasis on the four elements throughout *The Changing Light* serves as a metaphor of creativity in general (of genesis as well as of poesis). The spirit guide in "Mirabell" is referred to as a "mathematics master," and his lessons show how numbers serve as "CRUDE / FIGURES OF SPEECH," and as symbols of the five elements of the creation: earth, air, fire, water, and nature (320). The formulaic ratio 12:88 is a cipher of the soul itself, used to designate the relation between body and soul, angel and bat, psyche and environment (238). There are "Basic Formulas" for each individual soul—those of JM and DJ are provided for us, and they record the number of previous lives, the ratio of animal to human density, and a kind of "talent rating" (143). Certain soul densities, moreover, have numbers too (10 for the Jewish, 5 for the pentameter of the poet soul, and 14 for the Atlantean bat souls that dictate the poem). Also the fact that "THE ONE UNSPOKEN REVELATION MUST DWELL / IN THE NUMBER 5" (245) accounts for the five regular members of the Ouija board sessions: two living (JM and DJ), two dead (Maria and Auden), and one spirit (in three forms—Ephraim, Mirabell, and Michael). In "Scripts for the Pageant," the 5 is replaced by the 8, an octagonal configuration composed of the four mortal souls (JM, DJ, Wystan, and Maria), and the four immortal archangels (Michael, Emmanuel, Raphael, and Gabriel). The number twelve comes up during the ten lessons of the archangels, each one of the four having three natures (342).

These numerical formulas constitute a kind mythical mathematics of postmodernism, reminiscent of Charles Demuth's famous painting of the figure 5 (based on a poem by William Carlos Williams), or of Adrian Leverkühn's speculation with the numbers, notes, and elements of musical composition in Mann's *Doctor Faustus*. Keeping in mind that these numerical formulae serve as metaphors (at the very least) of poetic (if not of divine) creation, we might note other metaphors of the basic elements to which the world of *The Changing Light* is reduced. The hermetic notion of the four elements, in fact, becomes a basic structural principle of the poem as a whole, as well as the inspiration of many of its minuter beauties, such as the nine septets celebrating Mirabell's "UNION OF THE ELEMENTS / THUS: WATER (MM) EARTH (WHA) AIR (JM) FIRE / (MY POUR SELF) & LAST THE SHAPING HAND OF NATURE (DJ)" (159–61).[31] The entire poem is based upon this union: each of the major players in the poem performs the role of one of the elements; four of Mirabell's lessons are focused on the larger powers associated with the colors blue, red, yellow, and green (210f.); the colors of the "Minute intelligences that indwell" the DNA molecule are "red, blue, black, yellow, and white elements" (203); in "Scripts For the Pageant," each of the four archangels is associated with the elements, and with the five senses of God B, those five senses with which they endow the foetus in the womb, when Robert Morse is reborn in the "Coda" of the trilogy (532–41). Such alignments between colors, elements, archangels, senses, and basic properties of the world are characteristic of the hermetic tradition, which typically signifies the "succession of processes" in the opus by the different colors of the peacock's tail (Roberts 56).

The elements of the opus also include atoms and cells, frequent images of the basic constituents of creation throughout *The Changing Light*. Book 2 of the poem, "Mirabell," begins and ends with a vision of the cells as those minute particulars of matter which contain the intelligence of the whole system: it begins with the poet pondering "substances," "mitochondria," "Protons and Neutrons," "Polypeptides," "Enzyme, ion, what not, millionfold / (Down to the last bacterial organelle)" (110). It moves to Mirabell's proclamation that "THE ATOM IS OUR UNIT THE WHOLE GREENHOUSE / IS BUT A CELL, COMPLEX YET MANAGEABLE ALL MATTER / THERE4 IS PART OF THAT CELL," and that the sun itself is the single cell of a "HEALING CORPUSCLE" (210, 212). Finally, "Mirabell" ends with the angel Michael's description of God as "THE ACCUMULATED INTELLIGENCE IN CELLS SINCE THE DEATH / OF THE FIRST DISTANT CELL" (276). "Scripts for the Pageant" continues with Mirabell's evocation of "THE RADIANT CELLS ... PALATIAL ... LUMINOUS ... WEIGHTLESS DOMES" which the archangels inhabit (290). Mirabell's lesson moves rapidly from the cells of the mineral, vegetable, reptilian, and human realms—distinctions characteristic of the hermetic categories of the great chain of being)—to a vision of "THE STRUCTURELESS STRUCTURE OF THE SOUL CELL, / OR MORE PROPERLY THE SUBLIME STRUCTURE OF THE CELLS OF / GOD BIOLOGY" (290).

Each of these visionary passages presents the cell as that biological particle which contains the whole within itself. The cell, that is to say, is what I call a hologlyph, a hieroglyphic image which, like a hologram, contains the whole within each part (like the Aleph in Borges, or the cipher in H.D.). For Merrill's world in *The Changing Light* is a Blakean world of minute particulars, of grains of sand which contain the world. Arthur Koestler uses the word "'holons' for these subsystems which are both wholes and parts" (Capra 80).[32] Merrill, like many other postmodernists, is involved in a quest for such fundamental hieroglyphs, symbols which contain the whole in each smaller part. By the same token, the atom may be seen as the even more fundamental form upon which the larger structures of the whole are built, just as the entire earth may be seen as a single "NUCLEUS OF MINDS" (118). The poem represents the biblical Genesis as a "parable of fission," an allegory, in fact, of the creation and contention within the atom: Cain and Abel standing for its negative and positive forces, a conflict reenacted in subsequent generations ("Shem and Shaun, Rebekah's twins") by a sequence of "genealogical chain reactions" (116, 192). This elemental strife subsists on all levels of creation, from the smallest "froth of electrons," to the "brain's evolving cortex," to the "crust / World" of power stations created by the bat–winged souls of Atlantis (126).

A final way of figuring these basic elements— in addition to the use of letters, formulas, numbers, cells, and atoms—is to use geometric shapes (like the pyramid, which combines the point, the square, the triangle, and the quincunx). Perhaps the most popular geometric figure of hermetic speculation is the pyramid, to which Merrill devotes the long section of "Mirabell" dealing with Akhenaton's experiments (126). Near the end of the poem, a clever sonnet combines the pyramid with the simplest of geometric figures—the "Point of light" at the "apex" which represents the power and glory of the divine (in a way similar to the "point which became Thought, where all the figures were drawn" in Eco (*Foucault's Pendulum* 18), and to the Aleph in Borges. A similar synecdoche occurs in Merrill's sonnet on the diacritical dot in the arabic formula *bismallah*, a dot which Merrill calls the "Whole Point" (454), and which Stephen Yenser relates to the Sufi tradition, according to which the dot "is single in itself but embraces all phenomena" (299). As in Borges and Eco, the point symbolizes the "Divine Source ... the Prototype of the world (299). It is a hologlyph. But the base of a pyramid, beneath the point, is a square. Hence, JM's dream of a dance floor composed of four squares lit from beneath to form a "fifth that pulsed in the pitch–black terrain" is later glossed by Mirabell, who remarks that "YR SQUARE OF THE 4 / COLORS IS OF COURSE INFINITY" (204, 210). The color square, that is to say, is a hologlyph, a geometric figure which represents the whole system of time and space, the four elements of which cells, atoms, solar systems, and galaxies are formed. A related figure is the "MAGIC / PENTAGRAM UNDERLYING THE ENTIRE DUAL REALM / OF DENSITY," the mysteries of the whole system of seasons, suns, and elements contained in a single digit, the number 5 (230). The number 5 is also associated with the basic metrical unit of the poem, the iambic pentameter line (240). Furthermore, the square scratched in the mud by the first hominid is evoked as the first "CRUDE SYMBOL," which, like the "FIRST OF CHILDREN'S DESIGNS," figures the emergence of intelligence in our species (241). Later in "Scripts for the Pageant" the square emerges again in the form Sir Thomas Browne called the quincunx, as "NATURE'S 4 GENTLEMEN" (the archangels) "STAND FOURSQUARE," each corner representing an emanation from God B standing in the center.

In Sir Thomas Browne's famous essay, the quincunx becomes the fundamental figure of the creation, in all its forms. It is a kind of geometrical cipher, the key to the interpretation of the vast hieroglyphic of God's text, the world. Alchemical tradition typically strove to reduce the mysteries of the opus to a single figure which contained the whole within a minute particular (a hologlyph). For John Dee, this was the Monas hieroglyphica, a figure composed of a cross supporting a circle with a dot in the center and a crescent parabola intersecting the top. Like the squaring of the circle, with the use of the triangle, the Monas was for Dee the single "Figure conteyning all the secrets of the Treatise both great and small" (Fabricius 198). The Monas combines "the signs of the seven planets, plus the symbol for the zodiacal sign Aries, representing fire," and it is therefore "related to 'the stupendous fabric of the Hebrew letters.' It is a 'Cabalistic grammar'" (Yates, *Occult Philosophy* 83).

Merrill's quincunx is a typically witty variation on the theme: "In a work this long," he writes, it is "Madness to imagine one could do / Without the apt ideogram or two" (474). His ideogram comes with help of Yeats and the angel Gabriel, who instructs DJ to inscribe a double X on the board, separated by a convex arc at the base of the top and the top of the bottom X's. A horizontal line in each X forms a triangle within one half of each. Merrill notes that the whole figure has a "surprise resemblance" to *A Vision*, though in Yeats / The double cone, if I recall, gyrates" (475).[33] The figure represents man standing on the earth, arms upraised towards "REASON & LIGHT," the horizontal line forming the hourglass of time (with a "MINOAN WAIST"), the inverse shadow of which (doubling the X beneath the crescent) represents time (and the atom's) reversibility (474). The entire figure is hologlyphic, a part containing the whole—mankind, "TIME ITSELF. ALL HISTORY, YES, IN 4 QUICK STROKES OF THE SCRIBE'S HAND" (475).

If you set one of these X's "sideways," you create a related geometric figure (of Minoan origin): the "Twinbladed axe" which God himself (universal architect, ultimate patron of freemasonry) later inscribes upon the board in the form of the "Quincunx where ghosts of Five and Twelve perambulate" (493). This occurs in the last lesson of the "Scripts" as a kind of blessing, one appropriate to the completion of an Opus in which genesis and poesis are correlated. The figure is inscribed by moving the cup from "YES to NO to A to Z to YES," forming both a cross and a quincunx, and encompassing all of the letters and numbers which represent the basic elements of the creation (both of world and of text). Hence, Merrill uses the mythical geometry of hermetic and apocalyptic traditions to sum up everything the poem has to say about divine symmetry. A language of form (grand design, complete design, substance and sense, plan, no accident) is supplemented by a geometrical iconography of form, to create the kind of mythical mathematics so frequently found in postmodernism, which uses such symbolism to approach the mysteries of poesis and genesis.

The ultimate goal of the alchemical opus is apocalyptic: to recombine these fundamental elements, figured by the square, or quincunx, in order to create a perfected form of matter—a spiritual substance variously referred to as the earthly paradise, the elixir vita or the philosopher's stone. In *The Changing Light*, this seems to involve the insulation of the cell to protect it from the destructive powers of nuclear energy, so that new souls may be cloned to inhabit the earthly paradise to come. Maria identifies mankind's "IMMORTAL WORK" with the restoration of 'PARADISE" (455), which the alchemists took as their ultimate goal of the opus. The Great Work, as it was called, took place in the laboratory of the alchemist—Merrill's R/Lab, where Mirabell and the bat-winged souls of Atlantis proceed with their experiments on the human soul, cloning the energies of the immortal five to increase the densities of the great, and to immunize the souls of the many, in preparation for the day when a thermonuclear Paradise is reestablished on earth. These experiments are fundamentally alchemical, since they involve the transfiguration of the base elements of the material world, and the sublimation of the soul structure of cell and atom, which are "REFINED IN LIVE / ALEMBICS THRU THE CENTURIES" (497), in order to produce "A RACE PERFECTED AND / IMMORTAL" (439). As Jung points out, "immortality" was the "great hope of the alchemists," and it was typically symbolized by the "*elixir vitae*" distilled in the alembic (Jung, *Transference* 150).

Merrill's symbols for the completed opus include gems and the peacock, frequently associated in hermetic iconography with paradise and the philosopher's stone. Gemstones are sprinkled throughout *The Changing Light* as symbols of the opus (both alchemical and poetic). Mother Nature, for example, sets the scene for the penultimate pageant, in Lesson 9 of the "Scripts," with a lake, a well, and "GREEN TREES HUNG WITH UNCUT GEM." The image of the tree of life, planted in paradise, and hung with gemstones associated with the seven planets, is an old hermetic symbol of the completion of the great work—as for example in the magnificent plate by M. Merian from the 17th century, the *Janitor pansophus*, reprinted in A.E. Waite's *Museum Hermeticum* of 1893 (Fabricius 161). It shows a star–studded hermaphrodite holding a twinbladed ax at the center foreground, with seven large trees and twelve smaller behind him on a magic mountain, with the corresponding signs of the seven planets and the twelve houses of the zodiac inscribed on the trees. At the center of the circles of the macrocosm hovering above the hermaphrodite we find John Dee's Monas, beneath the four Hebrew letters of the Tetragrammaton. From these four letters the whole creation flows, just as the poem itself does: in *The Changing Light*, the alchemical opus is linked to poesis by the manipulation of letters, and by the compression of vast quantities of information "INTO THE SORT OF GEM" Merrill is so adept at fashioning (454).[34] This compliment comes from Auden's ghost by way of introducing a sonnet on the name of Allah, and it suggests that the many lyric forms Merrill weaves into his tapestry are like gemstones set in the crown on the peacock's head, poesis itself a matter of "transmuting the daily bread of experience" in the "smithy" of the soul, as Joyce puts it in *A Portrait* (221).

Like the gemstone (found in H.D. too), the peacock is a polysemous symbol frequently found in the hermetic tradition. In early Christian art the peacock symbolized the Resurrection, and, since it molts annually, came to represent the universe, full of shining stars and suns set on the deep blue of the firmament, like the eyes in a peacock's tail. In alchemical speculation, the technical term for the peacock's tail, "cauda pavonis," referred specifically to that stage in the opus, immediately after the mortificatio, when those numerous colors appeared in the vessel which announce the completed opus (Campbell, *Creative Myth* 501–03). This links the peacock to the cycle of the nekyia, since it appears immediately after the mortificatio, and the ocular symbolism of its tail plumes suggests that long lineage of mythical speculation which associates both birds and eyes with the underworld and the maze. The symbol of the peacock spreading its tail is to be found in one of the most splendid pages from the famous 18th century alchemical text, by Salomon Trismosin, known as *La Toyson d'or*, a later version of the *Splendor solis* (Roberts, Pl.IX). The plate could serve as an illustration for much of the action of Merrill's poem, for it shows us men and women in an earthly paradise, surrounding the peacock, which is suspended in the crucible in the center. They are engaged in the various activities associated with the afterworld of *The Changing Light*: picnics, music, poetry, reading, and love making. It is a masque of the dead, transfigured by the reduction to their elements, reborn as spiritual companions of the peacock.

Taken together as an image of transfiguration, these various motifs of the hermetic tradition—particularly the manipulation of letters, numbers, and geometrical figures—serve as Merrill's metaphor for poesis, that process whereby the ordinary details of daily life, of history, and of science are re–mythologized. The hermetic motifs confer aesthetic coherence and archetypal resonance upon a large, encyclopedic poem, in which the language of alchemy and Kabbalah is updated with reference to contemporary science, in order to produce a sacralized reflection of a secular reality. The poem combines the cosmic with the domestic, the vatic with the quotidian, the spiritual with the material. All of this links Merrill with his modernist precursors (like Thomas Mann, James Joyce, D.H. Lawrence, or H.D.), who also saw the alchemical opus as an allegory of poesis.[35] Merrill's hermeticism, however, emerges from these precursors in the same way that Rosicrucianism emerged from the Renaissance: the elegant mannerism of the postmodern Magus regenerates and transforms the "harmonious naturalism" of the modernist.[36]

Chapter 4
Voices From the Well

The single most important mythic symbol for the postmodernists was the descent to the underworld. In the wide range of postmodernist works in which the myth occurs, the central theme is the revelation of those fundamental ideas which give shape and significance to life and art, ideas for which the modernists developed a complex variety of terms. The underworld has from primordial times been linked to alchemy, the maze, and the Great Goddess, by such symbols as the crucible, caves, baths, and mountains. Hugh Kenner noted in his study of Pound that the *nekyia*, or descent to the underworld, may be the oldest of those myths upon which the modernists drew (147). The earliest literary version of the myth concerns the descent of the Sumerian Goddess Inanna through the seven gateways of the underworld, where she is killed by her sister Ereshkigal's eye of death and hung up on a peg for three days and nights before being rescued by her maternal grandfather Enki. The story was first inscribed in a Sumero–Akkadian script in about 1750 B.C.E., although it surely condensed a long oral and ritual tradition. Pieces of it were among the fragments associated with the stories of Gilgamesh and his journeys through the underworld, first translated in 1872, but much more of the story was recovered during the 1899–1900 digs conducted by the University of Pennsylvania. Then the spectacular findings of Sir Leonard Wooley, who directed the excavations of the Royal Cemetery of Ur, c.2500 B.C.E., were published at the height of the modernist movement (*Ur of the Chaldees* in 1929, and then the two volumes of excavation reports in 1934), and thence made their way into the work of Thomas Mann (among others), who was working on *Joseph and His Brothers* at this time. The Egyptian Books of the Dead, collated and transcribed by groups of priests in 1650 B.C.E. (but probably dating back to 3500 B.C.E.), also describe a journey through doorways and chambers from death to rebirth. Along with the Sumerian material, these books establish many of the key images and themes long to be associated with literary and religious redactions of the descent to the underworld: images such as mountains, doorways, chambers, shed clothing, and gates, and themes such as judgment, revelation, and renewal recur throughout the tradition, all the way up to the present. The complete details of the Egyptian *nekyia* were first published by Sir Wallis Budge 1904, at the beginning of modernism, while the primitive mythologies of the sun's night–sea journey were explored in the same year by Leo Frobenius in *Das Zeitalter des Sonnengottes*.[37]

While these major publications from Budge, Frobenius, and Wooley (spanning the years 1904 to 1934) brought the archaic imagery of the descent to the underworld into the mainstream of modernist mythography, literature, and art, exciting discoveries in philology and archaeology enriched the contemporary understanding of our Classical heritage. Oswald Spengler used the myth of the sun's descent to describe the modern world in his *Der Untergang des Abendlandes* or *Decline of the West* of 1923, perhaps taking the metaphor of the sun's "untergehen" or "going under" from Nietzsche's *Thus Spake Zarathustra*, in which it is a central motif (Kaufman 115). Furthermore, as Joseph Campbell put it, "Nietzsche was but twenty–eight when *The Birth of Tragedy* appeared in 1872—the very year when his elder countryman Heinrich Schliemann was unearthing Troy, to reveal within Homer's mythic world its core of historical fact" (*Occidental* 142), while it was during the years between 1921 and 1935 that Sir Arthur Evans published his four volume account of the excavations of *The Palace of Minos* on Crete. Such work greatly contributed to the Modernist's understanding of the mythic material of the Classical past, and often (as in Nietzsche, Frobenius, and Spengler) specifically focused on the imagery of the descent to the underworld. Similar breakthroughs occurred in anthropology: Jane Ellen Harrison's *Prolegomena*, of 1903, for example, focuses almost entirely on the Eleusinian mysteries and the story of Persephone's abduction by Hades. This story, recorded most fully in the Homeric Hymn to Demeter, is one of the most important and well known Classical myths of the descent in the work of Pound, Lawrence, Mann, and in many postmodernist practitioners of Eliot's mythical method, right up to Julio Cortázar and Eudora Welty.[38]

Hades is a place where the basic plan of their existence (i.e., their fates or destinies) is revealed: to the former by his mother, and to the latter by his father. It is also, as Ronald MacDonald has put it, a "burial place of memory," one where the fundamental stories of the tradition are stored: hence the extensive catalogue of noteworthy men and women in the *Odyssey*. The notion that the underworld is a place where the fundamental forms of existence and the archetypal stories are stored or revealed is one which recurs frequently throughout postmodernism, and is the aspect of Hades which I intend to emphasize in this book. The Classical term for these 'fundamental forms' is *eidola*, the Platonic word for the pure Forms or Ideas authored by God which provide a kind of cosmic blueprint for the creation. As James Hillman has recently pointed out, in his interpretation of the myth of the abduction of Persephone, "Hades has a hidden connection with *eidos* and *eidolon*, the archetypal intelligence given in images" (*Dream* 121), so that "The word *eidolon* relates with Hades himself (*aidoneus*) and with *eidos*, ideational forms and shapes, the ideas that form and shape life" (*Dream* 51). These fundamental forms manifest themselves in a wide variety of geometrical figures catalyzed by the descent. While these figures were frequently psychologized by the modernists (perhaps under the influence of Freud and Jung), postmodernists like Cortázar, Lessing, Pynchon, and Merrill turn to modern physics for metaphorical analogies in their descents. It is a move from the archetypes of the unconscious to the energy fields of subnuclear particles.

Jorge Luis Borges

The descent to the underworld is a central motif in the short stories of Jorge Luis Borges. These little gems exemplify the way the nekyia catalyzes the revelation of what Borges called "ancient forms, forms incorruptible and eternal" ('formas antiguas, formas incorruptibles y eternas') (*Labyrinths* 170; *Obras* 117). These "ancient forms" are represented by a variety of geometrical forms revealed at the climax of the descent.

In "The Aleph," the descent is into the cellar beneath the dining room in the home of Carlos Argentino Danieri, poet and first cousin of Beatriz Viterbo, with whom the narrator is still in love some five years after her death in 1929. It is the lure of the many photographs of Beatriz that eventually leads Borges to his descent into the cellar: the names Beatriz and Danieri surely meant to evoke Dante's *Inferno*. While objecting to the pedantry and pretentiousness of Danieri, the narrator is nevertheless drawn to the Viterbos home "one day toward the end of October," the time of the year associated with the Celtic underworld, celebrated as All Soul's Day in the Catholic Church, and as the Day of the Dead in Mexico. Danieri calls to say that the house which "would always stand for Beatriz" is going to be torn down. Carlos Argentino tells Borges that this is terrible because he will be unable to finish his long poem ("The Earth") "without the house because down in the cellar there was an Aleph. He explained that an Aleph is one of the points in space that contains all other points" (*Borges* 159).

The revelation of the Aleph is predicated upon a rather humorous version of the descent, here down a cellar stairway so steep as to have been forbidden the young Carlos Danieri, who, compelled by the suggestion that "there was a world down there," nevertheless takes the plunge, stumbling and falling before seeing the Aleph for the first time. When the narrator arrives at the house to see the Aleph for himself, he first addresses a portrait of his "darling Beatriz, Beatriz now gone forever" (*Borges* 160), before undertaking his descent (just as Dante's descent into the *Inferno* is preceded by a vision of Beatrice). Borges has his Virgil too: Carlos prepares him for the *nekyia* with a glass of pseudo–cognac and instructions. The scene suggests one of Poe's many versions of Hades (such as the "Cask of Amontillado" or "The Pit and the Pendulum"): Borges swallows his libation and descends the narrow stairway into a cellar which "was something of a pit" (*Borges* 160). After lying prone in a blackness rendered nearly absolute after Carlos shuts the trapdoor, Borges hilariously fantasizes a literal descent to the realm of the dead: he has been "locked in a cellar by a lunatic, after gulping down a glassful of poison!" (*Borges* 160). Immediately after the shocked suspicion that "*Carlos had to kill me*," the Aleph reveals itself to Borges.

That the revelation of the archetypal form of the Aleph succeeds a realistically portrayed descent to an ordinary place familiar to readers is absolutely characteristic of the journey into Hades in postmodernism. Equally typical is the sense of the revelation of all life's secrets in those places. The Aleph is "the microcosm of the alchemists and Cabalists" (*Borges* 160); "the only place on earth where all places are seen from every angle, each standing clear" (159); "one of the points in space that contains all other points" (159); "the first letter of the

Hebrew alphabet," which stands for "the pure and boundless godhead" (162), the source of all Creation. The Aleph, that is to say, is the *eidos* of all *eidola*, Broch's "*Urbild aller Bilder*," that ultimate pattern which gives shape and significance to all things. It is the part which contains the whole, a kind of 'hologlyph' of the universe analogous to what the Hindu's called the *bindu*, that ineffable point in space (Eliot's "still point of the turning world" and the "Fearful Sphere of Pascal," of which Borges writes in the essay of that title) where the Divine energy roars into manifestation, creating the world of phenomenality. Hence, when looking into the Aleph, Borges sees all minute particulars in their universality (the "awful omneity of all in each" as Coleridge put it), just as Dante, after his descent through the Inferno, sees "the universal form / that binds these things" as the "single volume" of a divine book "bound by Love, of which the universe is the scattered leaves" (*Paradiso* 33. 91–2; 86–7). Additionally, however, the Aleph is a source of inspiration, specifically providing the material of Danieri's poem about the earth, and a source of "the numberless texts" revealed to Danieri in his cellar. The descent into the underworld of the cellar, that is to say, is an image of *poesis*, a metaphor for the way texts are created: for it is in the cellar that Danieri, "the master," develops his pictures (*Borges* 159).

In "The Garden of Forking Paths," the key to the text which is in itself the entire world and all of time also occurs in the context of a journey to the underworld, although here Hades is set in a little train stop outside of London called Ashgrove. The hero of the tale, Dr. Yu Tsun, travels to this appropriately named destination (grove of ashes) by train at dusk on what he tells us is the day of his death. That Dr. Tsun "was going to the village of Ashgrove but bought a ticket for a more distant station" (*Labyrinths* 21) is a coy way of remarking that the journey is one that proceeds beyond the grove of ashes into eternity. The ferryboat of classical myth and of Dante has here been replaced by the train, upon which Dr. Tsun rides like "a man already dead" (22), fleeing the man who will be in fact instrumental in his death, one Captain Richard Madden. Getting off the train, Dr. Tsun asks some boys if he has arrived in Ashgrove, then gives them his last coin after they direct him to Dr. Stephen Albert's house: the way is long they say, but he won't get lost if turns left at every crossroad. All souls on their journey into the afterlife must offer a coin to Charon; hence, after doing so, Dr. Tsun immediately *descends* towards his end, going *down* some stone steps, then "*downhill*" along a solitary road in the darkness, details which evoke the imagery of Hades.

One of the oldest mythological images of the underworld which we know anything about is the symbol of the labyrinth, which appears over the gateway into Virgil's Hades in the *Aeneid*, and, much further back in time, at the entrance to the stone earthmound of Newgrange, outside of Dublin. As Eliade remarks, the labyrinth "was at one and the same time the theater of initiation and the place where the dead gathered" (75). Hence it is logical that Dr. Tsun, after arriving in Ashgrove and paying his coin for the crossing at dusk, should be reminded that the instruction to turn left "was the common procedure for discovering the central point of certain labyrinths" (22). The "central point" here is analogous to the Aleph, that place where all the various points on the compass of the world originate and terminate. As Dr. Tsun proceeds to this point where his destiny will be met, his ancestral past enlightened, and the mysteries of the world revealed, realistic details associated with the nekyia continue to assert themselves. The road continues to descend, and eventually forks "among the now confused meadows" to bring him to the "tall rusty gate" outside the "grove and pavilion" (23); similarly, the road Virgil has Aeneas follow diverges towards either Tartarus or the Elysian fields "beneath the ramparts of great Dis," with its "giant gateway" and "solid, adamantine pillars" (6. 715–730).

After being led across the threshold by a man bearing a lantern whose face is later described has having "something unalterable about it, even immortal" (26), Tsun experiences a sequence of revelations which eventually lead to murder and death on the gallows. The heart of these revelations has to do with the book and maze which Dr. Tsun's great grandfather, Ts'ui Pên, has famously left behind him. The maze, Dr. Stephen Albert (our immortal) informs us, is the novel itself, which Dr. Tsun has until now cursed as "an indeterminate heap of contradictory drafts" (24), and that novel turns out to be an image of time. One of the most persistent features of the nekyia retained by the postmodernists is the encounter with the ancestral past in the crypt of the underworld. Odysseus meets his mother, and Aeneas his father, in scenes set in the underworld where their fates are revealed. In Eliot, Pound, and Joyce all the great voices of their literary forefathers are echoed in complex patchworks of quotations.[39] Co–incidentally with this encounter with the ancestors is the notion of revelation: hence, Dr. Albert offers the great grandson of Ts'ui Pên "the explanation of the novel's contradictions" (26), and says that he has "re–established the primordial organization" of the novel, and hence of the world of time which is the hidden theme of the novel. This sense of "primordial organization" corresponds to that revelation of the informing archetype which shapes life and art associated with the nekyia in postmodernism. In Borges, the revelation provides a key to deciphering a text (Ts'ui Pên's *The Garden of Forking Paths*) which is in itself an "image of the universe" which "embraces *all* possibilities of time" (28). Like the Aleph, the text bears within itself the entire Creation (as the cabalists argued the biblical texts do). In order to decipher its mysteries, however, we must descend into that "humid garden ... infinitely saturated with invisible persons" where lurks the "enemy" of death and fate (28).

Another Borges story in which the deciphering of a cryptic text coincides with a realistically presented descent into the underworld is the detective story called "Death and the Compass." While this is not the place to explore the complexities of cabalistic speculation in the story, we can at least note that the revelation of the key to the sequence of murders which the protagonist Erik Lönnrot is investigating occurs in a ruined mansion which Borges takes pains to set in a postmodernist, urban underworld.[40] Like Dr. Tsun, Lönnrot arrives at the place of revelation and death via train, which takes him to the south side of the city into an industrial suburb which lies on the other side of a "blind little river of muddy water" surely meant to evoke Virgil's "Tartarean Acheron," just as the "turbid, puddled plain" and the dogs which populate the deserted landscape seem suggestive of the "melancholy marshland" which Aeneas encounters on the other side of the "whirlpool thick / with sludge" in the *Aeneid* (6. 578; 391–

92). Trees also inform the fabled iconography of Hades: "poplars and the drooping willow" outside the "crumbling homes of Death" in Homer (10. 482–84); oak forest, golden bough, and "myrtle grove" in Virgil (6. 275–282; 585); a dark wood in Dante; and the "black eucalypti" which surround the "villa of Triste–le–Roy" in Borges (83). The entrance to this appropriately name villa, "a rusty wrought–iron fence" and "insurmountable gate" which seems to swing open of its own accord (83) recalls the "tall, rusty gate" of "The Garden" (23), and both evoke the iconography of doorways omnipresent in descriptions of Hades: from Virgil's "giant gateway" and "sacred doors" which open with "hinges grating horribly" (6. 731; 760–61), to Dante's gates with "Abandon all Hope" inscribed above them; to Milton's doorway out of Pandemonium, guarded by Sin and Death; and at last to Borges' "insurmountable gate" which creaks open with a "laborious passivity" (83).

Once through the gateway and in amongst the eucalypti of the courtyard, it is appropriate that Lönnrot find a "two–faced Hermes" which casts a "giant shadow" (83), appropriate because Hermes is the guide of souls (*psychopompos*) to the land of the dead in the *Odyssey* (24. 1–15). To enter the villa, Lönnrot must descend to a vault and open a trap door at the far end, which leads up to the place of revelation and death. For in the villa, Lönnrot is accosted by Red Scharlach, who reveals the mysteries of the planned sequence of murders before killing the detective. That the secrets of plot informing the story are revealed in the underworld is consistent with the linkage between Hades and the *eidola* which give shape and significance to life noted above. And indeed, Lönnrot expects to discover that "Secret Name" of the cabalists, in which the "immediate knowledge of all things that will be, which are and which have been in the universe" is encoded (78). This refers to the "Tetragrammaton—the name of God, JHVH" (86) which Scharlach has used as the clue to the sequence of murders executed to lure Lönnrot to his death. Scharlach presumably has special access to the secret mysteries of names and letters, not only because he is a kind of debased cabalist, but also because he is a type of Odin, Norse God of wisdom and possessor of the runes, those "holy words" which "provide the necessary link between human beings and the other world" (Leeming 102). In Norse myth, Odin acquires the runes via a descent into the underworld: he hangs nine days and nights from the windy world tree, Yggdrasil, during which time he peered downwards and "grasped the runes" (Leeming 102). In "Death and the Compass," Red Scharlach tells Lönnrot that for "Nine days and nine nights I lay in agony in this desolate, symmetrical villa" (84), during which time the world is revealed to him as a "labyrinth, from which it was impossible to flee" (85). He then conceives the plan of weaving "a labyrinth around the man who had imprisoned my brother" upon which the plot of the story is based (84).

Borges uses the labyrinth, geometrical figures, and elaborate symmetries in his plot to suggest those "ancient forms, forms incorruptible and eternal" revealed in the underworld: the "equilateral triangle" sent to Treviranus; the four cardinal points of the compass on the paint shop sign where the first murder occurs; the "pointless symmetries" and "maniacal repetitions" of the villa (83); the "perfect rhomb" where a "punctual death" awaits Lönnrot (86); and the "diamonds" of yellow, green, and red which divide the sky above the villa (86). All of these figures are meant to suggest that symmetry in time and space (82) which comprises the universal order encoded in the Secret Name, which, like the Aleph and like Ts'ui Pên's labyrinthine novel, is a hologlyph, a part which contains the whole, and which is revealed to Lönnrot just before his death in an abandoned villa, belonging to the King of Sadness, Red Scharlach, Mafioso Lord of an industrial underworld.

Two other *invenciones* by Borges elaborate on the fable of the underworld, without however, strictly speaking, employing the mythical method, since they are set not in the ordinary context of daily life, but in fantastic landscapes of the imagination. In "The Immortal," the magnificent Piranesiesque temple where, the narrator tells us, "Everything was elucidated" for him (113), is reached by a journey which suggests the imagery of the *nekyia*. After wandering across deserts of black sand and encountering peoples "who worship only Tartarus," the narrator (later identified as Homer) collapses and dreams of a labyrinth with a water jug in the center. He awakens "in an oblong stone niche no larger than a common grave," dug out in the slope of a mountain, at the foot of which is "an impure stream ... clogged with debris and sand" (108). (Given the setting of this story in the ancient Near East, it is important to note that for the Sumerians, the Egyptians, and the Babylonians, the entrance to the underworld, through which the sun journeys nightly, is situated in the mountains).[41] Across from the mountain, and across the sluggish, stygian river is the City of the Immortals, where the narrator goes at sunset after drinking the "dark water" of the river, which reminds him of the "'black water of the Aisepos'" (108). Imagery of the descent continues on the yonder shore, as the narrator takes refuge from the sun in a cave, in the rear of which is a pit and "stairway which sank down abysmally into the darkness below" (109). He then finds himself lost in an infernal complex of circuitous chambers, each with nine doors linking and multiplying into a "deep stone network" (109) resembling the Cretan labyrinth below the Palace of Knossos. He finally discovers a well shaft leading upwards out of "the blind region of dark interwoven labyrinths into the resplendent City" (110). The imagery here suggests Dante's ascent up Satan's leg from the infernal pit to the purgatorial mountain. What follows then is that sense of the revelation of the "invisible design" or "secret form" of the world, of which the City is a "last symbol" forged by the Immortals (114; 113), which is the traditional climax of the descent in postmodernism.

Several other Borges stories are explicitly based on the descent to the underworld. "The God's Script" is set entirely in an infernal prison, vaguely Aztec in nature, in which a profound revelation of one of those "ancient forms, forms incorruptible and eternal" (170), with which we began our discussion, occurs. In the nearly absolute darkness of his prison, the narrator ("Tzinacácan, magician of the pyramid of Qaholom") meditates upon "a magical sentence" written by god on the first day of Creation. His reflections proceed from the "generic enigma of a sentence written by a god," to the concept of a "single word" in which the entire universe and the "sum of time" is contained (171). When the jailer interrupts the nightmare of being buried by grains of sand (an allusion to Blake's world in the grain of sand), the narrator experiences a vision, catalyzed by his eternity in the black underworld of the prison. Instead of an Aleph in the basement, a text in the garden, the Secret Name of God evoked by a charlatan, or a symbolic temple, he sees a hologlyph: it is Ezekiel's Wheel, a compound of water and fire which contains the "total fabric," "the intimate designs," and the "origins" of the universe (172–73). Once again, the revelation of these wheels within wheels, compounds of fire and water (the basic elements of the creation) suggests the imagery of Dante's *Paradiso*, where God manifests Himself to the spellbound poet in the form of three circles of differing color with a single circumference, exhalations of "pure fire," which the Dante contemplates "Like a geometer wholly dedicated / to squaring the circle" (33.115f.).

Leonora Carrington

Cooking cauldrons and descents into the underworld, as symbols of alchemical transformation, abound in Carrington's later novels, like *The Hearing Trumpet* of 1974 and *The Stone Door* of 1976. In *The Hearing Trumpet* the cauldron is associated with the Grail of the Knights Templar, a "Cup of Pneuma," a "Most Holy Vessel" (94) stolen from a hermaphroditic "subterranean Goddess" (91), to whom it must be returned.[42] When the aging protagonist descends into the basement beneath her nursing home, the Abbess of the abyss invites her to leap into a cauldron of boiling soup, from which she emerges refreshed and rejuvenated (138). In *The Stone Door,* the Goddess is called the Artisan, a practitioner of "the alchemy of Ivory" (41). She brings two little ivory dolls briefly to life with the help of an alembic "constructed of glass tubes and globes, all intricately connected in a system of branches," through which she circulates milk then mercury (39). Chapter 3 revolves around an alchemical game of cooking called "Animal, Vegetable, and Mineral" (52), and, in the final chapter, a sail is made by boiling the shrunken body of a dead alchemical King over a large cauldron, in which a Giant then boils a goat to make the mast and hull. Since the *vas hermeticum* is essentially a vessel of transfiguration, Leonora Carrington can call it "the Womb of the world, whence all things come" (*Hearing Trumpet* 137), while Thomas Mann can call it the "sepulchre," "the well guarded crystal retort wherein the material is compressed to its final transformation" (*Magic Mountain* 511). I discuss the Goddess symbolism of these two novels thoroughly in the appropriate chapter, and would like therefore to focus here on Carrington's use of the nekyia and alchemical motifs in her unique breed of surrealism.

As the title of the novel suggests, the partition between its two worlds is a stone door. It connects the mountains of Keschke in Hungary, from which the Danube springs, and an elaborately envisioned Mesopotamian underworld. The novel explores both sides of the threshold, which can be taken not only as the dividing line between the worlds of the living and the dead, but also between the conscious and the unconscious minds, since several of the characters move the plot forward in dreams and hallucinatory visions of the underworld of Mesopotamia. One such dreamer records her visions in a diary read by Amagoya at the beginning of the book. The diary records a dream about a woman wandering towards Hungary among Mesopotamian "tombs of all shapes and sizes, beautifully decorated and painted like tropical fish" (16). She meets a clay mummy who asks "What will you do if you can never get out of the country of the dead? The stone door of Keschke is jealously guarded" (17). Much of the plot then has to do with the efforts of this dream woman to get to and through the stone door of the underworld, while her male counterpart, Zacharias, moves towards her through a sequence of incarnations, dreams, and visions from Hungary, the side of the living. The two characters also represent two of the four elements of alchemical world, Fire and Air, seeking reunion.

Hence, the Hebrew King which the dream woman comes upon in her imagined Mesopotamian desert is both the dead alchemical king and the lord of the underworld. We learn this when the woman in the dream is asked to tell a story (a kind of dream within a dream) to the clay mummy who asks how she will escape the underworld. Her story recounts her meeting with a King with a "hermetic smile" in the desert, who is said to have "Dreams and nightmares" (21). The King gives the dream woman, Air, one of those geometrical figures which Carrington was fond of depicting in paintings like (among many others) "The Death of Giordano Bruno," Bruno, of course, being one of the greatest of the hermetic philosopher's of the Renaissance. The painting shows him suspended upside down in a kind of cauldron (like Leonora in *The Hearing Trumpet*), with several elaborately inscribed geometrical figures beside him, composed of interpenetrating pyramids, triangles, and circles. The Hebrew King in *The Stone Door* gives the dream woman "a small wooden wheel in the center of which was a spider," and then explains that "The eight legs of the spider are love and death. The eight spokes of the wheel are triumph, movement, and life" (22). The revelation in the underworld of such a symbol, one which combines alchemical motifs with icons of the Great Goddess, is typical of the literature of postmodernism: like the many figures (mathematical, musical, geometrical, architectonic, and cabalistic) of Borges, and Cortázar, these forms represent the eidola of Hades, symbols of those images which give shape and significance to life. This little wheel with the eight legged spider in the middle recalls the wheel vision at the climax of "The God's Script" by Borges, just as much as it recalls the importance of geometrical figures (circle, square, triangle, and octahedron) in alchemy, and the insectomorphic forms of the Great Goddess. Marija Gimbutas, for example, reproduces an eight legged Neolithic spider or bee from a cave wall in Sardinia, and an extraordinary little Middle Minoan seal embossed with an eight legged spider or bee (272; Figs. 423, 425). A Native American shell engraving shows an eight–legged spider with a large black cross on its back (Biedermann 316), and, curiously enough, the eight–legged spider appears in its web above the Monas hieroglyphica (a cross sustaining a circle crowned by a crescent) in an alchemical plate by Goosen van Vreeswyck in 1675 (Fabricius Fig. 170).

In the diary that Amagoya reads, the dream continues the next night with the dream woman walking along a road lined with rubbish and peopled by a "stream of beings" who she assumes to be ghosts. They appear in diverse geometrical configurations: some are "joined like siamese twins in two's or three's or in greater numbers, forming geometrical shapes and objects such as five–, six–, eight–, nine–, or twelve–sided polygons, triangles, squares, circles" (24). One has only to recall such alchemical plates as Michael Maier's portrait of the alchemist squaring a circle from *Atalanta Fugiens* (Fabricius Fig. 382), or the elaborate geometrical diagrams characteristic of the hermetic works of Robert Fludd or Athanasius Kircher, to remember how important such esoteric mathematics was to the alchemical tradition, lasting all the way to Dürer's famous portrait of the Melancholy angel with the intricate polygon beside her, and the Pythagorean square above her.[43] Carrington firmly situates such revelations in the Mesopotamian underworld: after the dream woman recounts her story of the Hebrew King and the ghostly geometrical forms, she sits down on a Druid's head to rest, and eats a "funeral cake" given her by the clay mummy as payment for her story (24).

The alchemical symbolism then continues, when a strange object comes along the dusty road running through the desert. It is an "Egg within the Star, the star within the Egg" which breaks open to hatch "a small white child who stood frail and luminous in the road" (27). He has a five–pronged crown of root and bone on his forehead, and announces that "All the colors on Earth have made me white; all the animals under the sky have made my body" (27). Like the philosopher's stone and lily in H.D.'s *Trilogy*, this divine homunculus is a 'hologlyph,' a small part which contains within itself the entire creation, all its colors and all its animals. The homunculus and the egg, of course, frequently occur in hermeticism as polysemous symbols of the prima materia, the philosopher's stone, and the athanor (a special kind of vas hermeticum or crucible in which the work proceeds). One of Michael Maier's plates from *Atalanta Fugiens*, for example, shows the alchemist brandishing a sword over a large egg on a table in front of a furnace (Fabricius Fig. 239). The dream woman needs "a language buried at the back of time" to communicate with this "embryonic body" (26), a secret language perhaps, as much like the symbolic scripture of the hermetic philosophers as the special language invented by Joyce in *Finnegans Wake*. The little dream embryo, or white child born from the star in the egg, then leads the woman to six horsemen, who hold aloft the eight–spoked wheel with the eight–legged spider in the middle, and say they have come to take the white child to the Hungarian mountains.

The dream woman herself finally arrives in these mountains on the third night, but she is blocked by the "great stone door on which was crucified an immense black parrot" which stares at her with "a hard yellow eye" (29). This image combines the symbolism of the doorway and the eye so frequently found in postmodernist portrayals of the underworld, portrayals which can ultimately be traced back to the seven doorways of Inanna (one of which shows a vulture peaking out) and Ereshkigal's eye of wrath, and to the Egyptian passage through doorways and the Eye of Horus in the Books of the Dead. The dream woman in *The Stone Door* knows she must "walk, swim, creep or sail through the mountain Keschke" (29), just as Gilgamesh must pass through the twelve leagues of darkness in the Mesopotamian epic. But the dream woman is blocked by the stone door, seemingly "lost forever in the country of the dead" with her own dreams, with a "Beast fed with the shade of a dry funeral cake," and in love with the "nightmare of a dead King" (31) who can be seen equally as Osiris or Hades as he can be as the alchemical King so often dismembered or burned in alchemical plates like Maier's Kings: one roasting in a kind of alchemical sauna

(Fabricius Fig. 200), one put in a coffin and chopped to pieces (Fabricius Fig. 356), and another devoured by a dog which is then burned in a fire (Fabricius Fig. 89), all from *Atalanta Fugiens*.

Carrington's ingenious narrative returns, at this point, to Amagoya, the woman reading the dream woman's diary, but the action remains surreal and visionary. Amagoya turns into a wolf and runs through a forest to the driveway of a mansion, where she finds a small golden cage with an ivory doll inside. She subsequently falls asleep with the doll cage in the snow, and dreams she is riding a bicycle with a hermaphrodite (an alchemical symbol of which Carrington was so fond in her work) running beside her to, carrying the golden cage with the ivory doll to what is called the Artisan's house (35). Here the alchemical mysteries proceed, again in combination with the symbolism of the underworld and the Great Goddess. The hermaphrodite says she found the golden doll cage beneath the body of a dead black dog, with Amagoya crying in the snow beside it. The black dog, of course, is as suggestive of canine guardians of the underworld from Anubis to Cerberus, but also of the black poodle in Goethe's *Faust* and the many wolves and dogs of hermetic lore recorded in the plates of Maier and others. The Artisan's house is full of dolls, and she takes Amagoya and the ivory doll, for which she has a matching twin, down into a basement laboratory reminiscent of the witch's kitchen in Grass. This basement is a "vaulted chamber which looked more like a kitchen" (38), and it is full of hermetic paraphernalia, like the "singing instrument," the alembic in which the Artisan circulates milk and mercury to resurrect the two dolls (39).

Among Carrington's innovations here is the female alchemist (the first in the literature?), no longer a soror mystica, or muse to a male hermit, but a kind of Goddess, one who describes herself as the mother of "many thousands of lost souls" (41). The operation which she performs upon the dolls in her singing alembic of "glass tubes and globes, all intricately connected in a system of branches" (39), is the one the alchemists called circulatio; it involves a "perpetual motion" circulating milk and mercury which the Artisan calls "the alchemy of Ivory" (41). The alchemy brings the dolls to life, and they turn out to be two of the base elements, and the two main protagonists of the novel: one doll identifies himself as the Jew in search of rebirth in order to find his "sister fire, who is also a Ram, a woman, and a gentile" (42). The other is sister fire, the woman blocked in the underworld at the stone door, crying let me in! She announces that she is "seeking my brother Air who passed through Mesopotamia in the form of a Hebrew King" (42). Hence the strands of this amazing narrative are woven together in the most extraordinary way. The Artisan responds to the female doll by saying that her brother must deliver her "from the dead" (42), and she then throws the dolls into the Fire, just as the alchemists roasted their dead kings and dogs to produce the philosopher's stone. Carrington has a "glittering green beetle and a speckled partridge" escape from the cinders and fly up the chimney (43). It is important to note that the scarab beetle, an Egyptian symbol of rebirth identified by Horapollo with Osiris, and a Christian symbol for the resurrection (Biedermann 300), also appears in the alchemical literature in connection with the elixir vita (Jung, *Psychology and Alchemy* 453). Its green color here links it with the emerald tablet of Hermes so important to Mann and H.D.

The Jewish male doll is, as it predicted, eventually reborn as Zacharias, the hero of the last chapters of the novel, in which Carrington continues to combine the journey to the underworld with a splendid variety of alchemical motifs curiously transformed by her unique breed of surrealism. The young Jew Zacharias is brought up in an orphanage, where he has dreams and visions of his soror mystica—in alchemical lore, the adept was guided during the opus by a female muse, a sort of Sancta Sophia or Anima Mundi, depicted by Maier in *Atalanta Fugiens* guiding the blind alchemist through the night (Fabricius Fig. 84). Young Zacharias and his dream "sister" watch a black ram with a "pair of golden scales" emerging from a pond (66), and proceed to slit its throat, with a black triangular stone, in the center of circle filled with polygons, which the 'sister' draws while chanting a litany of the four elements (66–67). Another song is a Hungarian ditty that will later provide the key to opening the stone door of the dead: "Open, Open little green leaf, great stone door" (67). In a second dream excursion, the little sister identifies Zacharias as "the white child, the wise King, the Jew, the Black Ram" (77), and tells him he must undertake the journey to Mesopotamia, that "huge arid cemetery, whose cities are tombs," where even "the wind is dead," and the air is infested with prayers like "black butterflies" (78). This visionary girl thus serves the traditional hermetic function of the soror mystica, guiding the alchemical adept through the night with dreams and visions, inscribing polygons which contain the whole secret of the Great Work, and chanting the litany of the four elements. This entire sequence combines iconographic details frequently associated with alchemy and the nekyia: butterflies, geometrical symbols, and doorways.

The last chapter focuses on the alchemical imagery of the sacrificed king, important earlier in the novel's portrayal of the Hebrew King in Mesopotamia (now identified with Zacharias). The journey to the stone door begins when Zacharias, now a poverty stricken adult, takes a job in a Chinaman's toy shop, and finds an "old music box" which plays the Hungarian ditty of his youth: "Open little green leaf, Come in through the golden doors" (87). He finds another "triangular box" covered with black feathers (suggestive of the parrot crucified earlier on the stone door) and containing a stone key "of Mexican workmanship inside" (89). These various strands of the plot come together when Zacharias surreptitiously opens a sealed packet during a train ride to Budapest, and finds the little ivory doll from the Artisan chapter inside (91). When the train is halted by a blinding blizzard, Zacharias rides off with the six horsemen seen earlier in the Mesopotamian underworld; one of them, Calabas Kö, sings of the stone door and of sister fire, and he gives Zacharias a "decagonal stone" (97).

They ride to a tavern where an alchemical king (old "Böles Kilary") dies after a black ram rushes out into the snow. The geometrical figures symbolizing the archetypal forms revealed by the descent into the alchemical underworld surface again here in the picture of the old king lying on a "sexagonal bier" wearing a "long black shirt exquisitely embroidered with scarlet letters, circles, and polygons" (98). The old wizard is apparently to be reborn as Zacharias himself, for he has the same face, and an old red–headed woman sings that the stone door will not open until the "Young Böles Kilary lets you into the country of the

Dead" with the "little green leaf" of the ditty (99). The old king cannot rise from the ashes, however, before the appropriate hermetic rituals of putrefaction and dissolution take place. That the king represents the philosopher's stone, however, is suggested by the stone polygons of the bier and sacrificial knife, and by the very stones of the tavern, volcanic stones as big as seven camels and three elephants "squashed into a great cube" (100), like the one Dürer's Melancholy sits beside. The stones of the house are holographic, the part which contains the whole, since encoded in them is all the "old mineral knowledge from the nine planets" (100). In alchemical lore, the metals of the earth were derived from each of the seven planets, and formed the material body of the incarnate soul as it "descends from heaven through the planetary spheres and acquires the qualities pertaining to each" (Edinger 134). Likewise, from the ceiling of the tavern hang "all the animal, mineral, and vegetable kingdoms in the universe," and the room is furnished with hermetic paraphernalia: "Bouquets of Egyptian mummies" in Greek and Syrian vases and "metals and jewels, heaps of jewels" scattered all over (101). It is a house of Hades, of Pluto, lord of riches, but also of alchemy.

The embalmers who arrive carrying jars full of sweet elixirs "for preserving the dead" perform the hermetic rituals of embalming ultimately derived from Egyptian alchemy (102). At sunrise, Zacharias sneaks upstairs into a "large granary" reeking of "embalming fluids" (104), with "A great stone jar in the corner" containing the King's entrails, and the mummified King, "shrunken to the dimensions of a newborn babe," hanging from the ceiling (104). It is pertinent to note the Classical sources of Carrington's surrealism here, as elsewhere in the novel: like Osiris, Hades was, both lord of the underworld and lord of the grain, since in Greece silos stored the wheat underground. Furthermore, at the climax of the climax of the Eleusinian mysteries, a child was born, just as, in the story of Isis and Osiris, the child Horus is born in the papyrus swamp, conceived by the phallus of the dead king. Hence, Carrington combines archetypal and alchemical motifs here to produce something uniquely her own, a kind of hermetic surrealism. Zacharias steals the "newborn" corpse of the dead King, and follows the black ram off into the forest, moving eastward towards the mountainous ravine where the Danube has its source.

Here a giant appears carrying the fleece of the black ram over his shoulder; rather like the golden fleece Jason pursues, this fleece represents alchemical mysteries (see Antoine Faivre). The giant has a harelip, and a dog's face, suggestive of the Egyptian Anubis, lord of the mummified dead, and patron of the alchemists (von Franz, *Alchemy* 42). He takes Zacharias into a filthy cromlech with bones scattered on the floor, and commands him to make a pair of pants, which Zacharias does by humidifying the shrunken body of Böles Kilary over a huge cauldron, until the body bursts in a shower of spices, which fall into the soup. The pants are made from the skin, and later serve as a sail for a boat which the giant makes from the body of a boiled goat. The giant instructs Zacharias to sail this boat on the river leading under Mount Keschke to the great stone door at the entrance to "Mesopotamia, the country of the Dead" where Zacharias will be reunited with his soror mystica, sister fire (111). This alchemical reunion of the elements, therefore takes the form of the hierosgamos, or sacred marriage, an archetypal symbol of the completion of the opus found in a wide range of alchemical illustrations, and most thoroughly and consistently explored in the *Rosarium Philosophorum*, the complete plates of which are to be found in Jung's *Psychology of the Transference*. As in the Rosarium, the hierosgamos occurs at the expense of the night–sea journey through the underworld, in alchemy represented by the putrefaction of the king and queen in the hermetic bath or crucible.

In *The Stone Door*, the hermetic nekyia is completed when Zacharias sails under Mount Keschke into a cavern populated by "luminous bodies" that so terrify him that he feels like he is "hanging in eternity with no beginning and no end, where life and movement no longer existed" (116). This is the nadir of the descent, and corresponds exactly to the journey of Gilgamesh under the mountains of Mashu through the twelve leagues of darkness, in the middle of which he cries out in terror. When Zacharias finally reaches "the great stone door feebly lit by a large luminous egg hung like a lamp on a pole," he is able to open it by singing the little Hungarian ditty, "Open, open little green leaf, Open, open great stone door" (117). As strange as the motif of the flowering rod and shrunken skin seem, they may have Classical prototypes in the Greek rituals explored by Jane Ellen Harrison: Carrington's ritual of flayed ram and goat skins may have its prototype during the Lupercalia in February, when two Roman youths girded themselves in the skins of slain goats, and rushed through the streets smiting women with strips of the hide, either to ward off the dead or to promote fertility (52); and Carrington's little green stem and leaf may find its precursor in the rhabdos of Hermes, a pliable twig he may be seen waving over a grave jar, for the purpose of either the "raising or the laying of ghosts" (44–46). Together with song (as in the myth of Orpheus), Carrington's rhabdos procures access to Hades: Zacharias plays a little pipe which bursts into a stem with "nine little green leaves" which crack the door open, and release the soror mystica from the underworld, along with a wild herd of white sheep, which Zacharias follows westward, back into life.

Julio Cortázar

Julio Cortázar also makes extended use of geometrical *figuras* revealed by the descent to Hades in his great novel *Hopscotch.* In spite of the daring manipulations of narrative form established by the alternative sequences of chapter progressions, the novel retains a structure informed throughout by the descent into Hades. The myth explores that process of breakdown and breakthrough which symbolizes the creative dynamics of *poesis* in the works of the first generation of modernists (Joyce, Lawrence, Mann, Eliot, et. al.). Cortázar shares with these authors that sense of paralysis, stagnation, anarchy and futility which compels a quest for new forms and new myths to redeem the Waste Land. But like James Merrill, Thomas Pynchon, and Doris Lessing, Cortázar brings the language and imagery of contemporary science into his version of the descent.

Hopscotch is structured by three interrelated descents which fall into the narrative structure of the hero journey (separation – initiation – return): the first is Horacio Oliveira's quest for La Maga, after she disappears following the death of her child Rocamadour in Paris; the second is related to the first, but takes place in Buenos Aires in the second section of the novel; and the third quest (the focus of section three of the novel) involves Oliveira and the rest of the members of The Club searching for the key to Morelli's apartment, and by extension the key to his theoretical writings. This key is initially presented in the metaphorical terms of the quest: "'You're looking for something you don't know,'" La Maga says to Oliveira in the beginning of the novel (76), and Gregorovius confirms this when he says that Oliveira "guesses that in some part of Paris, some day or some death or some meeting will show him a key; he's searching for it like a madman .... he is looking for the black light, the key, and he's beginning to realize that you don't find those things in libraries'" (33). The first and second searches end at the end of the second section of the novel when Oliveira 'finds" La Maga playing hopscotch in the courtyard of the sanitarium where he has a breakdown in Buenos Aires. Similarly, the third related quest reaches its destination at the end of the third section, indeed in the last pages of the last numerated chapters of the novel, when Oliveira and Étienne discover that the old man who had been hit by a car early on in Chapter 22 turns out to be Morelli himself. When Étienne and Oliveira visit him in the hospital, Morelli gives them the literal key to his apartment, which Oliveira sees as a "key to happiness ... a key to open Morelli's door .... A key, an ineffable figure. A key" which will lead to "something else," specifically to a "*découvrit l'auscultation*" (557). Morelli attributes this odd synchronicity which has brought Étienne and Oliveira to him to Hermes, the god of journeys and the guide of souls to the underworld.

These three quests, therefore, begin and end the book, thus establishing an archetypal form beneath the apparently random surface of its novelty. *Hopscotch* falls into the conventional form of the hero journey, with its quest and revelation, though a closer look at the mythic prototype of the descent to the underworld will reveal the originality with which Cortázar handles these archetypal configurations. It is entirely characteristic for the hero journey to be initiated by a crisis which leads to a departure and separation from a familiar environment: for the postmodernist hero, this crisis occurs in the form of a breakdown, whether it be a sense of spiritual paralysis in Joyce, of paralyzing obstacles to composition in Mann, or the death of parents in the early Lawrence. A similar sense of what Eliot calls the "anarchy and futility of contemporary history" permeates the Waste Land of Parisian culture in the opening chapters of *Hopscotch*, in which we see characters condemned to aimless wanderings, futile debates, and fragmented relationships. All of the members of the central group of characters in the Club are, like Joyce's Stephen Dedalus, expatriates in flight from the nets of family, state, and church: Oliveira, for example, is unruffled by "a letter from his brother, a solid–citizen lawyer from Rosario, who had filled up four onionskin pages with an account of the filial and civic duties which Oliveira had poured down the drain" (16). And the other members of the Club (Perico, Ronald, Gregorovius, Babs, Étienne) "were people who only wanted to escape the ordinary routine of buses and history" by wandering around Paris "outside the stream of news events, family obligations, and physical and moral burdens of any sort" (23).

In addition to the flight from civic obligations, the members of the club share that sense of the futility of the cultural past which Nietzsche had condemned as antiquarianism in his *The Uses and Abuses of History,* and which underscores Eliot's allusions in *The Waste Land.* Not only, for example, do Ronald and Gregorovius see themselves as "failures in the arts" who "were carefully killing themselves without worrying about anything" (45), but they also look upon the vast accumulation of cultural knowledge about the past in Paris as a "repertory of insignificant things" (59), preoccupation with which leads to a kind of "cretinism" (58). This attitude also results in Oliveira's ironic commentary on Berthe Trépat's hilariously evoked piano recital as "a useless and defeatist survival of ... artistic activities among groups of people equally defeated and useless" (106). It is from this sense of pervasive futility that the members of the club attempt to flee, and which initiates the separation stage of the descent.

Ironically, it is Berthe Trépat who announces the mythic key to one of the most important forms to the quest taken by Oliveira in the novel: "I also came to Paris, from Pau, quite a few years ago, looking for the golden bough" (114), she says to Oliveira as they walk home from the disastrous failure of the concert. The golden bough, of course, leads Aeneas into the underworld in Virgil's epic, and has come to be associated with the quest for regeneration of the Waste Land as a result of Eliot's notes to the poem of that name. In *Hopscotch*, the death of the baby and disappearance of La Maga compel Oliveira's descent shortly after the piano recital, during the extraordinary chapter in which the baby Rocamadour dies. As the baby lies dying in its crib, Ronald and Étienne discuss the "writings of the ancient seers, " and in particular the Tibetan *Bardo,* about which they say "Jung was all excited" (156–57). The *Bardo Thödol* describes the journey of the soul after death into its own underworld of mental forms. It is one of those documents crucial to Jung's formulation of the concept of the archetypes of the collective unconscious as mental forms analogous to Plato's *eidola*.[44] In this chapter, Ronald focuses on the "moment of judgment for a dead person" when "the King puts a mirror to his face" which reflects "the summation of all the dead person's acts" as a "projection of mental images" (157).

This synchronistic evocation of the *Bardo* as the baby lies dying, unbeknownst to all in the room apart from Oliveira, gives La Maga a glimpse of the ultimate patterns which shape and inform life, those *eidola* which James Hillman associates with Hades and the descent to the underworld. It is the revelation of these archetypal configurations that give shape and significance to life that constitutes the climactic moment of the postmodernist adaptations of the myth of descent in a large range of fictions, poems, and plays. La Maga's intuition of these patterns, therefore, announces the basic goal of Oliveira's ensuing descent, and places *Hopscotch* squarely in relation to the masterpieces of the mythical method in modernism: "She had understood enough," Cortázar writes of the revelation glimpsed by La Maga during the discussion of the *Bardo*; "a few pieces of the puzzle were in place, although it would never be as perfect as a kaleidoscope, where each crystal, each stick, each grain of sand arranged itself in a perfect, symmetrical, boring pattern, but with no problems" (158). As we will see, this aspect of the descent to the underworld—the revelation of those basic patterns like the kaleidoscope or the hopscotch court—falls in line with the myth of apocalypse as well, which by definition involves an unveiling of the secret patterns which inform the enigma of life.

Oliveira's quest following the death of the child and the disappearance of La Maga continues to be informed by allusions to the descent to the underworld. La Maga, in fact, is a kind of Persephone, a sorceress at home in those "metaphysical rivers" in which she swims (96). The imagery here suggests the Styx crossing and abduction of Persephone ("letting herself drop so that she can rise up all the better with the swoop"), as does the Atlantic crossing shortly following, at the end of which Oliveira gets a glimpse of La Maga on board ship among the boats in the harbor: she has led him into those metaphysical mysteries beyond reason to which he aspires.

But even before this decisive crossing to Buenos Aires, other episodes and allusions evoke the hero journey to the underworld, such as when Oliveira, speaking to Gregorovius about the arrival of the latter's mother Adgalle, talks about "the gates of assorted hells," and compares "The *nekias* of today" to "a trip on the Métro at six–thirty, or going to the police to get your *carte de séjour* renewed," or to a hole in the bathroom (179–180). The "hole in the bathroom" to which Oliveira refers in this passage had been or will be developed (according to the sequence in which one decides to read the chapters of the novel) in Chapter 57, the first chapter of the third section of the novel. In this chapter Oliveira describes washbasins as a kind of gateway through which one might return to the underworld of dreaming from which one has just ascended in the morning (one thinks here of Pynchon's toilet scene in *Gravity's Rainbow*). Oliveira uses the analogy to provide Étienne with an exegesis of a line of poetry Oliveira had written and attempted unsuccessfully to explain to his friend Traveler in Buenos Aires: the line reads "'Between sleep and waking, diving into washbasins'" (353).

Oliveira explains that when you wake up and stare into the mirror above the washbasin, it is "as if you were slipping down through that hole that carries off tartar, mucus, rheum, dandruff, saliva, and you let yourself go in the hope that maybe you'll return to the other thing, to what you were before you woke up" (354). The notion here that the return to the realm of the dream can be taken as a kind of descent, via the hole in the washbasin, into an underworld which contains the "remains of a paradise half–seen" aligns the "*nekias* of today" alluded to by Oliveira with the apocalyptic theme of a restored paradise as the goal of all our striving. But when one remembers that, in *Hopscotch*, it is as the result of sharing dreams that Étienne and Oliveira decide to visit the old man in the hospital, and that the old man turns out to be Morelli, who provides Oliveira with that key to happiness which will unveil the elusive pattern behind the anarchic surface of the novel ("*découvrit l'auscultation*"), then it becomes clear that the *nekyia* described by Oliveira link the dream and the underworld in a way consistent with perennial wisdom shared by many other texts in postmodernism: the descent via dream evokes intuitions of those metaphorical forms of the mind (the *eidola* of Hades) which give shape and significance to the anarchy and futility of life. It is the revelation of these archetypal configurations (kaleidoscopes, crystals, polyhedrons, hopscotch courts, etc.) towards which the novel as a whole continually moves.

Indeed, the first great climactic moment of revelation in the novel occurs appropriately in the last chapter of the first section, a chapter largely modeled on the descent into Hades, here updated to embrace the gritty details of life among the homeless in Paris. The chapter comes after the death of Rocamadour and the disappearance of La Maga, as Oliveira decides to wander the streets in search of her: his journey is immediately cast in the context of the descent to the underworld and the revelation of the archetypes. In the second paragraph at the beginning of the chapter, Oliveira acknowledges (to a cat in the street) that a certain "aesthetic requirement" to "complete the pattern" compels his quest for La Maga, and he identifies himself with Orpheus searching for Eurydice in Hades: "'But let's not forget about Orpheus. Maybe if I shave my head and cover it with ashes, go there with a tin cup like a beggar. I am no longer he that ye once knew, oh women. Tragedian. Mime. Night of *empusae* and *lamiae*, evil shadows, the end of the game'" (202). The "end" here meaning both conclusion, and purpose, in the apocalyptic sense of an ending.

The underworld of feminine demonia into Oliveira descends in the chapter will be the world of the destitute beggars along the banks of the Parisian Styx (the Seine), and his Eurydice a terribly smelling "*clocharde*" named Emmanuéle whom La Maga had pitied and spoken too. Oliveira finds Emmanuéle "there by the river, among the tramps" 9205) amid a "snoring that was coming out of the depths of the earth" (203), and he sees her as a perversely genuine "crystallization of desire" in what he calls his "kibbutz" (203). This filthy Eurydice emerges from under "piles of newspapers and burlap bags" (203) dressed like the mythical Sumerian Goddess Inanna in a black overcoat beneath which she is veiled in "four or five dresses and some topcoats and overcoats, carrying a bundle of red material with pieces of sleeves and a broken cornet sticking out" (206).[45] (The symbolism of clothing is always central to the descent). The couple then goes up into the city, crossing to "the other side of the Seine embankment, in the back of the lead RIP boxes where the pigeons were talking among themselves and fluffing up" (209). These realistic details evoke the underlying metaphors of the "*nekias* of today": a river crossing to a realm of coffins and soul–birds, and finally to a darkened arcade "along the Rue de l'Hirondelle," where the couple settles down to a ritual feast of wine and fellatio.

After two quarts of wine and several cigarettes, Oliveira has an extraordinary vision of his *clocharde* as a "Syrian goddess," and as "the Great Mother," abused by the soldiers of an enemy army who trample her, piss on her breasts, and masturbate into her eye sockets (209–210). This vision of a ritualistic humiliation of the Goddess by the forces of patriarchy soon becomes real when the police arrest and beat the couple, then throw them into a paddy wagon with some fairies: they do this when they find Emmanuéle sucking Oliveira's "*corpus delictii*" (213) as he imagines himself "buried in a pile of manure to cure himself of dropsy" like "Heraclitus the Obscure .... covered with shit up to the neck" (210). Such excremental imagery, as James Hillman notes, is characteristic of "descriptions of the underworld as a realm of murky or fecal matter" in Plato, Aristophanes, the myth of Hercules, Egyptian Books of the Dead, and a "*nekyia* text" translated by Dieterich to illustrate "the early Christian–Orphic fascination with purgation and with the underworld as a filthy hellhole of blood, dirt and shit" (*Dream* 183).

But within this excremental fantasy resides "an embarrassment of riches. Just this suggests an archetypal background in the richness of Hades, in Pluto's wealth" (Hillman, *Dream* 185). This wealth consists of the *eidola*, what Plato calls "the benefactory intelligence of Hades (404a), his 'knowledge of all noble things'" (*Dream* 121). In *Hopscotch*, the ritual pathologizings suffered by Cortázar's modern day Orpheus and Eurydice at the hands of the police leads dramatically to an evocation of that "archetypal intelligence given in images" that Hillman associates with Hades (121). As the fellatio progresses amidst the muck, just before the intervention of the police, Oliveira reflects "that perhaps the Obscure one had sunk himself up to the neck in shit without even having been sick, without having dropsy at all, simply to sketch out a pattern that his milieu would never have condoned in the shape of a message or lesson" (212). It is this revelation of an archetypal "pattern" beneath the pathologies of life that Cortázar's *nekia* ends on: riding to the station in the back of the police wagon, two of the central metaphors of the novel are clarified for the first time. The hopscotch court and the kaleidoscope become those images encoding an archetypal intelligence revealed at the climax of Oliveira's descent into Hades.

As Emmanuéle lies sobbing on the floor shouting "*Quand il reviendra, le temps des cerises,*" Oliveira ponders the mysteries of "spiral hopscotch, rectangular hopscotch, fantasy hopscotch, not played very often," which involves a continual ascent to and descent from Heaven (214). The "fantasy hopscotch" is of course the novel, with its leaping around between chapters laid out in a labyrinthine hopscotch court searching for the divine perspective that will unveil the pattern. Another such pattern immediately crystallizes as Oliveira watches the two "fairies" playing with a kaleidoscope: "Everything was so perfect, everything happening right on time, hopscotch and the kaleidoscope, the smaller fairy looking and looking, oh Jo, I can't see anything, more light, more light, Jo" (215). As the pieces fall into place, a pattern emerges that will shape our reading of the rest of the novel, giving us a glimpse of that key needed to continue the quest. The "Obscure one" emerges from the darkness with green eyes to reveal "patterns as pretty as can be," as "the squares" of the Hopscotch court open and "the labyrinth" unfolds, "like the spring of a broken clock." Hence, Oliveira's *nekia* in this chapter concludes with the revelation of the central metaphors informing the structure of the novel: hopscotch, the kaleidoscope, and the labyrinth.

This last chapter of the first section of the novel is balanced, with nearly exact symmetry, by Chapter 54, the second to last fully developed chapter of section two of the novel ("The Other Side"), hence indicating the sustained focus on the descent as the central myth shaping the narrative. The second journey begins after Oliveira departs from the apartment where he has been living with a woman named Gekrepten to live with his friends Talita and the Traveler in a mental clinic which they supervise. Yet this journey is related to the first section of the novel ("This Side") because both are compelled by the quest for La Maga, who disappeared after her child's death.

In this second climax of the novel at the end of the second section, Oliveira descends from his room on the third floor of the mental clinic (in which he and his friends Traveler and Talita are working) down into the morgue in the basement, which he calls a "refrigerated Hades, " though a Hades without a "Eurydice to look for" (320). The fact is that the Orpheus–Eurydice paradigm for the conclusion of the first section has now shifted to the Hades–Persephone paradigm for the conclusion of the second. This is indicated by Oliveira's remark, as he stops by the shaft of the freight elevator to look into "the black depths" of the "Phlegrean Fields" in the basement that "he was at the edge of the pit, the hole of Eleusis, the clinic wrapped in sulfurous vapors, the descent" (316). The allusion here is to the Eleusinian mysteries, those religious rituals performed yearly just down the road from Athens and devoted to the reenactment of the abduction of Persephone by Hades, Lord of the Underworld, and the ensuing search and rescue of Persephone by her mother Demeter.

This shift from the Orpheus–Eurydice to the Hades–Persephone pattern results in correlative variations in the narrative and thematic structure of Chapter 54. This second '*nekia* of today' begins as Oliveira, at 11:00 PM, sits looking out the window at the hopscotch figure in the courtyard of the clinic. As Talita (his friend Traveler's wife) walks out into the courtyard for a second time in a few minutes to play a game of hopscotch, Oliveira sees her as La Maga (whose disappearance he suspects has been by drowning into the realm of the dead). As he watches Talita–La Maga play hopscotch, he feels everything "coming back into order." The phantom girl picks up a "flat stone out of the several that Number 8 kept piled up next to the flowerbed," and she appears not in the "ash–grey blouse and a skirt that most likely was white" worn by Talita, but as a "figure in pink that came out of somewhere" to hop on one leg "like a pink flamingo in the half–light" (314). These precisely observed details are richly suggestive of the Hades–Persephone complex: before La Maga–Talita appears, Oliveira feels "imprisoned," but as soon as she plucks a pebble from the flowerbed, his fantasy impels him towards the last Parisian lover buried in his mind. In the original version of the abduction of Persephone, recorded in the Homeric "Hymn to Demeter," Persephone (like La Maga in this scene) inadvertently opens the gateway to the underworld by plucking a lotus flower from the field of poppies (pink?) in which she plays with her nymphs. Even the duality of Talita–La Maga's appearance is appropriate, since in the myth Persephone is both her mother's daughter and the bride of Hades, and will alternate between those two identities forever. Hence, the "ash–grey blouse" worn by Talita in this scene at the clinic suggests Persephone's association with death as the bride of Hades, while the "figure in pink" that Oliveira sees as La Maga would suggest the freshness of new life associated with Persephone's return from the underworld with the first blossoming poppies of the Athenian springtime.

The whole scene in Chapter 54 occurs around midnight, when the inmates of the clinic, like Number 8, are all "giving in to the effects of a cubic centimeter of hypnosis," most likely a sugar cube laced with a soporific drug dispensed after dark by Talita, who is the pharmacist of the clinic. This would make Talita the Queen of the Night, dispensing sleep to her initiates, just as the neophytes of Eleusis most likely received a psychotropic beverage at the beginning of the mysteries.[46] Hence Oliveira, as the Guard on duty at midnight, becomes the Lord of the Night, making his rounds to check up on the inmates along the "silence and half darkness ... of the corridor with its closed doors" (315), "Stopping by the shaft of the freight elevator" which leads down into the "black depths" of the "Phlegrean Fields," turning to look down "the straight line of the hallway to the end, with the purple light from the bulbs on the frames of the white doors," and then foolishly hopping down the hallway all the way to "the first door," beside which he lets "himself slide down" in exhaustion. I quote these details here to emphasize the importance of doorways in Cortázar's *mise–en–scene*, which suggests the possible influence of films like *Nosferatu,* Cocteau's *Beauty and the Beast* and *Orpheus*, or Bergman's *Wild Strawberries*, in all of which the imagery of doorways, corridors, windows, portals, and the like plays such a crucial role in the realization of underworld settings. Cortázar even adds the detail of the half–open door, which B. Haarløv studied as *A common symbolic motiv with Roman sepulchral sculpture* (n. 32 in Hillman, *Dream*: 226): in this scene, Oliveira pauses at Number 5's room to calm him down, and then leaves "the door half open because he was on to his tricks" (315).

Through such doorways as this, Oliveira fantasizes a "Passage" through the "hole of Eleusis" down into the pit, and it is at this moment that Talita arrives with a glass of lemonade. While discussing Oliveira's vision of Talita as La Maga in pink (exchanged, by the way with her "ash–grey blouse" as she passes between doorways leading into the courtyard, just as Cocteau's Beauty exchanges peasant rags for noble riches when the Beast carries her through the doorways into her room for the first time)—a color associated with the pajamas of the inmates—Oliveira confesses feelings of being possessed, in a "shamanistic trance, on the point of jumping into the hole to put an end once and for all to conjectures" (317). The shaman was a master of what Mircea Eliade calls "Archaic Techniques of Ecstasy," primary of which techniques was the journey to the underworld. Cortázar connects shamanism at several points in *Hopscotch* with writing, suggesting a correspondence between *nekyia* and *poesis*.

In this second section of the novel, for example, before working in the clinic, Oliveira worked in the circus, imagining himself like a shaman beneath the tent pole (a symbol of what Eliade calls the *axis mundi*, or passage point between worlds) looking up at "Sirius in the center of the black hole and he speculated about the three days when the earth is open, when the manes ascend and there is a bridge between man and the hole on high, a bridge between man and man" (267). In the present chapter in the clinic Oliveira again sees himself in a "shamanistic trance," but this time descending: "In the circus it had been just the opposite, a hole up above, the opening in communication with free space, an image of consummation; now he was at the edge of the pit, the hole of Eleusis" (316). Later, in the third section of the novel, a note from Morelli explicitly links the descent with shamanism and suggests that both are metaphors for the dynamics of creativity, i.e., of *poesis*. Morelli says that "Writing is sketching my mandala" (402).

The Mother Goddess of the current scene in the clinic is, of course, Talita–La Maga, who after the lemonade on the fourth floor tells Oliveira that the hole he had fantasized jumping into during his shamanistic trance "ends in the basement: There are cockroaches and colored rags, she says, and everything is "dark and damp, and a little beyond is where the dead people start" (317). (We should remember that La Maga, like the *clocharde* Emmanuéle of the previous *nekyia*, was fond of collecting red rags and red thread, as if stitching their Ariadnean way through the labyrinth of Paris). After further discussing Talita's resemblance to La Maga, and imagining what clothing La Maga might be wearing when seen again ("She'll be naked," Oliveira says, like the disrobed Inanna in the Sumerian *kur*), the freight elevator mysteriously ascends from the basement. Oliveira and Talita jump up and run over to open its door, and "An almost cold breath of air came out," odd given the stupendous heat of the night. Inside the elevator stands the old lunatic Don Lopez, petting his hallucinatory pigeon "that had been white once and that the continuous caressing of the old man's hand had turned ... ash–grey" (318). The old man appears in this scene very much like the wise Wotan of Norse myth, who won his wisdom from Mimir's well in the tangled underroots of the World Tree Yggdrasil.

After the Old Man is sent to bed, Oliveira and Talita agree to go down into the basement on the freight elevator "to have a look" (319). The imagery of doorways, so prevalent in postmodernist *nekyias*, is immediately precipitated as the couple steps through the doorway of the elevator: "There wasn't a living soul in the basement, but one of the doors of the freezer was ajar and a beam of light was coming out through the opening. Talita stopped in the doorway, with her hand to her mouth, while Talita went over" (319). Oliveira then imagines a conversation having taken place between the old man with the recently dead Number 56; then, "while closing the door of the freezer," an epiphany of sorts occurs, like "a vomit of memory," as Oliveira remembers telling La Maga–Talita about "the hopscotch, his fear in the hallway, the tempting hole," and reflects that this moment "was all like an ending ... the re–entry into the human family .... the return of the prodigal son (of a bitch)—into the arms of easy reconciliation, and from there the even easier step into the world, into the possible life, into the time of his years, into the reason that guided the actions of Good Argentines" (320).

Hence, quite conventionally with respect to postmodernist *nekyias*, the climax of Oliveira's descent into this "refrigerated Hades" coincides with a rebirth into a possible life and with the revelation of an archetypally human pattern by which to lead that possible life: "the reason," as he says, "that guided the actions of Good Argentines" (320). Indeed, from the beginning Oliveira had that sense that "everything was coming into order" (314), that "Everything (in a manner of speaking) had an explanation" (314), and that the confusion of La Maga and Talita "explains it all, right down to the last detail" (315). All the pieces of the puzzle, all the colored chips of the kaleidoscope, fall into place in the basement, as those "ideational forms and shapes, the ideas that form and shape life," the *eidola* of Hades, are revealed (Hillman, *Dream*: 51).

As a result, Oliveira immediately enacts the role of Lord of this domain by opening the "freezer and taking out a bottle of beer, king of the castle" (320). In the Eleusinian mysteries, what follows the descent is the sacred marriage of Hades and Persephone; hence, here in the basement next to a "freezer of corpses" (321), Talita takes pity on Oliveira, who sees her entirely now as his lost Parisian lover La Maga, whom he now kisses in his refrigerated Hades, a world in which "one could have died of drowning in a river ... and appear in a Buenos Aires night to reproduce on the hopscotch the very image of what they had just attained, the last square, the center of the mandala" (321–22). This passage makes clear Oliveira's fantasy, touched on in the climactic *nekyia* in Chapter 36, that La Maga had drowned herself in the Seine, and has now returned as Queen of the Underworld for connubial reunion with Oliveira "with a face floating in dirty water" in the basement of the clinic (321). And she brings with her that sense of revelation "from the center of life," of having attained the last divine square of the hopscotch court only pointed towards in the earlier Parisian *nekia*, which becomes an image of wholeness achieved within the self at the "center of the mandala" (322).

In the third section of the novel, among the so–called "Expendable Chapters," the mythic focus gradually combines the *nekyia* with the apocalypse. In Chapter 96 of the third section, for example, when the members of the Club enter Morelli's apartment, Ronald says "'Did you bring the drinks, Babsie? An obolus for Charon, you know. Now the door will open and the magic will begin, I expect to get something out of tonight, it's like the feeling of an end of the world'" (434). The imagery of the doorway is a crucial link to the iconography of the hero journey: it opens halfway in this first chapter of section three, and completely by the end. Here the crossing of the threshold into the underworld of the apartment requires a payment to the ferryman Charon, and evokes the imagery of doorways connected with the nekyia, which is here conflated with the apocalyptic notion of "'an end of the world.'"

What Ronald seems to expect, in fact, is the discovery of some text, like the "tablet of Ur" reproduced on the walls of the apartment (435), that will provide the key to the deciphering of Morelli's theoretical writings. Charon is mentioned in connection with Morelli again later on in Chapter 113 as a liminal figure leading to revelation, who accepts cigarettes, a sugar skull, or a "*Kindertotenlieder*" as payment for the "unforeseeable trip on the black waters" (476). This sense of Morelli as a threshold guardian of revelation continues right up to the end of the numerological sequence of chapters in section three. Chapter 154 forms a kind of climax, both to the novel and to the section, which stands in symmetrical balance with the *nekyias* ending sections one and two. When Étienne and Oliveira visit the old man in the hospital who turns out to be Morelli, he gives them the key to his apartment after being offered cigarettes. Then he significantly evokes Hermes, the guide of souls to the underworld and the patron god of artists who presides over the synchronicities which have led Oliveira to Morelli. Morelli gives Oliveira a package to deliver to "Paku. Publisher of *avant–garde* books, Rue de l'Arbre Sec. Did you know that Paku is the Akkadian name for Hermes?" (556). Like Thomas Mann, Morelli then suggests that Hermes is also the god of a special kind of literary craft, a "winged fabricator of subterfuges and lures" (557). This suggests a relationship between the *nekyia*, *poesis*, and *hermeneusis*, since the key Morelli gives Oliveira promises a kind of revelation, a literal apocalypse or uncovering: "'*dans cet hôpital,*" Oliveira muses to himself, "*Laennec découvrit l'auscultation:* maybe still ... A key, an ineffable figure. A key" (558).

All the pieces of the puzzle, all the colored chips of the kaleidoscope, fall into place during the riverside tryst with the *clocharde*, in the basement of the mental clinic, and in Morelli's apartment. In those *temenoi*, the "ideational forms and shapes, the ideas that form and shape life," the *eidola* of Hades, are revealed (Hillman 51). The geometrical *figuras* employed to symbolize this revelation are "the hopscotch" and "the center of the mandala" (321–22). These are figures which, like the Aleph, the labyrinth, the Wheel, or the Tetragrammaton in Borges, are revealed at the climax of scenes which combine the ordinary details of daily life with allusions to the descent to the underworld. Both Latin Americans are practitioners of Eliot's mythical method, postmodernists for whom the *nekyia* became a symbol of *poesis*, of that creative process by which the elemental forms of fiction which give shape and significance to art and life are revealed. As Cortázar has his alter ego Morelli remark, in one of his meditations on the processes of literary creation, "by writing I go down into the volcano, I approach the Mothers, I connect with the Center" (402).

Thomas Pynchon

The revelations precipitated by the descent into Hades have persisted in several recent works based on the mythical method, in which we find new conceptions of the eidola derived from science. In Thomas Pynchon's *The Crying of Lot 49*, for example, the heroine Oedipa Maas is portrayed both as Persephone and as Inanna, as she journeys through the underworlds of Los Angeles and San Francisco, trying to find out why a former lover (Pierce Inverarity) has willed her his estate (the riches of Hades?), and in search of the key to an elaborate mail conspiracy which she stumbles upon in the process. Pierce has left behind an "organized something" after his "annihilation" (56) which she intends to get to the bottom of, beginning with a journey southward to a suburb of Los Angeles, where a sense of those patterns shaping her experience from an invisible realm immediately crystallizes in the "ordered swirl of houses and streets" which she sees as "circuit cards" (14). She notices in "both outward patterns a hieroglyphic sense of concealed meaning" (15) quite typical of the postmodernist intuition of shapes and patterns revealed by the nekyia, but original in the adaptations of the metaphor to contemporary suburban and scientific terminology. Shortly after this urban epiphany, Oedipa is seduced in her motel by Pierce's lawyer, who takes nearly an hour to strip her down, removing "six pairs of panties in assorted colors, girdle, three pairs of nylons, three brassieres, two pairs stretch slacks, four half–slips, one black sheath, two summer dresses" (23). The scene combines, therefore, motifs from the abduction of Persephone and the unveiling of Inanna, and holds out the process of revelation as well. Before she passes out, Oedipa sees an advertising map on TV offering "some promise of hierophany: printed circuit, gently curving streets, private access of the water, Book of the Dead" (20). Thus Oedipa's descent into "the underground of the unbalanced" (which is Los Angeles!) begins with the promise of "revelations in progress all around her" (29), from the "hieratic geometry" of circuit and housing tract, to the postal symbol of the Tristero conspiracy, which she sees amidst the graffiti of a bar near an electronics plant, "thinking: God, hieroglyphics" (34). It is in this same bar where the "sinister blooming of The Tristero" begins that Oedipa once again enacts the unveiling of Inanna, as she watches a deathly striptease dancer shed "breakaway gowns, net bras, jeweled garters and G–strings" until she stands naked with her "luminous stare locked to Oedipa's, smile gone malign and pitiless" (36) as the "eye of death" with which Ereshkigal killed the naked Inanna in the Sumerian *kur* (Wolkstein and Kramer 50–60). After another one of her lovers dies later in the novel, Oedipa again returns to the metaphors of the Inanna complex: "They are stripping from me," she says, "stripping away, one by one, my men" (105). The novel then closes still holding out the promise of revelations that push Oedipa "out over the abyss" (105): revelations from an invisible world taking shape in circuit cards, binary computer switches, the chemical reactions of Maxwell's Demon, and the patterns assumed by the "hieroglyphic streets" (107).

Pynchon's *Gravity's Rainbow* is modeled throughout on the nekyia: it includes descents into a tube stop in London (3f.); down a toilet bowl 63f.); into the rivers along which a ship of fools called the *Anubis* travels (459f.); down into the salt mines where launching pads of the V–2 rocket are in the works; into the seven basement chambers of parapsychological research labs (231f.); and into the subterranean network of SS Grail Brother Temples high up in the German mountains of madness (566f.). That Pynchon was aware of the Sumerian prototype of his diverse unveilings and descents is suggested not only by the seven chambers under the White Visitation which he forces his old General Pudding through, before he encounters the elaborately made up eyes of Katja, his "Queen of the Night" (143), but also by the typical Pynchonian pun which occurs in the section where Slothrop pursues the terrifying death Goddess Gretta to Bad Karma, a town along the Rhine, where he encounters the burning of her "scrutable eyes" while the "Kur–Orchestra" plays (478)—*kur* being the Sumerian word for underworld and mountain, for which Mann, in the *Joseph* novels (also in debt to Sumerian myths), borrowed the Babylonian equivalent, *bôr*. In the grotesque scene at the White Visitation, General Pudding is forced to "negotiate half a dozen offices or anterooms before reaching his destination" in the seventh room, where Katje awaits him. He sees her as "Domina Nocturna ... shining mother and last love" (232): she is naked underneath a black uniform and her eyes have been heavily made up during "an hour at her vanity mirror with mascara, liner, shadow, and pencil, lotions and rouges" (233). She looks like that other Queen the of the Night, the Sumerian Goddess of Death Ereshkigal, who "fastens the eye of death" upon Inanna after she passes through the seven gateways of the *kur*, or underworld. The disgusting ritual of coprophagia which ensues evokes a traditional linkage between excrement and the underworld which we find from Aristophanes (in the *Frogs*, Hades is a swamp of flooding sewage), to Dante (in the second circle of the *Inferno*, the Gluttons are submerged in filth), to Thomas Mann in the *Joseph* novels (57), and on to James Hillman (*Dream* 183–85).

Like Leonora Carrington and Umberto Eco, Pynchon also weaves together a complex of motifs from the Grail legends into his portrayal of the underworld. L. E. Sissman calls *Gravity's Rainbow* "a parody (and an updating) of the Grail legend" (139), while Douglas Fowler suggests that all the major characters in the novel pursue various versions of the Grail (167), and notes particularly that the rocket Slothrop is searching for "is of course nothing less than the Grail itself" (183). As one of Slothrop's friends in the Zone puts it, "grails themselves come in plastic these years, a dime a dozen, penny a gross" (321). The narrator muses that "even as determinist a piece of hardware as the A–4 rocket will begin spontaneously generating items like the S–Gerat Slothrop thinks he's chasing like a grail" (275). And Ombindi, the leader of a group of black commandos the Nazis bring into their ranks to intimidate the Allies, remembers an epiphany in his African village hut "of a grail slipping through the room, radiant, though the jokers around the table be sneaking Whoopee Cushions into the Siege Perilous, under the very descending arse of the grailseeker" (321). And even though one of the minor characters tells Slothrop that the rocket "is no Grail, Ace, that's not what the G in Imipolex G stands for" (364), the Grail imagery persists. Imipolex G, the chemical used in the rocket sealings, was used in experiments conducted upon Slothrop as a child, when his erections were conditioned by the smell of plastics made from the chemical.

That chemical becomes the blood of the Savior in Pynchon's dark vision of the Grail. Greta Erdman, one of Slothrop's many lovers in the novel, remembers being taken during the last days of the War to a Nazi Castle with "black and broken towers" (486). In progress is "a meeting of nobles in the Castle" who are in fact members of the complex hierarchy of technicians in control of the rocket program. Greta sees them "through the windows of the board room ... at a round conference table, with something in the center" (487). A seance is being directed by "An elderly man who used a cane, a notorious spiritualist" who seems magically to have materialized the ectoplasmic substance on the round table: it is "a heavy chalice of methyl methacrylate, a replica of the Sangraal" (487). Here then is Pynchon's Grail Castle in a Nazi version much like Leonora Carrington's: we have a crippled king and brotherhood seated at a round table with the Grail in the center, a chalice containing the rocket's vital fluid, Imipolex G, not the Blood of Our Savior.

Pynchon's association of Nazism and the Grail brotherhood of Templar Knights is to be found not only in Umberto Eco's later novel, *Foucault's Pendulum*, but also in Syberberg's film *Parsifal*, in which the Grail procession is ornamented by swastikas. Recently, Edward Whitmont (who suggests that the Grail quest is the "Myth for Our Times") demonstrates the same troubling affiliation between Hitler and the Grail legends (149–78). This led Hitler to the formulation of the SS as what he himself called a "fraternity of templars around the Grail of the pure blood" (qtd. Whitmont 163). They met in "Grail castles for the purpose of cultivating a pure race" (163), a historical fact which Pynchon, Carrington, and Eco have all responded to in their updating of the descent into Hades and the Grail quest.

All of the descents in *Gravity's Rainbow* are motivated by the quest for that "reason" behind the patterns (434) that yields a "Destiny with a shape" (362). The long slide down the toilet bowl of the Roseland Ballroom, for example, is typical: Slothrop sees the shit on the sewage walls congeal into "patterns thick with meaning, Burma–Shave signs of the toilet world, icky and sticky, cryptic and glyptic" (65). General approaches the same mysteries at the end of his *via scatologica* when he sees Katja as "blessed Metatron ... keeper of the Secret" (231). The term "Metatron" is cabalistic, and refers to the revelation of the angel which follows the passage through the seven halls of the Greater Hekhaloth (Poncé 37). The angel's name is "Metatron, the Prince of the World," with "eyelashes of lightning and eyes of flaming torches" (Poncé 38). It presides over the "*yetsirah*, the world of formation" (Poncé 65). Hence, Pynchon's version of the mystical journey through the halls of the otherworld leads to the revelation of that angelic power which governs the world of form. This world of hieroglyphic secrets, which alternately take on cabalistic, chemical, mathematical, statistical, and scatological forms, eventually assumes the shape of an international cartel "cutting across every agency human and paper that ever touched it" (566). Slothrop, having been the guinea pig of an experiment that conditioned his infantile erections with Imipolex–G, a chemical used in the V–2 rockets, carries the secret dealings of the cartel within him as a "personal doom ... always to be held at the edges of revelations" (566).

Doris Lessing

The revelations of Hades also assume geometrical, scientific and political shapes in Doris Lessing's novel, *Briefing for a Descent into Hell*. The novel casts the psychotic hallucinations which the hero Charles Watkins undergoes during a mid–life breakdown into the form of a journey across the water on dolphin back (shades of Yeats) to supernatural island from another world. As the psychiatric doctors madly administer drugs, Watkins experiences a profoundly disturbing sequence of revelations (a sequence which I suspect owes a great deal to R.D. Laing's account of a psychotic breakdown in *The Politics of Experience*). Lessing develops an elaborate vocabulary of metaphors for the eidola revealed in the Hades of the human unconscious, many of them derived from modern physics and crystallography. Watkins hallucinates a mysteriously potent "circle in the square" of the island city to which he has journeyed, and sets about clearing it of carnage in preparation for a space landing on the next full moon (54). The circle in the square is an old alchemical symbol of wholeness which preoccupied Jung in his studies of the mandala, circular diagrams which he interpreted as representations of wholeness; we also find the problem exercising the talents of Hans Castorp during his last years on *The Magic Mountain*. The action in Lessing's novel continues to focus on the revelations in the piazza, where a purgatorial flame gives Watkins a new body which vibrates like an intense crystal vortex directly over the center of the squared circle (93). The geometrical symbolism, which recalls the figures of Cortázar and Borges, yields to architectural and lithographic imagery, as the outer "city of stone and clay dissolved, leaving a ghostly city" (93) much like the "ghostly paradigm of things" Yeats evokes in "Among School Children." Lessing describes this paradigm as a "pattern and a key and a blueprint for the outer city" (93), and as an "inner pattern or template," or "inner blueprint" upon which the city is modeled (94). The emphasis here on the City as a metaphor of that wholeness revealed as the climax of the nekyia recalls both "The Immortals" of Borges and the radiant city of which Jung dreamt after the death of his friend, Hermann Sigg (*Word and Image* 91f.). Lessing's rendition of the archetypal forms then moves more deeply into the metaphors of the maze and of physics, as the "inner blueprint" of the city itself dissolves into the many celled honeycomb of a larger Mind (96). Lessing calls it the "inner structure" of things and compares it the "white blaze of the Crystal," to the "colored glass in a mosaic," to a "dance" which binds "the inner pattern of light with the outer world," to a "great web of patterning oscillations and quiverings," to a "delicate mesh" of "pulsing patterns," and finally to a web of "frightful necessity, imposing its design" on stars and atoms (96–105). The passage is extraordinary, and shows how consistent the linkage between Hades and the eidola has been in postmodernism, producing a diverse and flexible vocabulary of images and events modeled on the nekyia. The novel concludes with a Gnostic version of the descent much like the one we found in Mann's "Prelude" to *Joseph and His Brothers*: Charles Watkins joins a "Descent Team" created by the planetary powers for the purpose of fulfilling and redirecting the "pattern" of human history (127). Like the Messiah in Mann's Gnostic parable, Watkins must go down into life as if descending into "a Poisonous Hell" (130), but his purpose is to wake "up those of us who have forgotten what they went for" (132).

Umberto Eco

Umberto Eco's recent novel *Foucault's Pendulum* illustrates the continuing relevance of the descent to the underworld as catalyzing the revelation of archetypal forms and geometrical shapes. Eco creates a wide variety of synonyms for the eidola of Hades, revealed by a sequence of descents in which the major characters discover the key to the plot of the novel. The plot has to do with the deciphering of a parchment which encodes a Templar Plan stretching over some 666 years to take control of the World by mastering an underground energy sources. The main characters in the novel, Casaubon and Belbo, uncover the basic form of the plan through a sequence of descents: into the labyrinthine chambers beneath the city of Provins, into the caves of a mining museum in Munich, into the crypt of the cathedral of Tomar, into the belly of a periscope in the Museum des Arts et Métiers in Paris, and into the sewers of that same city where the action of the novel is resolved.

The first descent is the most important, since it leads to the revelation of the basic plot, both of the Templar Knights and of the novel. Significantly, the revelation comes in the form of a parchment of manuscript which needs to be deciphered. The manuscript was first discovered in 1894 by a spelunking dragoon named Chevalier Edouard Ingolf of Petersburg, who descended with another chevalier named Laforge into "A network of tunnels—real catacombs" preserved beneath the city of Provins since "prehistoric times" (125). Every building in the town "has an entrance to a tunnel" through its cellar, and all the tunnels taken together form a complex maze of "columns and vaulted ceilings," cellars "with ogival vaults," and "Room after room, deep in the earth, covered with ancient graffiti" (126). There are "Hieratic drawings of druid origin" and "Catharist symbols which suggest that the Knights formed a "new, underground Templars" after the execution of Jacques Molay in 1344. The most important entrance to the labyrinthine underworld of tunnels and rooms is through the "big Gothic building, the Grange–aux–Dîmes, or tithe granary" in the very center of town, where the Templars collected their tax and stored it in the "network of passages" underneath (126–27). The brave dragoons (Laforge and Ingolf) descend into the "subterranean rooms, on the second level below ground, and then go further down through "unknown tunnels" and "mysterious passages" to a "great hall with a fine fireplace and a dry well in the center" (127). (The passage recalls both the network of rooms beneath the city in "The Immortal" of Borges, and the fountain in the center of the spiral dance in Mann's portrayal of Joseph's wedding ceremonies). A week later the dragoons return with ropes to lower themselves down into the well (eleven meters deep), at the bottom of which they discover "a big room with stone walls, ten meters square and five meters high" (127). Though it is not definitely known what they find here, Colonel Ardenti (who tells the story to Casaubon and Belbo) concludes that Ingolf "must have found a gold case studded with precious stones" which he sold in Paris in 1935 and then disappeared. Ardenti also surmises that Ingolf "found a parchment in the case" (129), and it is this parchment which the Colonel has copied and which, when deciphered, reveals the Plan of the Templars and establishes the Plot of the Novel. It occurs in the section of the novel called Binah, the cabalistic Sephiroth in which "all forms are already formed" (158). These forms are the eidola of Hades, the essential shaping forces of the novel: nekyia=poesis.

Casaubon undertakes the second revelatory descent in the novel, this time into the artificial caves of a mining exhibition in Munich, where he is doing research on metallurgy. He spends his nights in "the immense crypts where elderly mustached gentlemen in lederhosen played music," and his days wandering through the "tunnels," "elevators," "narrow passages," and "bottomless pits" of the exhibition at the Deutsches Museum. Strolling through the darkness, despairing of ever seeing the light of day again" (305), Casaubon meets Signor Salon, his taxidermic neighbor from Milan, who tells Casaubon about a house in Paris, near the Métros of the Gare de l'Est and Gare du Nord, which stands "at the mouth of the underworld" (307). Threshold imagery dominates the description, for the door to the phony façade of the house "conceals the door of doors, the point of departure for the journey to the center of the earth" (307). Down there, Salon continues, "the Masters of the World exist," the rulers of the subterranean realm of "Agarttha, the underground headquarters of the King of the World, the occult center of the Synarchy" (307). The underground Kingdom is both a refuge and a place of revelation: there, in the "secret dwelling place of the King of the World," anarchy becomes synarchy, "senseless riddle" becomes "Design," as the Templar knights supervise the "occult direction of history" from the "underground cities" where they have taken refuge (310–11). Keys to the puzzle of the novel fall into place here in the artificial underworld of the Deutsches Museum: Hades rules from below, the secret governor of history and the source of all synarchy.

More pieces of the puzzle are revealed to Casaubon during his descent into the crypt beneath the castle of Tomar in Portugal, where the Templars "had withdrawn after the king and the pope saved them from trial and ruin by transforming them into the Order of the Knights of Christ" (381). It is in this chapter that Casaubon begins to identify the various groups and individuals associated with the "occult direction of history," a bizarre conglomeration that devours everyone from Christopher Columbus and Francis Bacon to Ben Franklin and Adolph Hitler. This revelation begins in the castle complex when Casaubon enters "the church of the Templars, which had an octagonal rotunda reproducing that of the Holy Sepulcher" (381), and then proceeds "down into the crypt" (382). He goes down seven steps and passes beneath seven keystones, each in the form of a rose, one larger than the next, with the last set over a well" (382). While Eco connects these rosettes to the Rosicrucian Manifestoes of the early 17th century, we should note that the passage through seven thresholds has been characteristic of the nekyia since Inanna shed her seven veils during her descent to Ereshkigal, Goddess of Death. Eco also explicitly connects Hades to geometrical symbolism (the "octagonal rotunda"), and to the labyrinth in this passage, for the guide takes Casaubon to see "a little garden designed like an elegant French maze" after they ascend from the crypt (383).

The final descent in the novel reveals the members of the occult group Casaubon and Belbo have lured into their Plan by baiting them with details of the Templar plot which they have in fact made up. In the third to last section of the novel, called Hod, we return to the setting of the first, as Casaubon climbs out of the periscope he was hiding in Chapter 1, and descends a staircase in the Museum des Arts et Métiers to the nave, where he sees the members of the group entering through a cubic pedestal in the transept. He then runs to the sentry box, where he falls down into a fetal position, and sinks "slowly into the embrace of the Subterranean World" (580), where the climactic revelations of the novel occur. Entering slowly, Casaubon sees the various members of the Tres, the "Templi Resurgentes Equites Synarchici, the triune and trinosophic mystical and most secret order of the Synarchic Knights of Templar Rebirth" (584). Last of all comes Signor Aglié (the elderly impostor of the Count de Saint–Germain of the novel), leading Lorenza (Belbo's faithless Sophia) "by the hand, as if escorting a soul along the path of Hades" (586). All the grotesque revelations of occultism occur here in the center of the mandala, as the mediums enter trances and exude the ectoplasms of Edward Kelly, Heinrich Khunrath, and the Comte de Saint–Germain (589). While I do not want to scrutinize the "mighty Secret" revealed by this occult assembly (591), I do wish to point out simply that Eco creates a mandala here on the transept pavement where the nave intersects the apse, a geometrical figure analogous to those forms of revelation we have witnessed in other postmodernist underworlds. Surrounding the central axis of the pendulum's circle (to which Belbo is tied), which hangs from the center of the transept, Eco places three mediums on chairs, who are then surrounded by four dervishes who whirl through the ritual at each of the four corners. This gives us seven hierophants and the circle, triangle, and square of alchemical computations, forming a mathematical figure much like the ones that so preoccupied Cortázar.

The novels of Cortázar, Pynchon, Lessing, and Eco bring the iconography of the nekyia up to date, and regenerate the conventions with curious doses of a kind of archetypal but scientific terminology: for the pulsating webs, meshes, quiverings, and crystallizations with which Lessing endows her underworld blueprint recalls the Oriental myth of Indra, whose net of gems, each facet reflecting the other and bearing within itself the whole system, is so suggestive of the newly dubbed "holographic universe" of contemporary physics, in which each particle of matter bears within itself the dancing burden of the whole.[47] It forms a pattern which we only seem to be able to perceive when thinking, reading, or writing about the otherworld. After Casaubon leaves the nave of the Museum, he sees such patterns everywhere surrounding him in the streets of Paris, which he has regained via and descent into and emergence from the sewer system. As he walks through the little maze of streets in the Porte Saint–Martin, he sees "windows," "portals," "arcades," "doorways," a "line of arcades," "a new door," and "an old door" all leading down into the Mundus Subterraneus from which he has just escaped, and from which he imagines the Masters ruling the world (602–06). The cityscape he traverses is typical of the urban mazes and underworlds that Joyce and Cortázar, and such Modernist film makers as Cocteau and Bergman, force their protagonists to tread.

Derek Walcott

Derek Walcott's marvelous poem, *Omeros*, demonstrates the continuing influence of T.S. Eliot's "mythical method" on the literature of postmodernism. Both the narrator in the poem and its central characters reflect upon those Homeric parallels which link the present to the past in their efforts to establish a history for the Caribbean island of St. Lucia. The retired British major Plunkett, veteran of the Montgomery's North Africa campaign against Rommel, searches for "parallels" linking the poem's central female character, Helen, and Homer's *Iliad* into a "net of myths," a "webbed connection" (95). The basis of the parallel revolves around the Battle of Saints, fought on April 12, 1782, the English under Admiral Rodney, versus the French, commanded by Le Comte de Grasse (in the *Ville de Paris*), in the channel between Dominica and Guadeloupe. The Battle of the Saints was part of the historical conflict between the Dutch, the Spanish, the English, and the French for control of the colonies on the islands of the Lesser Antilles, and generally for the trade in the Indies. Sugar and slaves were involved, so that Walcott incorporates elements of the African diaspora into his portrait of postcolonial St. Lucia. The language of the poet–narrator of the poem continually draws our attention to the narrative device of Eliot's mythical method: he speaks of the "Homeric repetition / of details, their prophecy" (96), and of the "Homeric coincidence" (100) linking the island's present to its past, and conferring that "shape and significance" upon the poem which Eliot suggested was the aesthetic result of the method ("Ulysses" 681). Walcott however also expresses what Harold Bloom would call an "anxiety of influence," when he asks "Why not see Helen / as the sun saw her, with no Homeric shadow" in order to "enter that light beyond metaphor" (271). The same anxiety is implied in the long conversation with ghost of Homer in Chapter 7, and in the notion that Homer is a possessive ghost to be exorcised (294).

The character names and basic structure of the narrative, however, demonstrate the omnipresence of Homer and Walcott's reliance on Eliot's mythical method, with a particular emphasis on the descent to the underworld. The names are mostly Greek—Helen, Achille, Hector, and Philoctete (wounded by Hercules arrow, left on Lemnos, retrieved and healed by Aesculapius to defeat Troy). Other characters clearly have epic prototypes, like the blind sage Seven Seas (Tiresias, or Homer himself), and the pagan healer Ma Kilman (a Cumaen Sybil) (242). Furthermore, the versification employs epic prototypes: Virgilian syllabics (12 syllable lines throughout, in varying, flexible metres), and the tercets of Dante (sometimes, but not always with the linked stanzas associated with terza rime). Of the conventional formula associated with the epic, we have sea–voyages, battles, dream visions, bird imagery, communion with ancestors, and, most prominently, five descents into the underworld at key points in the poem: Achille diving to the wreck of the *Ville de Paris* (43–47); the poet communing with his dead father (67–76) and mother (165–68); Achille's sunstroke, dream vision, and night–sea journey to Africa (125–60); Ma Kilman's quest for the healing herb in the dark grove of her ancestral deities (235–48); and the poet's trip on a fishing boat with Homer and subsequent ascent of Soufrière, seen as the Inferno (285–94). The sequence of descents forms the skeleton of the poem's narrative, and employs many of the iconographic motifs we have noted in a wide range of other postmodern texts (threshold imagery, ocular symbolism, geometrical figures, encounters with the ancestral past, birdsong, and sea–voyages).

The first of these descents occurs when the native fisherman, Achille, dives to the ruin of the *Ville de Paris*, in search of treasure to win the heart of Helen, and, more deeply, in search of "salvation and change" down there in the wreck (44). Like Gilgamesh, whose journey to the underworld culminates on the ocean floor, Achille drops down into the depths like a "canvas–bound carcass," with a "stone heart," and a cinder block tied to his heel (44). As he falls "for fathoms towards his fortune," he wonders if Helen's love was already "dead," and he feels the "cold of the drowned entering his loins" (44). The ocular and threshold images consistently associated with the nekyia (from Inanna to Oedipa Maas) emerge as the diver reaches the ocean floor: he imagines the "coins of light pouring from the galleon's doors" as "the eyes" of Iberian kings; fishes swirl around him with "goggling eye–bulbs"; the "corpses" of sailors drowned "in the crossing" peer out at him with "bubbles of eyes"; a "moon–blind Cyclops" counts "The ransom of centuries" behind "mossy doors"; and "silvery mackerel" swarm through the "swaying cabin–doors" leading into this world of the "dead," a world not "meant for the living" (45–46). The ocular imagery is emphatically combined, in this passage, with the threshold symbolism characteristic of the descent into the underworld: as James Hillman has pointed out, "One epithet of Hades was 'he who closes the door,'" and Hercules must be adopted by "a God–father, Pylios, a doorman," before he can pass through the gates of Hades (*Dream* 180). The association linking Hades with treasure may also be archetypal, as the granaries of Pluto, god of wealth, were underground

The second nekyia in Walcott's poem employs threshold imagery and geometrical symbolism to portray an encounter with the poet's ancestral past (the dead mother in the *Odyssey*, the dead father in the *Aeneid*), a motif immemorially associated with the journey to Hades. The encounter archetypally leads to the revelation of the pattern shaping the hero's destiny (the homecoming of Odysseus, or the founding of Rome). In *Omeros*, the meeting between the poet–

narrator and his dead father focuses on Walcott's vocation, while the imagery of the dream–like hallucination is a composed of fresh variations on the threshold motifs and geometric configurations so frequently evident in postmodernism. The nekyia begins with the poet's return to his childhood home in Chapter 12, when he sees his father's ghost step through the "angelic mirror" of his mother's wardrobe, and then pass towards him, "framed in the quiet window" of the room (68). The father's ghost walks through the printing machines now in the room, and he holds a book in "his transparent hand" (68): it is the same book in which the poet found his father's "verses" as a child, the book which determined the boy's "life's choice" and his "calling" (68). Hence, the journey to the world of the dead serves as a metaphor for poesis, linking the verses of the dead father with those of his living son. The father is therefore muse and mentor, a "lucent body" "patterned in shade" who leads the poet–narrator through the chambers of the past (picturing the past as a house and city of dead ancestors, as do Borges, Cocteau, and Lessing).

As the poet walks among the "brown phantoms" of the dead, in the little Caribbean port where he grew up, the threshold imagery of mirrors, doorways, and windows shifts to those geometrical motifs which figure the poet's search for form and inspiration. The ghost of the father leads the poet past the shadows cast by "long–stemmed pillars" to "a green square cut in smaller squares," where "water sprang in plumes / from the curled, iron–green fountain at its centre, / though its gates were shut under pluming cabbage palms" (70). One of the most consistent features of those modernist works which employ the mythical motif of the descent into Hades is the discovery of a water source at the center of a geometrical figure, like the one Walcott evokes here (a large square composed of smaller squares with a fountain in the centre): we find this, for example, in Mann's great biblical tetralogy, when Joseph celebrates his nuptials with Asenath; in the infernal palace at the centre of the Imperial labyrinth in Hermann Broch's *Death of Virgil*; and in the water jars which refresh the "Immortals" in the story by Borges of the same title.

It is from this centre that revelations proceed, this time of the poet's ancestral past, as the father points out the long lines of women carrying coal up long planks to the steamers docked in the harbor of St. Lucia (for many years a small coaling station of the British Empire). The revelations combine the imagery of the "inferno"—in the "Hell built on those hills" of the coaling station, where the "infernal anthracite is quarried" (74)—with geometrical figures of poesis: the poet sees the lines of slave women as "black pyramids" moving beneath a sky etched with the "studded diagrams" of the constellations, and he is instructed to hear in the rhythms of their footsteps the "ancestral rhyme" of his poem. The nekyia, that is to say, becomes a figure of poesis. The father's ghost appears in a house cluttered by printing machines, holding a book of verses (67–68), and he then serves as the poet's mentor, teaching his son, from beyond the grave, to imitate the rhythm of "one bare foot after the next" in the "staggering feet" of his verse; to use the "couplets" of the twin "wooden planks," which connect the steamers to the dock, to lift his poem "higher than those hills of infernal anthracite"; to find his metres, rhymes, and couplets in the "slow ancestral beat" of "those multiplying feet" which carry the coal down the mountainsides and up the gangplanks (75). It is a very beautiful moment of revelation, one which transforms the inferno of slavery into a temenos (a sacred space), or crypt, where the ancestors speak, and the young poet struggles to "give those feet a voice" (76). After his instruction, the threshold imagery returns, as the father's ghost walks back "through a pillared balcony's alternating shade" into the deepening shadows of the underworld (76).

The third nekyia in the poem is the most thoroughly developed, and it leads us more deeply into the underworld of the ancestral dead. Allusions to Homer and Virgil enrich the long passage, which begins at the end of Book 2 and proceeds through all of Book 3. The journey begins at sea, as Achille imagines his canoe being pulled toward Africa, the ancestral homeland of the dead, by a "sea swift" (125), which he calls "*l'hirondelle des Antilles*" (126), and which he imagines as a hummingbird towing the boat with "electric wings" (130). He sees the bird as a kind of Hermes figure, "mind–messenger" of a "god's orders," leading the soul of Achille homeward (131). The swift evokes the uncanny omniscience of the soul, shooting "ahead of each question like an answer" (130), with "the whole world / globed in the passing sorrow of her sleepless eye" (127)—she is what I would call a 'hologlyph,' a symbol in which a small part of the world contains the whole. It is archetypal for the journey to Hades to combine the theme of revelation with the ocular symbolism of the swift's "sleepless eye." Her prototype is perhaps to be found in the *Aeneid*, Book 6, in which Aeneas follows the twin doves of Aphrodite to the "jaws of foul Avernus" (145), but the affiliation between birds and the souls of the dead is ancient, and widespread, forming a kind of archetypal aviary of Avernus. Among the Egyptians alone we have Isis, as the Goddess of death, sitting on the sarcophagus with outspread wings; Mut, the mother goddess of the tomb, depicted as a vulture, bearing the Ankh in its talons—the Egyptian cross with the loop enclosing a lapis lazuli eye; and the Ba soul of the dead, typically depicted in papyri as a human–headed bird (Reed 14, 92). Going further back to the Sumero–Babylonians, we find Enkidu's vision of the dead "clothed like birds with wings for covering" (92), and the bird–beaked figure sitting inside a ceramic plaque, representing the door to the underworld, associated with Inanna's descent (Wolkstein and Kramer 190). In fact, as noted before, the symbolism of the soul as a migratory bird may well take us all the way back to the ritual burial sites of the Paleolithic, such as Mal'ta on Lake Baikal, where six flying geese, carved out of mammoth ivory, were found in a child's grave (Campbell, *Atlas* 1.1.72).

But the archetypal symbolism of the bird embraces both the nekyia and poesis, since birdsong has traditionally been recognized as a metaphor for poetry. According to the Egyptians, the very letters of the alphabet were a gift from the Ibis or Heron headed deity, Thoth, who becomes the Greek Hermes, patron of poetry (Drucker 58). Robert Graves traces Welsh traditions linking the flight of cranes to the origin of letters back to Hermes, who "is credited with having invented the alphabet after watching the flight of cranes" (234). Derek Walcott follows the same line of mythological tradition, consistently linking bird song and flight to poesis and the nekyia. The narrator of the fiction is seen as a "phantom" (28), and we discussed the vision of phantom father as the poet's muse or mentor above (74). Later in the poem, we will find the dead Homer and poet singing on ferry boat to the underworld (286), and the idea linking the poet's "craft" to the building of a canoe, and the canoe to his own coffin, is a frequent motif in *Omeros* (159; 227; 321). It recalls Eliot's notion, in *Four Quartets*, that "Every poem is an epitaph" (58). By the same token, the motif linking birdsong to poesis is sustained throughout the poem: in the night–sea journey to Africa the poet evokes "the bird whose wings wrote the word / 'Afolabe' in the letters of the sea–swift" (159). Later in the poem he alludes to a "flotilla of swallows memorizing an alphabet" 192), notes that "frock–tailed sparrows are / tagging notes to pediment" (182), and pauses outside the Boston Museum to smoke "on the steps and read the calligraphy / of swallows" (183).

As Achille watches the sea swift towing his canoe towards Africa, he performs the sort of ritual which the epic tradition has lead us to expect in portrayals of the nekyia. It is midday, for the sun is vertical to the mast, as Achille furls both oars and lays them, "with ritual / solicitude," down into the "the grave of" his canoe (127). Then he scoops sea water with a calabash cup, "sprinkles the scorched sail / stitched from old flour sacks" (128), and pours it "streaming over his boiling skull" while pulling "at the knots in the sail" (129). The precisely observed actions of this "ritual / baptism" (129) summon the spirits of the dead: first the "noble and lugubrious names / under the rocking shadow" (127–28) of the boat, the dead sailors of Caribbean folklore and history—Winston James; an old drunk called "Always Soused"; "Herald Chastenet, plaiter of lobster–pots"; Dorcas Henry; and Midshipman Plunkett, whose death during the Battle of the Saints is powerfully recorded in the poem. Then the dead appear as "corpses wrapped like the sail" (129), until, finally, when Achille cuts his hand on the ropes binding the sail to the mast, while struggling to "loosen its burial knots," he is mesmerized and gripped by "pious horror," as "the ghost of his father's face" appears "at the end of the line" (130).

All of these ritual details are significant, enriching the surface realism with mythological symbols derived mostly from the *Odyssey*, Book 11, when Odysseus summons the Kimmerian shades with a necromantic ritual taught him by Circe. It is the same ritual Pound evokes in Canto 1: digging a trough in front of the cave, pouring the blood of a black ram into the pit, and then sprinkling the blood with milk and honey, wine, and barley (186). Similar rituals occur in the *Aeneid*: the Sybil pours wine upon the brows of the black steers (147), and while in Hades, Aeneas "sprinkles / his body with fresh water" at the threshold gates forged by the Cyclops (159). While not sticking as slavishly to the details of Homeric and Virgilian necromancy as Pound does, Walcott nevertheless cannily cloaks the "ritual" Achille performs to summon the shades of the dead with epic figures. Like Aeneas, he pours water on his head, and encounters the spirit of his dead father; and like Odysseus, he uses water and grain (Walcott evokes the "flour sack" of the sail) to consecrate his invocation. Other motifs in the ritual take us farther afield: the image of the drowned "Herald Chastenet, plaiter / of lobster pots" (127), and Achille's pulling at the "burial knots" of the sail, both focus on the symbolism of weaving and unknotting, Classical and archetypal sources of which can be adduced here. Bachofen, for example, discusses the symbolism of Ocnus the rope plaiter, a figure frequently found depicted in

Roman mortuary artifacture (51–65), and linked to the liberation death brings to that soul which has unwound, or unknotted, the "crude fabric" of its body (65).

Similar motifs occur in the story of "Eros and Psyche" in *The Golden Ass* of Apuleius: when Psyche descends into the underworld, she throws barley bread soaked in honey wine to Cerberus, passes quickly by a lame ass driver, and then proceeds on her journey across the river Styx, ignoring a dead man floating on the surface, who tries to get in the ferryboat (shades of Achille's father), and passing by some old women at work weaving, with whom she does not meddle (139). These are surely the fates; like Ocnus—with whom Marie Louise von Franz equates the lame ass driver (101)—the fabric they weave is the life of the body, which is unwound by death. The more prominent source for Walcott's imagery is perhaps Dante, but the particular motif of the knot, evoked by Herald Chastenet, the lobster–pot plaiter, has a widely diffused basis in folklore, as opposed, perhaps, to the epic. As the drowned man's name suggests, the act of plaiting, followed by the "loosening" of the "burial knots," prefigures (heralds) the liberation of Achille's soul from his body, so that he can conduct his journey to Africa, the ancestral home of his dead. Ananda K. Coomaraswamy traces "the 'universal form of the knot' spoken of by Dante (*Paradiso* XXXIII.91)" back to "Plato's 'golden cord' (*Laws*, 644)" and "so to Homer's 'golden chain' (*Iliad* 8.18f.)," all images of those solar threads which bind the various forms of the universe into the network of the creation (27–28). In India, the incarnate soul, bound to the body by the "'knots (granthi) of the heart,'" becomes the liberated soul in death—when it is released from "the bonds, knots, or nooses" of life, the soul is said to be "Nirgrantha, 'whose knot is undone'" (28). Images of knots abound in Dante, but perhaps closer to Walcott's *Omeros* we have Yeats, who, in "Byzantium," another great poem depicting the journey to the underworld as a sea voyage, evokes the unwinding of the "mummy cloth" as a symbol of the divestiture of the body of fate, which binds the soul to life. In *Omeros*, the motifs of weaving, death, and the bird flight of the liberated soul are beautifully woven together in the picture of Maud Plunkett stitching all of the birds of the island into a quilt, which she suddenly realizes is her shroud (88–89), the "silk" which we will later see "draping her bier" (267).

Along with the archetypal symbolism of weaving, knots, birds, the sea–voyage, and necromantic ritual, Walcott concludes Book 2's initiation of the nekyia with geometrical figures: while his boat passes "under the geometry / of the hidden stars," Achille ponders "the great design / of the triangular trade" linking Africa, the Azores, and the lesser Antilles (130). History becomes a sequence of ricorsi, of "circled epochs" (131), rather like the gyres, but here, the "swift's flywheel" (131) leads Achille back to Africa, his place of "origin" (130), the homeland of his fathers. The circular figure of the whirring "flywheel" of the swift's flight recalls the "hum / of the wheel's elbow" which stops earlier in the poem when the poet encounters his own father's ghost in the house of his childhood, which is filled with the machines of the "printery" (67). That earlier nekyia uses the cessation of the wheel's turning to represent what the loosening the "burial knots" implies in this scene: the end of life, which the soul experiences as a liberation.

Allusions to Yeats (and other modernist precursors) persist in the first chapter of Book 3, devoted to the passage to the yonder shore of Africa, to which Achille returns in quest of his ancestral origins. Achille paddles "from the other world" up an "endless river" which unreels "those images that flickered into real mirages" (133); it is a "branch of the Congo" which sloughs "its old skin like a snake / in wrinkling sunshine" (135). He is guided to a village of "the dead" (136) by a "skeletal warrior," who plays the role of an African Charon (133). Here Achille encounters the ghost of "himself in his father" Afolabe (136), and is himself transformed into "the ghost / of a name" (139), at home in "that dawn–sadness which ghosts have for their graves" (141). The poet recounts Achille's passage "under the flat keels of whales, / under the translucent belly of the snaking current," which takes him across three centuries, passing "huge cemeteries / of bone" along the way (142), until he arrives "home" to be reunited with his father. These passages evoke biblical and literary prototypes of the nekyia: Jonah in the belly of the whale; the Prodigal son "lost" in the far country; Conrad's infernal Congo, also described a snake on an old map; Yeats's "images that yet / Fresh images beget" in "Byzantium"; and Eliot's brown river god, littered with its "cargo of dead negroes" in the *Four Quartets* (40). As in Eliot's great poem, the underworld is a place of apocalypse, where the end meets the beginning, where the past and the future merge in a present which embraces all of history. Here Achille comes "into his own beginning and his end" (134), just as Eliot does, led homeward by "the swift whose wings" figure the "crucifixion" (134).

But Walcott's underworld is not only a place of atonement, where father merges with son, and future merges with past, nor only a place of revelation, where the pattern of historical destiny is revealed: it is also an inferno (a place of suffering), and a temenos (a place of transformation), where the sacred rites of poesis are performed. The village is infernal because slavery takes root there: first the village is attacked and fifteen slaves are taken out of doors "like open graves" (145), to be crammed beneath the "iron door" of the hold on a slave ship, where the dead are tossed overboard like palm trees, "the ribbed corpses / floating, riding, to the white sand they remembered" (149). The details of Walcott's powerful narrative recall the iconography of the nekyia: the doors in these passages; the knotted "arc of a net" of arrows, forming a "mesh" which binds the villagers into slavery (144); the "emerald net" of the surface to the sea, beneath which Achille walks on the ocean floor (142); the "net / of vines" from which Achille struggles to unrope himself, as he flees the slave traders, only to be looped in the heel by the "piercing chain" of a "thorned vine" (148); the "criss–crossed net" of fate, written in the life lines of "their palms" (150); and, finally, the fishing "nets" at the end of the pier, from which the "eyes" of the dead sear "through his skull" (147). Walcott stitches eyes all through his tapestry of the underworld: here the dead villagers drowned in the net, but also Achille's own tear–filled "eyes, where the past was reflected / as well as the future" as he listens to his father (139); Achille's "blind eyes" staring up from the mud after the vine trips him (148); the "eyes" of the slaves on board the ship, showing "dried fronds in their brown irises" (149); the "eyes like pots left out in the rain" over which the iron door of slave ship's hold slides (149); the "cold eye," like "a globed window," of the kingfish Achille's mate catches on the return crossing to St. Lucia (157)—which parallels the "sleepless eye" of the swift at the beginning of the nekyia (127)—and the "eyes sore as embers" in the burned white skull of the village poet (146), who is elsewhere referred to as "the seed–eyed prophet" (143), the "white–eyed storyteller" (139), and the "seed–eyed, tree–wrinkled bard" (140).

These last images remind us that the underworld is not only an inferno, but also a crypt, where the ancestral voices are to be heard, ringing in the well; and a temenos, a place where poems are made, and submitted to the sacred memory of the village bard. It is therefore appropriate that Achille's father Afolabe instruct his son in the mysteries of names and words (137–39), and that the narrative of Achille's sojourn in the otherworld of the ancestors should repeatedly evoke the tribe's Omeros—its "blind," "white–eyed," "seed–eyed" "storyteller," "prophet," and "bard." He sings the songs of tribal memory to the tune of "a balaphon's whine" (139), and he chants to the beat of "blurring ankles" during the dance and feast in celebration of Achille's homecoming (143). His song blends with Walcott's own, recording the history of the tribe, and celebrating the power of men as "born makers" (150): of wicker basket weavers, sculptors of antelopes, bow makers, armorers, potters, and painters. The climax of Achille's nekyia, therefore, celebrates the powers of poesis specifically, and, more generally, the creative instincts of Homo faber, man the maker. The geometrical figure Walcott uses to represent man's shaping instinct in this passage is the circle, as opposed to the square containing smaller squares evoked during the poet–narrator's communion with the ghost of his father in the earlier nekyia. When Achille arrives in Africa after his journey beneath the sea, he climbs a hill above the village to find "that sacred circle of clear ground / where the gods assembled," and there he "recited the gods' names" (140). And when the slaves return across the water to their Caribbean captivity, they do so under "circling suns" (151).

The kind of poesis which the nekyia inspires, in the epic tradition at least, involves large visions of the historical life of the tribe: Odysseus sees all the great men and women of Greek history, past and present, among the shades which throng towards the blood–filled pit; Aeneas receives a vision of the future of Rome from his dead father in Hades; Dante speaks with a vast host of historical and mythological characters as he treads the circles of the Inferno. Similar moments of omniscient revelation have been recorded by thanatologists interested in what Carol Zaleski calls near–death narratives, literary and clinical versions of which typically involve those panoramic visions of historical destiny we know from the epics of Homer, Virgil, and Dante. Another critic, Ronald MacDonald, has used the phrase "burial place of memory" to describe the classical underworld, for that is the place where the great stories of the ancestral past, present, and future are stored. Hence, it seems fitting that Walcott conclude Achille's netherworld journey with an overview of three hundred years of the African diaspora. As he walks under the sea back home to St. Lucia, he sees all the "important epochs" of the tribal dispersion inscribed on the "parchment" of the sea surface far above him: the rise and fall of governments, Jesuits burning in Veracruz, a Sephardic Jew fleeing the Inquisition in Lisbon, to be reborn in

Lima, and Curaçao, a black man frozen in the Pyrenees under Napoleon, Queen Victoria with "orb and sceptre," Wilberforce struck by lightning, Darwin in the Galapagos, and Madrasi from Calcutta and Bombay in the fatal hold of a ship off the Cape of Good Hope (155–56). It is the kind of historical catalogue readers of the descent to Hades in the epic have come to expect, and Walcott consistently includes such breadth of vision throughout the course of *Omeros*.

Achille's nekyia ends, like Odysseus, when he awakens off the shores of the island. He finds himself "cradled in the bow" of his canoe (157), curled up "like a foetus" (158), with a huge blue albacore lying at "fresh at his feet, its eye like a globed window / ringing with cold, its rim the circular river / of the current that had carried him back" (157). Eye, circle, globe, fish, bird, rebirth, and canoe: an iconography of the nekyia, for, as the poet–narrator says, "a wave rhymes with one's grave, / a canoe with a coffin" (159). Achille is reborn from his journey with a new sense of his identity, with a new name in fact, given him by "the bird whose wings wrote the word 'Afolabe,' in the letters of the sea–swift" (159). Like the souls in "Byzantium," he is escorted back across the water by dolphins (159), and arrives home with a prayer for "His Virgin Mother" and a blast of the conch shell (160). To complete the historical catalogue begun earlier in the nekyia, Walcott concludes this section of the poem with another kind of descent: after his return, when Achille recuperates from his ordeal in Seven Seas' back yard, he finds a stone head in the "dead leaves" (163). It lies at the base of a "pomme–Arac" tree, with an iguana in the leaves of its branches, and a "dog barking around the trunk's base" (163). It is a timeless afternoon, "one of those Saturdays that contain centuries, / when the strata of history layered underheal [...] can lie in a quartz shard" (163). In this case, the centuries encoded in the quartz 'hologlyph' stretch back not to the African, but to the Aruac past, the native inhabitants of St. Lucia, pre–Columbian and even pre–Carib, the cannibal tribe who first terrorized the island. The face of the rock Achille finds glares up at him "from its disturbed grave," with "blank circles for eyes" (163–64). Terrified by the "Stone–faced souls" that peer up at him "with their lizard eyes," Achille hurls it over the oleander hedge (164).

This is a marvelous passage, one which replaces the metaphor of diving, with the metaphor of digging, to represent those mysteries of poesis inspired by the nekyia. (The archaeological symbolism of a layered history which the poet uncovers is one we find also in *The Anathemata* of David Jones). It is also a marvelous example of Eliot's mythical method, combining precisely observed, realistic details with a strong undercurrent of mythological symbolism. Once again, we have the combination of ocular and geometrical imagery ("lizard eyes" like "blank circles") (164). The stone head Achille finds at the base of the Arac–pomme in the garden may suggest the "enigmatic zemis," tri–pronged idols which have been "recovered from sites scattered throughout the Antilles," buried in garden plots to fertilize the ground, for they were the heads from which the yucca tree was said to grow (Campbell, *Atlas* 2.3.312–13). But Walcott puts a lizard in the branches of his Aruac apple tree, and a nameless dog barking "around" its base, motifs which suggest Biblical and Minoan sources. Garden, fruit tree, serpent, and death certainly bear Biblical associations; but the dog barking in circles at the base of the tree recalls the dog at the base of the tree of life on the famous "Ring of Nestor," a representation of the Mycenaean afterlife, dug up from the beehive tomb at Pylos by Sir Arthur Evans, who suggests that the "dog–like monster" is a "forerunner of Cerberus," the dog which guards the entrance to Hades in Greek myth (Campbell, *Occidental* 52). As always in *Omeros*, Walcott employs this suggestive iconography of the nekyia in a spontaneous, intuitive manner, without being enslaved by the correspondences which enrich his poem.

The motif of the nekyia does, however, serve as a basic structural device throughout the poem, linking the various episodes together into a coherent aesthetic whole. Book 3 ends, for example, with the a variation on the journey to the otherworld, when the poet visits his aging mother in the "Marian Home" where she is being cared for: she is a described as a "fledgling," with a hand as "frail as a swift," and a "cotton halo" fanning her "shrunken crown" (165). Returning from this twilight world to the village—walking past "children with bat–like cries" and among "shadows" that 'cross' the poet in the signs of a "black language"—is like being "transported" into "another country," the language of which is "untranslatable" (167). In fact, Walcott's "village whose fires flickered in my head / with tongues of a speech I no longer understood" (167) recalls Eliot's statement that "the communication / Of the dead is tongued with fire beyond the language of the living" (*Four Quartets* 51). As the poet closes the "door," which leads into and out of this underworld of shadows (168), metaphors of weaving and knotting are once again evoked alongside the threshold symbolism of the nekyia. The poet hears the distant breakers crashing in the surf "with a sound like tearing cloth / ripped down the stitched seam, a sound Mama made sewing / when, in disgust, she'd rip the stitches with her mouth" (168). Like Achille loosening the burial knots of the sail in the earlier passage, the combined imagery of knitting and unknitting in this passage evokes the dual symbolism archetypally associated with weaving: in the *Odyssey*, Penelope sits weaving the shroud of Laertes, which she unknots at night, a symbol of the lunar cycles of birth and death, creation and destruction (Campbell, *Occidental* 163–64). By closing a passage about his dying mother with a description of her ripping up the stitched seams of her sewing, Walcott cleverly employs the same kind of imagery which fascinated Bachofen in his discussion of Ocnus the rope plaiter, sitting with the donkey at his feet, nibbling away at the "crude fabric" of the departed soul's body.

Walcott ends this passage, and all of Book 3, with one final motif derived from the archetypal iconography of the nekyia. The poet sees a "stuttering moth" in his hotel room, the "swift shadow" of which he then notices rippling on the surface of the "emerald lagoon" outside the window, with a "canoe, nearing the island" in the foreground, and a sail in the distance, which he describes as a "hooked butterfly / on its flowering branch" (168). David Jones uses the symbolism of the mast as a cross in *The Anathemata*, and H.D. uses the motif of the cross as a flowering rod in *Trilogy*. Along with these symbols of the resurrection, Walcott includes the motif of the canoe reaching the yonder shore, and the lovely motif of the moth, or butterfly. In Cretan art, we see butterflies rising beside the horns of consecration on a Late Minoan III sarcophagus, and, on a really splendid pithos from Late Minoan I (c.1400 B.C.), "A double–axe–

shaped butterfly with a head of concentric circles emerges from a vessel of some kind (center); she is flanked by growing plants and bull's heads, from between whose horns emerge lily–headed butterflies" (Gimbutas 275). The motif continues to appear as "the double–axe shaped butterfly" on Mycenaean vases (Gimbutas 274–75; Figs.431–32). Chrysalis and butterfly also appear, famously, on the beautiful "Ring of Nestor" mentioned above, where two butterflies and two corresponding chrysalises in the upper left compartment of the world tree represent "the resurgence of the human spirit after death" (Campbell, *Occidental Myth* 51). This is a fitting symbol to conclude Book 3 of *Omeros*, which is entirely devoted to the descent to, and return from, the underworld.

The next nekyia of note occurs in Book 6, Chapters XLVII to XLIX, which describe Ma Kilman's quest for the herb she will use to cure Philoctete's festering wound. Earlier in the poem, Walcott had referred to Ma Kilman as a "sybil, obeah woman / webbed with a spider's knowledge of an after–life" (58), and he frames her journey to the "dark grove" (237) where the healing herb grows, with the tombstones of the cemetery: she walks "past the stones with dried palms and conchs, where the buried / suffer" on her way up the goat path (238), and returns "past the crunching goats, where the buried / lie under the cement stones" on her way back down (246). The allusive framework for this passage to the otherworld is not so much Homeric as Virgilian: Ma Kilman is the Cumaean Sybil of the Aeneid Book 6, who directs Aeneas to follow the twin doves to the tree where the golden bough grows, the light of which will lead him through the gates of Hades to the land of the dead. Hence, Walcott refers to Ma Kilman as a "furious sybil" (237), a "caverned prophetess" (243), and a "spidery sybil / hanging in a sack from the cave at Cumae" (245). The herb she gathers for her "sybilline cure" waits beneath the "citron / sprig of a lime–tree," upon which a swift sits (235), like the doves perched on the treetop in the dark grove where golden bough grows in the *Aeneid* (145–46).

Ma Kilman's netherworld journey evokes the threshold and weaving imagery we have seen earlier in the poem, along with the revelation of the language, history, and deities of the ancestral past. She leaves home wearing a black hat with a "berried fringe," stepping down the "concrete step / of the rumshop's back door," catching her finger as she rams the hinge shut, and crossing herself as she walks out the "gate" (236). She recites "her own litany / of berries" as she walks, echoing Keats, but replacing his "rosary of yewberries" with the beads of her herbal lore: "Hail Mary marigolds," "mild anemone / and clear watercress," "anthurium," "the thorns of logwood," "aloe," "the hole in the daisy's palm," "roadside tisane," and "the buds of green sugar–apples in the sun" (236–37). The herb she seeks for the cure of Philoctete sits beneath "the nodding palanquins of umbrella yams" in the "dark grove" of the mountain, "its pronged flower" springing up "like a buried anchor" (237). The mulch in which the herb is rooted stinks like gangrenous corpses rotting in the grave, "its rage / festering for centuries," the flower reeking "with corrupted blood" and seeping "pustular drops instead of sunlit dew / into the skull" (244).

A more funereal flower is not to be found, and it is found only with the guidance of the ancestral deities who inhabit the haunted grove. Walcott replaces the twin doves of Virgil's Venus with ants, "generations of silent black workers"

(244) who lend Ma Kilman "their language" (245), and whose cries and trail lead her from the Catholic Church to the pagan grove where the herb grows (238). Ma Kilman sees the ants as "the ancestors of Achille, / the women carrying coals after the dark door / slid over the hold" (239, 244). The grove to which they lead her is guarded by "gods in the leaves," whose names she has forgotten, deities like "Erzulie, / Shango, and Ogun," who swarm "in the thicket" and who are "subdued in the rivers of her blood" (242). These gods inhabit the "restless shade" of the grove, having migrated from Africa like "swallows," and having escaped Christianization (242). They are "unburied, for three centuries dead," but their power and rituals remain alive, "concentrated / in the whorled corolla of that stinking flower" beneath the umbrella yam (242). The weaving motif combines with bird imagery in this otherworld journey, as Ma Kilman hears the pagan gods screeching like bats and "building a web overhead," like a "net that entered her nerves," with "crisscrossing stitches" (243).

To find the healing flower, Ma Kilman performs the ritual of divestiture, frequently associated with the descent into the underworld (to be found in Cocteau, Merrill, and Pynchon, among others). She unpins her hat, removes her henna wig, and unbuttons "the small bone buttons / of her church dress" (243–44). The imagery of unpinning and unbuttoning in these lines correlates with the loosening of the burial knots and the ripping of stitches in the earlier scenes, motifs to which Walcott now adds the related notion of unwinding, or unreeling film. Ma Kilman continues her ritual invocation of the pagan deities of her African ancestry by rubbing dirt on her "mossed skull" and in her hair, by praying "in the language of ants and her grandmother" (243–44), and by scraping the earth with her fingernails (244). Then she screams so loudly the sun puts "clouds to its ears as her screech reeled backwards / to its beginning, from the black original cave / of the sybil's mouth" (245). This unreeling is a ricorso, a return to ancestral origins which shakes Philoctete "up from the bed of his grave" (245). The poet's sybil has retrieved that herb from the land of the ancestral dead, inhabited by her grandmother, the ants, and Yoruban deities—Shango is the god of thunder; Ogun the god of smiths (Bonnefoy, *African* 143–44). The herb will enable her to raise Philoctete from the grave of his sickbed.

To do so Walcott introduces another motif familiar in the literature of postmodernism—the cauldron, or sacred vessel of transformation, variations of which would include Lawrence's "bath of birth" in *Women in Love* (301), the cauldron in which Adrian Leverkühn is boiled in oil in Mann's *Dr. Faustus* (354), the Black Witch's pot in *The Tin Drum* (98), and the cauldron of the Abbess in Leonora Carrington's *Hearing Trumpet* (136). Even Freud uses the metaphor, when he describes the underworld of the id as "a cauldron of seething excitement" (Hillman, *Dream* 18); and Jung follows the lead when he compares the immersion in the alchemical bath to a "*descensus ad inferos*" (*Transference* 83). Mythological variants of the symbolism would include the cauldron Medea cooks an old ram in (Matthews 46); the child in a cauldron in an Attic vase (Kerényi 23); the Pietrosa bowl and the alabaster serpent cup of the Hellenistic mysteries, which contains not one, but sixteen people (Leisegang 194f; Campbell, *Mythic Image* 388); the Gundestrup bowl, inscribed with warriors being dipped into a cauldron (Davidson 76; Cunliffe 108); King Matholwch's magic cauldron, in which he cooked his dead warriors (Green 58); the Pietrosa Bowl, and the Chinese Yu Vessel of the Shang Dynasty, which portrays a jaguar devouring a head with no body (Campbell, *Mythic Image* 126). Walcott's genius adapts the archetype to the specific context of postcolonial St. Lucia by baking Philoctete in a cauldron "from the old sugar–mill" (246), so that an instrument of oppression becomes a healing vessel of transformation: like the Celtic warriors of the Dagda, like Jason's old father, like the men on the Gundestrup bowl, Philoctete emerges from Ma Kilman's bath a new man, like Adam, with his "first clay's innocent prick" glistening in the light of the first day (248).

The last journey to the underworld in *Omeros* adapts elements derived from Homer and Dante to portray the inferno of the slave and sugar trade, and the processes of poesis which redeem them. It begins at sunrise, as the poet narrator steps out onto his hotel balcony, and sees what looks like a coconut shell bobbing in the surf. When it drifts towards the shore, a dog comes racing its shadow along the surf line, yapping at the shell, which alternately appears to the poet as a "floating head" (280), a log, a "foam–headed fisherman" (281), and, finally, as "the blind stone" head of Omeros, the poet's muse and mentor, who stares off at the sea with "empty eyes" (282) as he leads Walcott on his last nekyia in the poem. The oracular head floating towards the shore recalls Orpheus, the archetypal poet associated with the descent to Hades, decapitation, and (like the coconut shell rolling in the surf) fishermen: Robert Eisler was the first to establish the analogy between Orpheus and Jesus as fishermen of souls (Campbell, *Creative* 24). In *Omeros*, the poet follows the "marble head" up the hill and then down to a canoe waiting for them in a cove for which "no wanderer could have chosen a better grave" (281). While walking past "the grove / where the sybil swayed," and on down to the canoe in the cove, the poet–narrator turns ghostly, "no shadow" underlining his "being," and "every line" of his palm turning "transparent" (282).

It is a "black canoe" with a "grizzled oarsman" serving as its Charon, holding the prow while the poet wades aboard with an "untroubled weightlessness" (285). The poet remains transparent, as the "oarsman seemed to stare through" him, and the oars pass unnoticed through the bodies of the bathers in the surf (285). Walcott's Charon is a "charred ferryman," black as coal, a "legendary oarsman" with a "gravedigger's breath" (287), and he rows the "strange crew" past the hotel out to a cove where a "ghostly fleet" floats "at anchor" (288). Echoing Eliot's "familiar compound ghost" of "Little Gidding" (53), Walcott describes the ferryman as a "comfortable, / common, familiar apparition" (287). While the apparition rows the canoe through "the rotting fleet in a dead silence," the blind Omeros revolves "irisless eyes" (288), and he challenges the poet to a singing match in praise of the island. The nekyia, that is to say, becomes a journey of poesis, as the dead poet's "Greek calypso" inspires the "thin voice" of the living poet, who sings of mountain pools, springs, and "screeching" birds stitching a musical "tapestry" (286). The metaphor Walcott uses for versifying here (stitching) recalls the motifs of weaving and knotting, consistently found, during the various descents in the poem, as images of poesis.

After beaching the canoe, Homer yields to Dante, leading the poet, like Virgil in the *Inferno*, into the circle of the fraudulent and the malicious. The "blind guide" leads the poet through the "sulphur of hell" to the "Pool of Speculation," where the heads of colonial investors "gurgled in the lava of the Malebolge (289). Among the "spectres / that the forge of the Malebolge was bubbling with" the poet finds "Hector in hell," with a "charred face" and a "spiked hubcap" for a shield, and the ghosts of Bennett & Ward, two young Englishmen who failed in their efforts to transmute the mountain's sulphur into gold—as we are told earlier in the poem, when Major and Maud Plunkett undertake their own pilgrimage through the "gate of sulphur" to the Malebolgian springs, whose "smoke signaled the thunder of the dead" (59). Once again, Walcott's language evokes the ocular iconography of the nekyia: the sight of the speculators bubbling in the "forge" of the "pool's sluggish circle" brings tears to the "eyes in the stone head" guiding the poet (290), whose own eyes are "seared" by the "scorching light that had put out St. Lucia's eyes" (289). Along with Hector and the speculators, the poet also sees the poets suffering in the pits of the Malebolge, "Selfish phantoms with eyes / who wrote with them only," seeing only the surfaces of things (293).

Placing the poets in hell also reinforces the linkage between the nekyia and poesis established in the rest of the poem. For the journey inspires the poet's reflections on the nature of his "craft," which he compares to swifts stitching "shadowy spires" on a screen, which they have "ravelled and unravelled," like the "unthreading foam" of the surf (291), hence using the same metaphors of birdsong and knitting found in the other descents. Walking through Hades, another key metaphor of poesis is made explicit, as the poet compares his craft to an "odyssey," in which the "'I' is a mast; a desk is a raft," and the pen is an oar dipping its "beak" in the white foam of sea and page (291). These analogies reinforce the frequent pun linking the poet's "craft" to that canoe in which his own journeys to the netherworld are performed. For the poet, like the epic hero, must descend to the valleys below, to the burial places of memory—the house of his childhood, the shipwrecks sunken among the reefs, the African village where the blind bard sings, and the coves, caverns, and sibylline groves of his own island. In these temenoi the ancestors recite the unwritten history of the Caribbean diaspora—unwritten, that is to say, until Derek Walcott went down among the dead to retrieve the real treasure of the *Ville de Paris*.

James Merrill

"Admittedly I err by undertaking / This in its present form," Merrill writes in the first line of the "Book of Ephraim" (3), announcing the central myth of poem as a whole: for the poet is an undertaker, one who attends the dead on their passage; the poem is a crypt, where ancestral voices echo; poesis, therefore, is an "undertaking," one which allows the dead to speak. Through the medium of the Ouija board, Merrill incorporates the many voices of dead friends (Maya, Mimi, Maria, Wystan, Chester, Hans, Robert, George), family members (Charles Merrill, Matt and Mary Jackson), and the ancestral precursors of the poetic tradition (Homer, Dante, Milton, Blake, Goethe, Yeats, Stevens, Rimbaud, Proust, Hardy, Campion, Colette, Austen, Congreve, Stein). "ALL THE DEAD" clamor to speak (257) through the mirror, and at least two of them are compared to classical shades: Robert to Sir Orfeo (452), and Maria to Proserpine (517).

Mirabell celebrates the seances at the Ouija board, which produce the poem, as a way of "MAKING YR RAFT FAST TO THE SHORES OF THE DEAD" (265), thereby using a metaphor we also find in Derek Walcott (whose "craft" is both "canoe," "coffin," and poetry itself). In fact, Merrill presents the underworld literally as a place where poems are made, and recorded, a burial place of memory: there Auden dictates his stanzas, masques, and couplets; there Flagstad sings an aria by Strauss, specially composed for the occasion (358), Marvell composes wonderful couplets (381), and the Muses perform in masque (400f.); there Robert Morse appears to compose his first "otherworld symphony," (418), like "Orfeo / Singing to damned" (452); and from there derive the inspirational visions of Homer, Dante, Milton, Blake, Yeats, and even Eliot, whose *Waste Land* is said to have been 'ghost written' by Arthur Rimbaud (219). Even the archangel Michael, and God himself participate in these otherworldly rites of poesis, the former trying his hand at couplets, and the latter singing an odd song at the climax of the "Yes" section of "Scripts for the Pageant" (360). This section closes with the two sestets Wystan composes to evoke God B's song, which he compares to an aria from *Tristan*, sung by a homesick tenor, high up in the rigging above the ship below (365).

Merrill weaves many of the icons of the nekyia into this tapestry of poesis—ornithological, canine, and ocular, in addition to the clothing and threshold symbolism frequently found in postmodernism. As we have seen, Faust's black dog initiates the journey, but 741, the bat–winged soul from before mankind, quickly assumes the role of psychopomp —here a kind of benevolent vampire, even though he and his kind represent the dark forces buried within the atom (like Merrill, the physicist Jacob Bronowski also used the metaphor of the "hidden underworld" to describe that inscrutable realm of the nucleus revealed by the research of Einstein and Niels Bohr (123)). Since the underworld is a temenos, as well as a crypt, this bat is miraculously transfigured into the peacock (157–58), whom Merrill names Mirabell. This fits in well with the traditional iconography of Hades, which from "The Descent of Inanna, to the Epic of Gilgamesh, to the Egyptian Books of the Dead, to the Celtic Islands of the Blessed, has represented the souls of the dead as birds. We find the motif also in Yeats, Eliot, Leonora Carrington, and H.D. Other kinds of birds fly through the pages of The Changing Light—particularly the owl, sparrow, eagle and phoenix, which a lovely interlude of couplets, recording a dinner chat with George Cotzias, evokes (298–300). This interlude links the birds of the underworld to their poetic lineage (Boccaccio, Poe, Keats, Wagner, and Dante), and to their traditional role of interlocution with the realm of the spirit: George tells JM about a hallucinatory woman who whispered him the secrets of black holes (the ash left by the Phoenix), and about "the song / The Phoenix sings throughout eternity," both of which he heard once under general anesthesia (299).

By using the peacock, however, Merrill manages to integrate the ornithological symbolism with the ocular, and to firmly root both in the iconography of death and resurrection, with which this particular bird is associated—in both the hermetic and the Christian traditions (Campbell, *Creative* 501–03). The ocular motif, aroused by the thousand eyes on the peacock's plumes, surfaces again during the first visions of the archangel Michael, whose "GOLDEN EYES" emanate a "SERENE WHITE BRILLIANCE" as they fix, alert and calm, upon Maria and Wystan, who are "LIFTED TO THE LEVEL OF HIS FACE" (207). Perhaps the most moving example of the ocular symbolism in the underworld explicitly linking it to the moment of death occurs in the section on suicides in "Scripts for the Pageant," in which the Angel of Death, Gabriel, appears with "*Eyes opaque as minium*" (329), and gazes lovingly into the eyes of the suicide, like a "MOTHER GAZING INTO THE EYES OF A BABE" (333). Maria, who confesses she took her own life in this scene, stands abashed in Gabriel's presence, unable to "MEET" his "EYE" (334). The ocular motif surfaces again, when Akhenaton slowly opens his "painted eyes," like a mummy emerging from a trance, to celebrate those "EYES" (the combined "4 EYES" through which both he and Nefertiti look simultaneously) which worship Michael, in the form of the sun. Akhenaton tells us, before returning to his "DREAMING SHUTEYED" self, that he and his twin sister were "BORN EYES OPEN" (337). The ocular symbolism continues to be associated with the underworld throughout the "Scripts for the Pageant," as when George Cotzias appears with a "black eye–hole" drilled into a mirror gleaming on his wet brow (398), or when he describes the shock of his meeting with Mother Nature in terms of having been "ZERO'D IN ON BY THOSE EMBER EYES" (404). Even Mohammed appears "*eyeballed like an ox*" during the pageant of the Old Masters (Jesus, Mercury, Buddha, and Mohammed) (450). Finally, the passage devoted to Wystan's descent to the burning core of the earth explicitly links the ocular symbolism with the nekyia: as he goes with Gabriel on "the down elevator ... INTO EARTH A PURE / WHITE LIGHT, THE NEGATIVE OR 'EYE' OF BLACK / BURST ON US" (457). As in the Sumerian "Descent of Inanna," the nadir of the descent opens the black eye of death.

Along with ocular and ornithological motifs, Merrill's poem incorporates the divestiture and threshold symbolism so widespread in the mythic traditions upon which postmodernism draws so heavily. Like the Sumerian Inanna passing through the seven gateways of the kur, or like Oedipa Maas in Pynchon's *Lot 49*, the souls of the dead are gradually divested of their earthly attributes, as poet and reader pass with them through a sequence of doorways—those lessons which progressively elevate us to the very gates of heaven. As Auden puts during one session, in response to JM's anxious response to the news that Maria has been stripped of her human soul by radiation therapy, all of the souls who dance the in the "MASQUE" of the dead "WERE BEING / EACH IN TURN STRIPPED REDUCED TO ESSENCES / JOINED TO INFINITY" (209). Maria even goes so far as to say "THE STRIPPING IS NO (M) [no metaphor] / ENFANTS: ALL MY OLD DREAMS OF SOUNION / HAVE LIKE BLACK WORKCLOTHES VANISHED FROM THE CLOSET" (237). For Auden, this stripping process will eventually lead to his absorption in the mineral elements of earth, when (as JM puts it) "he'll doff his dim / Red shift (the mufti of a star's retreat) / To vanish into quarry and tar–pit" (306). Optimistically speaking, these "RETURN TO THE ELEMENTS," by which both Auden and Maria are "stripped of personality," prepares them for becoming "Part of what those angels know and are" (309). Hence, divestiture leads to a kind of re–investment: Maria has put off her old workclothes and "'wet look' raincoat'" to put on her bat wings, euphemistically described as an "OLD BLACK DRESS QUITE CLINGING AND SEXY" (208).

Although JM continues to protest Maria's divestiture ("isn't it taboo to strip the soul / From the raw power it shields?), Mirabell points out that the entire necromantic seminar which the poem as a whole records "IS THIS STRIPPING PROCESS," by which JM and DJ are prepared for increasingly unnerving revelations (211), until, like the souls of the suicides "STRIPT OF IDEA AS MORALITY IS SHED" (333) face Gabriel's "opaque" eye of death. This passage links the seminar's stripping process to poesis itself, since the seminar is the poem. JM later elaborates on the "stripping process" as one storyteller's like Tolkien knew about, for a tale survives by feeding on "its personages' lives" (218). Auden later reiterates the linkage with poesis: faltering over a couplet, he compares himself to "AN OLD CARDINAL WHOSE LATIN'S GONE / NO DOUBT THE STRIPPING PROCESS"; to which JM responds by asking if Wystan is "Changing clothes each session, like Maria? " (252). While Maria tries on "THE WHOLE RANGE (LOVELY PALE ROSE TODAY)", Wystan is more masculinely restricted, changing from a "COMFY BATHROBE INTO RED / A CHANCERY JUDGE ALL BUT THE WIG!" (252).

The stripping motif continues to symbolize the nekyia throughout the "Scripts for the Pageant," as when the black souls of Hitler and Caligula are "STRIPPED LIKE GEARS" (451), or when Psyche threatens to unveil herself (450), or when the mortal soul sheds its last item of clothing, its "SPANKING NEW PINK SKIN" (472), like Marsyas in Dante (473). It therefore seems appropriate that JM and DJ appear so scantily clad at the otherworldly church service—which summons Jesus, Buddha, Wagner, Mercury, and Mohammed—that the angels complain of their "NUDITY" (446). A final instance of the linkage between the nekyia and divestiture occurs in Robert's description of his death, which follows the general outline of the near–death narratives studied by Moody, Ring, and Zaleski: at the moment of death, he looks down at his body, and then passes through "THE GENERAL BLACK" towards the starlight, into which he finally steps "BAREASS / THRU SAND AND WATER OF YR MIRROR GLASS" (498). Furthermore, during the angelic lessons which follow Robert's death, "THE VARNISH" of his former self is "STRIPPED AWAY" (499), until the "pilgrim soul" (as in "*The Tibetan / Book of the Dead*") is drawn towards the "apparitions / Of copulating figures" that lead to its reincarnation (501). This rebirth leads to reinvestiture of the soul, "CLAD / IN 'TRAVELING DRESS'" as "THE TRAIN CHUGS AWAY" (510). Even Michael uses the clothing symbolism associated with divestiture, when he admits his secret transformation from Ephraim to archangel with the words "I UNDID THE SLAVE LIKE A ROBE" (550), and when he subsequently refers to that robe as a "SUMMER SUIT" (551).

Merrill links the divestiture and threshold symbols of the nekyia by putting the experiments in the Research Lab "Behind closed doors" (140), and by comparing the sequential lessons of the poem to a progression towards "THOSE GREAT DOORS" (175) at the end of the journey. Along the way, the poet passes through a series of doorways, at each of which a veil is removed. As in the Sumerian story, there are "seven veils" to be stripped before the soul stands naked in the presence of the sun, like an atom stripped of its froth of electrons (192). It is this nakedness towards which the lessons of "Mirabell" gradually aspire, stripping down poet and spectral guides until "NO VEIL REMAINS (OR ONLY ONE) / TO SCREEN OUR SENSES FROM THE SUN" (259). The doorway symbolism which the shedding of the veils implies is firmly established throughout the poem's nekyia. The "gates of clay" Old Matt stands above during his wife's interment gradually yield to the higher doors of the afterlife: Ephraim is referred to as a "DOORKEEPER," reduced to "PEERING THRU THE CRACK" when Mirabell takes over the lessons (218), though Mirabell also calls himself "THE LATEST DOORKEEPER" (222). This passage explicitly incorporates divestiture and doorways into its itinerary of the poet's passage through the otherworld: Mirabell tells JM that he must change "THE CLOTHS SHROUDING THE FUTURE FROM U," so he can traverse the fifteen lessons left till he stands "Before the Doors" (222). Mirabell also calls these ultimate doors of revelation "THE GREAT DOORS OF THE OPERA" (217), and later uses threshold imagery to remind JM of his own limitations, when he says that "WE WHO FALL AT THE FEET / OF MEANING MAY BUT LEAD YOU TO THE DOORS" (225). Mirabell also confesses that his lessons are subject to the approval of higher powers, when he says that "AT ANY MOMENT WE CAN BE EVICTED THE DOOR / SLAMMD BEHIND US" (257).

Later, in "Scripts for the Pageant," Michael instructs Gabriel, the angel of death, to "FASTEN THE DOORS" behind him as he enters the schoolroom at Sandover (337), where a new "TURNKEY" (380) will take over—Uni, a unicorn who constantly appears latching and unlatching the gates, or shyly listening to the lessons inside the classroom. It is during one of these lessons that Mirabell explicitly evokes the mirror as a door with four frames, through which the spirits come and go (as in Cocteau). Later, when "Two still–warm shades" (Robert Lowell and Maria Callas) arrive, they find the "schoolroom door / Ajar," and enter to "take refuge from the shock of Heaven" (508). In the trilogy's concluding "Coda," Uni warns that after Robert Morse's reincarnation JM "WILL FIND OUR NURSERY DOOR / SWINGING ON ITS HINGES" (537). As we have noted, this linkage between doorways (sometimes "Ajar") and the nekyia (whether conceived as death, or as the descent of the reincarnated soul into the underworld of life) is archetypal: curiously enough, the half–open door, so often found in postmodernist versions of the nekyia (Cocteau, Bergman, Eco, Weir), was a common symbolic motif in Roman sepulchral sculpture, and, as James Hillman reminds us, "One epithet of Hades was 'he who closes the door'" (*Dream* 180, 226). Throughout *The Changing Light*, these doorways demarcate the journey of the soul on its passage through the labyrinthine chambers of the underworld.

Chapter 5
Re–Figuring Revelation

Apocalypse means "uncovering" or "unveiling" (from *apo*, from or away, and *kalupto*, to cover) and carries the connotations of "doom" and "revelation." The Book of Revelation combines this dual sense of an ending: the end as the destruction of the world, and the end as the revelation of its ultimate form and meaning. Jacques Derrida has recently addressed the apocalyptic themes of "découvrement" or "dévoilement" in a manner that suggests their relation to the myth of the descent to the underworld in the previous chapter (13). Essentially, what is involved is a stripping down ("l'idée de mise à nu"), an apocalyptic unveiling ("de dévoilement précisément apocalyptique"), and a subsequent revelation of the tetragrammaton ("découvrement de YHWH"), the four letter figure of the name of God upon which all Creation is based (14–15). Derrida is primarily interested in what he calls the oracular voice ("la voix oraculaire") of philosophers whom he terms mystagogues (33), to whom alone the secrets are revealed or unveiled ("La révélation ou le dévoilement du secret se réserve à eux") (27), and in the themes of circumcision and castration implied by scenes of divestiture in the Old Testament, in which the unveiling allows us to see that which had remained covered the way clothing covers the body or the way the foreskin covers the penis ("découvrement qui laisse voir ce qui jusque–là restait enveloppé, retiré, réservé, par exemple le corps quand on enlève le vêtement ou le gland dans la circoncision") (15). Our focus, however, will be on the symbolism of disrobing and the revelation of the archetypal forms of the imagination, often using geometrical symbolism, more in the line of Renaissance Neoplatonism than Neo–Freudianism.

The apocalypse—like the entrance into and departure from the labyrinth, the descent into and return from the underworld, the return to and rebirth from the womb–tomb of the Great Goddess, or the submersion into and emergence from the alchemical bath—is a circular journey of descent and return: it ends where it began. It involves a circling back to the beginning at the end of time (ricorso), a manifestation of the archetypal forces shaping human life and history (revelation), and an ensuing reconstruction and renewal of the world in transfigured form (recreation). Several of the modernists, in fact, conflated the descent into Hades with the imagery of the Apocalypse: Lawrence in *Apocalypse*, Eliot in *Four Quartets*, Mann in *Doctor Faustus*, and Hermann Broch in *The Death of Virgil*. In doing so, they continued a process of conflation which is rooted in the earliest prototypes of the apocalypse, and which flourished during the Middle Ages and which was revived by the Romantics.

The essential characteristics of the myth of the apocalypse upon which I wish to focus are those which it shares with the archetypal configurations of the maze, the Goddess, alchemy, and the underworld. First of all is the theme of the ricorso, particularly strong in apocalyptic thinking based on the famous words of Jesus, "I am Alpha and Omega, the beginning and the end, the first and the last" (Rev. 22: 13). These are very nearly the last words of the Bible, and typologically oriented critics from the late Middle Ages onward have shown how the imagery of Revelation, the last book in the Bible, circles back to the imagery of Genesis, the first book in the Bible, which it completes and fulfills. The notion of the return to the origins of the beginning at the end of time is a recurrent refrain throughout the literature of postmodernism, a theme upon which many variations are played, from David Jones to Julio Cortázar. The circling back to origins implies and makes possible a new beginning at the end of time, a recreation of word and world which is the basis of poetic creativity. The millennial renewal which follows the annihilation of the world in Revelation, and the reconstruction of a new heaven and a new earth, became, for the Modernists, not only an image of hope during and after the two major wars of our century, but also an image of renewed personal and artistic creativity: out of the ashes, the Phoenix did rise, again and again.

Along with the images of ricorso and recreation, is the notion of revelation of those fundamental forms of life and the imagination which makes renewal possible, whether on political, personal, or aesthetic levels. In *Revelation*, after the destructive calamities visited upon the earth by the opening of the seven seals, Jesus appears as the archetypal force giving shape and significance to life, while after the devastations unleashed by the blowings of the seven trumpets, the New Jerusalem descends as the archetypal form of life for all eternity. During the Middle Ages, the Gawain poet went into magnificent detail in his description of the Heavenly City; in his poem the *Pearl*, it appears with its four walls with three gates on each side and twelve steps of different stone as a base, with a crystalline light and river running out from the throne in the center where Jesus sits. This kind of orderly figure of a four sided square centered upon that source of all existence which gives shape to life is typical of the multiplicity of geometrical metaphors. For Borges, Cortázar, and Merrill, numbers and various kinds of figurations (musical, mathematical, architectural, geological, etc.) are used to suggest the ultimate revelation of the archetypal forms of life which shape our experience of the world. But the apocalyptic geometry of postmodernism is more intricate than that of modernism: complex polygons replace the simpler figures of the circle and the square; and scientific perspectives (coming from the new physics) are increasingly incorporated into works concerned with sacralizing the modern world, without submitting it to religious dogmatism.

David Jones

All of the mythic allusions Lawrence, Mann, Broch, and Kazantzakis evoke in their Apocalypses suggest various metaphors for poesis also prevalent in postmodernism: ricorso, revelation, and recreation. In *The Anathemata*, not published until 1952, but written between 1938 and 1945 by the Welsh poet, David Jones, during the same years as *Four Quartets, Doctor Faustus, The Death of Virgil,* and *The Odyssey*, we find myths of the Great Goddess, the Apocalypse, the Nekyia, and the Maze all combined to produce one of the most powerful meditations on aspects of creativity in our century.

The Anathemata is much concerned with ricorso, the return to the original forms of creation at the end of time (59), for the purposes of recreation. The first section of the poem, "Rite and Fore–Time," focuses on first things from aesthetic, historical, geological, archaeological, and anthropological perspectives. It evokes the first sculpture, the first pottery, the first cities, the first ports and quays of London, the first defended hill sites, the first burial sites, the first migrations, the first domestications of animals, the first argosies, the first sacred wells, the first martyr, the first of the Welsh Kings, the first landscape formations, the first numbers, and the first geometric forms. This preoccupation with first things to which the poet returns continues in the sections called "The Lady of the Pool" and "Mabinog's Liturgy," which focus on the first sacred sites in London and Wales upon which the first Christian churches were built, and upon the earliest rituals which became the basis of the Christian liturgy. This obsession with first things is contextualized by allusions to the myths of the underworld, alchemy, and the apocalypse, for the poem begins with the quest for symbols suitable to serve as a effective signs during our era, which is described as the end of a chapter (49). These signs are to be found by bringing the ancient forms back to life through a process of "recalling" the dead.

A great deal of the poem is then devoted to this other aspect of ricorso, the "recalling" of a variety of archetypal prefigurations of British argonauts, Jesus, and the Virgin Mary. Ulysses, Noah, and Manawydan (141) all serve as prototypical argonauts, while an encyclopedic catalogue of Christ figures is evoked: the sleeping lords of Celtic myth (like Arthur); the Norse Wotan, who hangs from the windy tree; Osiris of the barley grain, and his son Horus; John Barleycorn of British ballad fame; Peredur of the Mabinogion; the Welsh Cwledig; the Roman Paterfamilias; Triptolemus of the Eleusinian mysteries; Dionysus; Adonis; Jugatinus of the noose; and even the sacrificial bear of the Tlingits and Gilyaks! Perhaps most beautifully amplified is the image of Jesus as the male god who replaces the Lady as the Lord of the Fountain, the source from whom all waters flow (235–38).

All of these prototypes, to which the poem circles back, are seen, most fundamentally, as embryonic forms in the womb of the Great Goddess (74), a central figure throughout the poem. She is the earth, and she inhabits the sacred rivers, seas, and pools of pagan, Celtic, Classical, and Christian times, precursor of the Virgin Mary. Her most archaic prototype is the Venus of Willendorf, beautifully evoked by Jones (60), but an elaborate array of more recent precursors populate the pages of "The Lady of the Pool": Helen of Troy, Selene, Calypso, Gwenhwyfar, Chrétien's Lady of the Fountain, various naiades of pool and stream, Artemis, Persephone, Flora Dea, Bona Dea, Blodeudd, the Vestal Virgins, Chloris, Morgan le Fay, Miriam, Maia, Minerva, and the mother of Constantine who found the wood of the Cross. To indicate this line of transmission, Jones poetically expresses a fact well known to archaeology: many of the oldest churches of Europe sacred to the Virgin were built on Celtic sites where the Goddess was worshipped. Jones particularly evokes the crypts of the Great Goddesses, in the old churches of London, where the Virgin was later to be worshipped (127). The implication is that poetic, as well as religious creativity, involves a ricorso, a return to the matrix from which all mythic imagery derives, for the purposes of renewal. As Jones puts it, the arts germinate from the spirits of the dead, just as the grain of Demeter emerges from the grave to produce the crops (230).

In addition to the notion of the return to the Goddess, Jones develops other metaphors to describe this poetic process of revelation and recreation. In his preface to the poem, Jones says at one point that his craft is like "making a kind of coat of many colors, such as belonged to 'that dreamer' in the Hebrew myth" (34), and at another that the poet is like a hunter pursuing his quarry into the forest, "where the 'forms' lurk that he's after" (20). The tailoring analogy recalls Carlyle's *Sartor Resartus* and the "shearsman of sorts" in "The Man With the Blue Guitar" by Stevens, while the hunting metaphor evokes the vast realm of Celtic legend in which animals like the stag, boar, or rabbit lead deeply into the otherworld of the forest. Of the two, the trope of clothing and divestiture play a central role in such passages of *The Anathemata* as the glorious description of Guenevere at Mass on Christmas Eve in "Mabinog's Liturgy" (193–202), some parts of which are devoted to the robe of glory Christ assumes at the moment of His Incarnation (193). The clothing imagery is particularly important because it surfaces in the allegories of poesis of most interest to Jones: the Mass and the Apocalypse.

Like Joyce, David Jones saw the "transubstantiation" effected by the mystery of the Mass as a metaphor for the way the poet manipulates "archaeological and anthropological data" to produce a "permanent mythus" (82). Hence the centrality of the ritual of the Mass in the poem, a ritual which involves raising up valid symbols as an offering analogous to the poet's task. For, as Jones notes in his "Preface," the intention of both Mass and poem is "to 'uncover'; which is what a 'mystery' does, for though at root 'mystery' implies a closing, all 'mysteries' are meant to disclose, to show forth something" (33). The metaphor of uncovering here is sustained throughout the poem, and relates to the myth of apocalypse. The covering and uncovering of the chalice which occurs during the Mass is analogous to the 'covering' of bones by burial and the "uncovering of the bones" associated both with archaeology, poesis, and the apocalypse. Ultimately it is the archetype which is "uncovered," a prototypical form in the mind of God which prefigures the splendor of the forms of the future (78). Jones speaks frequently in the poem of uncovering, such as when the Lady of the Pool compares the Merlinesque figure of John Dee to John of Patmos, John of Patmos (136), or when he alludes to the Word of John Donne uncovering all things at the end of time (236).

These references suggest a connection between apocalypse and resurrection, the bodies of the dead being "uncovered," 'recalled,' or 're–membered' during the ceremony of the Mass, and at the end of time. These notions become central metaphors of the poet's task, who recalls the dead from their sleep in order to make his offering of efficacious signs acceptable. Jones suggests that the Goddess Proserpine "stands for death in general, so then for that particular death, indeed particularly for that death which is 'shown forth' and 'recalled' in the Eucharist," a ritual which, Jones continues, should be "regarded as a recalling of the dead" (76). This too is the poet's priestly task of recalling and transforming the dead (81). The process may also be considered a remembering, an "anamnesis," defined as a "'recalling of things past,'" or "'re–presenting' before God an event in the past so that it becomes *here and now operative by its effects*'" (Dix, qtd. 205; Jones italics). Elsewhere Jones notes that "the whole Mass is an *anamnesis*" (209).

The suggestion here is of a sacred form of recollection which gathers together the shattered fragments of the past in order to "make it new" (the task of poetry, as Pound put it). The fragments are made new by a creative act of *memoria* which moves backwards through historical time to the primordial archetype of all creation in the mind of God, shattered vestiges of which reside in the soul of the individual poet (Hillman, *Myth* 168–172). Hence the cabalistic notion of reconstructing that which has been broken or shattered in the past (tikkun) goes along with the metaphors of apocalypse, resurrection, and recalling which Jones uses as allegories of poesis. The priest, for example, breaks the communion wafer then lifts it up whole at the altar. The poet pieces the elementary fragments of an archetype together, like an archaeologist reconstructing shards of pottery (78). Although the archetype has been fractured, it is the poet's task to bring it back to life by assembling the pieces of the broken bowls (90). The language Jones used here is very close to the cabalistic conception the *shevirah*, the shattering of the *Sephiroth,* or bowls which God formed to contain his light, but which exploded under the strain. The shattered sparks fall "into the realm of demonic *kelippoth* or shells" to create human souls, whose task is called *tikkun,* the "reformation of the *Sephiroth*" (Poncé 81–82). Jones returns to this metaphor in a letter about "a pewter teapot of vigorous form" which, like the holy city, is "composed of so many parts—united in one" (Lowery 33). Poetry, then, is a matter of the "interjoining" of fragmented parts, a reunion of elementary forms, to create a living work of art (33).

This task is only made possible by recalling the ancient prototypes (232), by finding the archaic correlative of each contemporary circumstance (149). With these lines, Jones rewrites Eliot's definition of the mythical method, with which we began, as "a continuous parallel between contemporaneity and antiquity" (681). It is the poet's task to uncover the archaic prototypes of the past, now, at the end of time, and in doing so to recall them to life. Eliot compared a poem to an epitaph, but it is also an epiphany, a revelation of those elemental forms upon which all creation is based. For, as David Jones suggests, poesis ex nihilo is impossible, for poetry can only proceed by the recollection of archaic prototypes (79).

Gabriel García Márquez

Two recent Latin American novelists (Márquez and Cortázar) have applied the myth of the Apocalypse in classics of postmodernism which employ similar vocabularies of *ricorso* and *revelation*. *One Hundred Years of Solitude* is saturated with biblical imagery throughout; taken as a whole, the novel recapitulates the complete cycle from Genesis to Revelation, a cycle reenacted in each generation of the Buendía family as well. The theme of the apocalypse forms the basis of the structure of the novel, as well as informing the vocabulary of its images. In a sense, the novel is an original refiguration of the Bible (a kind of Midrash, in fact), though with an ironic reversal of the myth of the apocalypse. As in the other works discussed, the rhythm of the return to origins (*ricorso*), and the disclosure of those fundamental forms which give shape and significance to life and to art provide the central focus of this refiguration.

The catastrophes unleashed upon the earth in Revelation find their parallel in the progressive degeneration of the Buendía house, which eventually yields completely to the one hundred year assault of scorpions, leeches, termites, cockroaches, and red ants (suggestive of the locust plagues of the Bible), and to the deluge, desiccating winds, and "biblical hurricane" (suggestive of the terrestrial turbulence of the last days) at the end of the book. In addition, we find a detailed sequence of apocalyptic analogies: there is a kind of Armageddon in the Banana company sponsored massacre of three thousand or so Macondians (though an Armageddon which the Anti–Christ, the American corporation of gringos, wins); a scarlet Whore of Babylon in the figure of Pilar Ternara and the other prostitutes of the novel (who, however, are celebrated as the sort of Goddesses Lawrence argues come in to Revelation through the back door!); a cosmic Mother and Child pursued by the Dragon (though here the dragon succeeds, in the form of the red ants who devour Aureliano's baby after Amaranta Ursula dies in childbirth); a Beast of the Apocalypse in the angelically deformed animal the priest refers to as the Wandering Jew (the citing of which was a traditional sign of the imminence of the Second Coming, but here only of the final collapse of Macondo); an 'Isle of the Birds' such as the one from which John of Patmos delivered his prophecy in the "Fortunate Isles" from which Amaranta brings hundreds of canaries on her return from Brussels; and a Book of Life in the form of the text left behind by Melquíades which Aureliano finally succeeds in deciphering as the novel ends.

While these details keep us alert to the biblical nature of the novel's imagery, Ursula's recurrent allusions to the idea of the *ricorso* as she observes the unfolding history of her family in the passing of the generations alerts us to the extent to which Márquez has relied on the biblical paradigm as a means of giving his narrative structure and coherence. When Ursula is reminded of her husband by the plans of José Arcadio Segundo to bring a boat up the river, she remarks "It's as if time had turned around and we were back at the beginning" (199), and Aureliano Triste's railroad "confirmed her impression that time was going in a circle" (226). Such remarks punctuate the novel, and keep our attention focused on the *ricorso*: When José Arcadio Segundo incites the banana workers to strike, as Colonel Aureliano Buendía had continually spawned the insurrections of the radicals, Ursula says "It's as if the world were repeating itself" (303), and later when the same José repeats the words of his father, Ursula "shuddered with the evidence that time was not passing ... it was turning in a circle" (341). The combined concept of the cyclical return to the beginning and what Ursula calls the "progressive breakdown of time" (251) is summed up in the words of the illegitimate Great Mother of the whole line, Pilar Ternera, when she says "the history of the family was a machine with unavoidable repetitions, a turning wheel that would have gone on spinning into eternity were it not for the progressive and irremediable wearing of the axle" (402). It is with Pilar's "zoological brothel" that time in the novel closes, "turning back to its earliest origins" (400) in a reversal of Darwinian evolution similar to that envisioned by Hermann Broch.

In Revelation, Jesus announces the *ricorso*, by saying "I am the Alpha and the Omega, the beginning and the end, the first and the last" (22: 13). With these words the Bible circles back to the lost paradise of Genesis, a process of restoration frequently alluded to in *One Hundred Years of Solitude*: there is the "paradise of misery" which the red ants inherit at the end of the novel (417); the "paradise of disaster" in which Aureliano and Amaranta Ursula consummate their incestuous but somehow innocent love (411); Pilar Ternera's brothel of the "Golden Child," in which "ways of love that man had left behind forgotten in the earthly paradise" are revived (400); the "decadent paradise" that follows the return of the would–be Pope, José Arcadio, from Rome, when he restores his mother Fernanda's bedroom to its original effete splendor (378); the "paradise of shared solitude" which Aureliano Segundo and Petra Coates find during the "rites of poverty" which unite them in the final days of their extra–marital marriage (345); and the "paradise of disemboweled animals" and mechanical toys in which the grand patriarch, José Arcadio Buendía spends his last lucid days (76).

Following the biblical paradigm, all of these are paradises recovered at the end of lives which look back to their beginnings. Each generation, in fact, reenacts the rhythm of Paradise, Paradise Lost, Paradise Regained which M. H. Abrams has called the apocalyptic circulatio. In each case, as in the biblical model, the Fall coincides with the discovery of sex and death, which catapults the protagonist into adult life (metaphorically envisioned as the underworld), and which is eventually reversed by a movement towards redemption or a return to the conditions of the hero's origins or early life. In the case of Colonel Aureliano Buendía, for example, we see his childhood years of reverie and exploration in the laboratory of Melquíades (where he spends his time laboriously making little golden fishes) yielding to the agitation of love (when he becomes aware of his brother José Arcadio's nocturnal sojourns to Pilar Ternera), marriage (when he becomes obsessed with the virginal Remedios Moscote), and finally to the war (when he is transformed from Aurelito to Colonel Aureliano) which entangles most of his adult life and destroys him as a human being. The circle is completed by his return to the laboratory, where he spends the rest of his days innocently employed in the production of golden fish, a process which restores his sense of peace (if not ultimately his humanity lost during the war years). The sense of the biblical circulatio of Fall, Exile, and Redemption is reinforced by the geography of Colonel Aureliano's journey: he begins and ends his life in Macondo, but spends most of the intervening years in the jungles of the revolution. A great deal of text is devoted to this central section of his life, when after his departure from Macondo he becomes completely dehumanized and demoralized by the war.

Other biographical narratives in the novel reiterate the same basic pattern of departure, initiation, and return (a pattern Joseph Campbell called the hero journey, but which here refers explicitly to the biblical circulatio of a descent into hell followed by a redemptive *ricorso* to the place of origins). José Arcadio (Colonel Aureliano Buendía's brother), for example also begins and ends his life journey in Macondo, the departure from which is imagined as variant on the biblical fall and exile, and the return to which is eventually perceived as a movement towards redemption and the restoration of the lost paradise. His fall begins with the discovery of sex with Pilar Ternera, and his exile from Macondo occurs while watching a gypsy side show about "the man who had been turned into a snake for having disobeyed his parents" (33), whose cage José Arcadio is last seen pushing out of the town on a cart in the company of the gypsy girl whom he has deflowered the night before (34). The biblical affiliation of the Fall, sexuality, and the serpent is obvious, if also originally handled. José Arcadio's years of exile are spend wandering the high seas in search of "adventures in remote countries" (94), all of which involve spectacular images of mortality: cannibalism in the Sea of Japan, a slaughtered sea dragon in the Gulf of Bengal, and the ghost of pirate ship in the Caribbean (94). This world of wandering and death is analogous to the underworld of the war years for Colonel Aureliano, but José Arcadio's redemption comes in the more domestic form of marriage, hard work, and sacrifice for his brother (whom he saves from execution with a shotgun in his hand), as he attempts to rejoin the family and the community of Macondo in his last years.

The next generation of Buendía's also traverse the circular journey, with some curious variations arising from the mix up of the twins Aureliano and José Segundo. Aureliano Segundo begins life in the innocent paradise of books in Melquíades' room, where "the air seemed fresher than in the rest of the house" (188), and where Aureliano Segundo sets about "deciphering the manuscripts" under the ghostly tutelage of Melquíades himself, who converses with the boy every afternoon. Meanwhile, the innocent youth of Aureliano's brother José Arcadio Segundo is spent preparing for his first communion under the spiritual guidance of Father Antonio Isabel. The Fall for both brothers coincides with the awakening of sexuality and their encounter with Petra Cotes, who begins as the mistress of both and ends up as the life–long consort of Aureliano Segundo: after making love to her, Aureliano leaves the laborious task of deciphering the manuscripts and enters a wild life of dissipation with Petra, while José Arcadio departs into the shadowy realm of cock fights and then labor unions. The underworld of the former is simply the fornication and gluttony of daily life, while for the latter it is the train ride with the three thousand dead slaughtered during the massacre of the strikers against the banana company. José Arcadio Segundo escapes from this nightmare by returning home and hiding in Melquíades' room, where he spends the rest of his life in "seraphic" pursuit of the meaning of the mysterious text over which Aureliano Segundo had labored as a youth (by now it seems certain that the twins have in fact been mixed up, since José Arcadio Segundo has memories of having spent hours in the room where his brother had been seen reading). This return to the innocent purity of spiritual quest is a kind of redemption, paralleled by the transformation of his brother Aureliano

Segundo, who spends his last years working so hard to restore his lost fortune that he becomes as lean and trim as a youth, and discovers true love with Petra during the "rites of poverty" (344) and "paradise of shared solitude" (345) which replace the wild orgies of their midlife.

The apocalyptic cycle is again enacted in the last generation of the family by Aureliano Segundo's children. José Arcadio travels from Macondo to Rome (where he is meant become the next Pope, but where he actually falls into the ways of vice associated with degenerate life in that city) and then back to Macondo, where he attempts to reconstruct "a decadent paradise" by restoring his mother's room, surrounding himself with children, and indulging in vaguely pederastic orgies. Meanwhile, his sister Amaranta Ursula is sent off to a convent school in Brussels by her father and mother, where instead of the cloistered life planned by her mother she leads a wildly romantic life with her husband Gaston, whom she meets after he crashes his airplane on school property, and who then introduces her to the sophistications of country club life in old Europe. Her return to Macondo, like her brother José Arcadio's return from Rome, yields to a kind of ironic reversal of the restoration of "the lost paradise of the deluge" (414), as she consummates an incestuous affair with her nephew Aureliano (illegitimate son of her sister Meme and Mauricio Babilonia), with whom she had cavorted as a child during the years of the rainfall. Aureliano himself undergoes a more narrowly confined circulatio, which takes him from the room where he has been confined since childhood, busy working on the manuscripts under the direction of the ghost of Melquíades, to the streets of Macondo (particularly to the bookstore where he buys a Sanskrit grammar and to the brothel of the Golden Child, ruled by Pilar Ternera, into which he is driven by the lovemaking of Amaranta Ursula and Gaston in the thin–walled rooms around the lab of the wizard), and finally after the affair with his aunt back to the room where he at last deciphers the manuscripts.

Hence, each generation of the Buendía family repeats the biblical paradigm of the *ricorso*, with its rhythm of Paradise, Paradise lost, and Paradise regained. The narrative cycle provides the same kind of structure and coherence which unifies the various episodes of Bible, which is similarly held together by a typological series of figurative hero journey cycles which enabled allegorical exegetes to link such scenes as Joseph in the Well, Daniel in the lion's den, Jonah in the belly of the whale in the Old Testament, to such scenes as the Prodigal Son among the swine in the far country and Jesus in limbo after the Crucifixion in the New Testament. In each case, there is a departure, a metaphorical descent into hell, and a return towards a promised land of the beginning, a mini hero journey cycle within the massive embracing frame of movement from Genesis to Apocalypse. Northrop Frye suggests a circular model (175) as well as a sequence of fallings and rising returns in the form of a U–shaped sine wave (171) to describe this basic narrative structure in the Bible, while Gabriel Josipovici refers to the progression and repetition of similar circular journeys as "items in a series," invoking a mathematical analogy.

In Márquez, this constant rhythm of *ricorso* moves progressively towards revelation. Each generation of the family involved in work on the texts of Melquíades brings the final day of deciphering one step closer, but that day becomes the day of doom, ending the family line and destroying the city of Macondo. That which is *ciphered* at the beginning of the novel (the text of Melquíades put into code) is *de–ciphered* at the end (when Aureliano breaks the code), a symmetrical parallelism which links the processes of reading and writing to the root notion of apo–calypse as an unveiling of something which has been veiled in the beginning. Hence, Márquez exploits the image of the Book in St. John's Apocalypse, with its seven seals which, when broken, gradually fulfill the prophecies of the preceding prefigurations going all the way back to the beginnings in Genesis. It also becomes gradually clear why Márquez has consistently portrayed Melquíades throughout the novel with a large–brimmed hat shaped like a raven's wings: these details allude to the Norse master of mysterious codes, Wotan, who wanders the globe accompanied by two ravens named Hugin (thought) and Munin (remembrance) which are the source of his omniscience (Biedermann 281),. Wotan is conventionally depicted (as in Wagner's *Ring* for example) as a wanderer wearing a broadbrimmed hat, who moves freely between this and the other world, and who earns the capacity of deciphering the runes of wisdom by hanging nine days and nights from Yggdrasil, the World Tree of Norse myth (Davidson 243–47).

The Buendía family begins to move closer towards the generational task of deciphering the mysterious runes of the texts of Melquíades when José Arcadio Segundo retreats to the old man's room after the massacre of the banana company strikers and manages "to classify the cryptic letters of the parchments" into "an alphabet of forty seven to fifty–three characters" (355). He dies shortly thereafter, but Aureliano (the bastard child of Meme and Mauricio Babilonia who was said to arrive in Macondo in a basket, like Moses) confirms these results and announces to the ghostly Melquíades that he has discovered the language in which the parchments had been written, "Sanskrit" (362). The ghost with his characteristic "crow's–wing hat" continues to visit Aureliano from the far shores of the dead until, assured that the texts will be deciphered before they "became one hundred years old" (362), his spiritual tutorials become increasingly infrequent, until he fades away altogether, to meet his "ultimate death" on the sands of Singapore (363). Before Melquíades dies, however, he tells Aureliano that he will find a Sanskrit primer (the key to the code's cipher) on the shelves of a Catalonian's bookstore, "between *Jerusalem Delivered* and Milton's poems" (362). An apocalyptic location! Between Paradise Lost and Paradise Regained!. Once the text is translated into Spanish, however, Aureliano finds that "the lines were in code" (369), which delays the ultimate revelation of their meaning long enough for the affair with Amaranta Ursula to begin, just when the parchments "were beginning to reveal themselves as predictions in coded lines of poetry" for which Aureliano must still find the final keys (397).

It is not until the instant when the ants devour his child after the death of Amaranta Ursula that the "final keys were revealed to him" (420), which enable Aureliano to decipher what he finds is "the history of the family, written by Melquíades, down to the most trivial details .... He had written it in Sanskrit, which was his native tongue, and he had encoded the even lines in the private cipher of the Emperor Augustus and the odd ones in a Lacedemonian military code" (421). To complicate matters, Melquíades had devised a "final protection" by concentrating "a century of daily episodes in such a way that they coexisted in one instant" (421). Not only is the end in the beginning, but both end and beginning are contained in each moment of the narrative, and in the encyclical structure of both syllable and generational biography. As the "whirlwind" of a "biblical hurricane" descends on the city, Aureliano "began to decipher the instant he was living, deciphering it as he lived it, prophesying himself in the act of deciphering the last page of the parchments, as if he were looking into a speaking mirror" (422).

Each generation, then, repeats the circular journey of the biblical paradigm, until finally the *ricorso* yields to the *revelation* of the keys to the text. For Lawrence the fundamental forms revealed by apocalypse were the mythical images pagan antiquity; for Broch, the crystalline archetypes of the *Urbilder*; for Eliot, the "patterns" which redeem and 'transfigure' the past; for Mann, both the archaic images of the underworld and the mathematical mysteries of musical figures revolving around the number twelve; and for Borges and Cortázar, a wide range of geometrical configurations, like the Wheel, the mandala, the rose, and the kaleidoscope. For Márquez, the figure which gives shape and significance to life and which is revealed by apocalypse is the Book itself.

Julio Cortázar

Among more recent novels, few have achieved such notoriety and acclaim for literary innovation as Julio Cortázar's *Hopscotch*. Yet, in spite of the daring manipulations of narrative form established by the alternative sequences of chapter progressions, the novel retains a structure informed throughout by the apocalypse. The myth explores that process of breakdown and breakthrough which symbolizes the creative dynamics of *poesis* in the works of the first generation of modernist writers (Joyce, Lawrence, Mann, Eliot, et. al.). Cortázar shares with these authors that sense of paralysis, stagnation, anarchy and futility which compels a quest for new forms and new myths to redeem the Waste Land. This complex notion of the apocalypse is most thoroughly developed in the third section of *Hopscotch* , among the so called "Expendable Chapters," which are permeated by what Cortázar calls the "nostalgia of a lost paradise" (162). The aspects of the myth of apocalypse most relevant to the novel include the reconciliation of opposites, the notion of revelation, annihilation and recreation, and, most importantly, the idea of the restoration of a lost paradise. Often these aspects work together in single key passages.

The theme of the reconciliation between opposites in relation to the apocalypse derives primarily from Christ's announcement in Revelation that he is "Alpha and Omega, the beginning and the end" (22:13), a statement which links Genesis to Apocalypse in an elaborate typology of analogies. The mystical *coincidentia oppositorum* is a theme so pervasive in *Hopscotch* that it is impossible to cover all incidences of its occurrence in the text.[48] One of the most direct, and typical, statements of the theme comes appropriately, very near the end of the novel, in Chapter 144. In this extraordinary erotic prose poem, which Cortázar calls an "Orphic hymn" (542), he celebrates cunnilingus as a return to the "hub of the wheel of origins" where "the initial and final figures are sketched," and where "everything becomes alpha and omega, *coquille*, cunt, *concha, con, coño,* millennium, Armageddon" (542). But even less thrilling moments, such as "a walk through the suburbs," can yield that sense of the union of the opposites and produce "the growing suspicion that only the alpha can yield the omega, that all insistence upon an intermediate period—epsilon, lambda—is the same thing as spinning around with one foot fastened to the ground" (495). This selection from Chapter 125 continues to identify the central theme of the novel as an apocalyptic quest for "that conciliation, let's say reconciliation" that will not deny either pole of the elaborate dialectics Cortázar establishes in the novel. It must be an "immanent" apocalypse "with no sacrifice of lead for gold, cellophane for glass, the least for the most .... It's not a question of perfecting, of decanting, of redeeming, of choosing, of free–willing, of going from the alpha to the omega. *One is already there*" (497).

This conciliation unites Earth and Heaven without annihilation but retention of the former; it is a ternary logic that bypasses the Hegelian dialectic in a way Douglas Robinson sees as characteristic of versions of the apocalypse in American literature as a whole. The American breed of apocalypse, Robinson argues, characteristically has it both ways: "American iconoclasm is iconically mediatory; images of nature are negated apocalyptically not in order that they might be thrown out, but that the writer might incorporate and transform them into the mediate ground for visionary contact" (8). This tendency yields what Robinson calls a "ternary logic of intercession, in place of Hegel's binary logic of supersession .... to allow writer and reader to perceive the opposites (earth and new earth, present and future) *in* opposition without subsuming or supplanting them" (8). Hence, in the American breed of apocalypse as Robinson sees it, *this* world may in fact obstruct our access to ultimate revelation; it is not, however, "destroyed by fire but is itself converted into the mediatory icon of Christ, the self–unveiling veil that reveals by standing between" (9). The veil is to be made transparent by a shift in vision effected by art, not to be destroyed by cataclysm.

Cortázar refers to this replacement of the dialectic with a "ternary logic" in Chapter 86 in the following terms: "binary reasoning might be replaced with an analogical consciousness which would assume the shapes and assimilate the inconceivable rhythms of those profound structures" (410). Such an approach would surpass the "purse sized dialectics" of the Judeo–Christian tradition (383) with a sort of trialectic that unites the opposites without negating either pole. In fact, the novel as a whole is structured according to this principle: the first two sections are balanced in a symmetrical duality ("From the Other Side" and "From This Side") that the third section ("From Diverse Sides") transforms into a triad, since it is integrally connected to both of the first sections by the chapter sequence Cortázar suggests at the beginning in his "Table of Instructions." Yet it forms a separate unit on its own according to the numerological sequence of the chapters (so that section neither subsumes nor is subsumed by the first two terms of the dialectic). And what is true of the overall structure of the novel is true of also of its minuter parts, in which a dialectical logic continually yields to a logic of triads. In terms of the characters, to cite just one example, we have Oliveira–La Maga–Gregorovius in section one balanced by Oliveira–Talita–Traveler in section two, and by La Maga–Oliveira–Pola in section three (Chapter 108). As

Gerald Martin suggests, Cortázar adds this third section "as if to offer the opportunity of some dialectical escape from the oppositions which leave the human prisoner pacing endlessly back and forwards" (203).

Hence the duad, the triad, and the circle become versions of those geometrical figures which the narrative often evokes as metaphors of that ultimate pattern shaping life and art into meaning, to be revealed either by *nekyia* or by apocalypse. The general term for such patterns in the novel (which include, circles, polyhedrons, crystals, circles, mandalas, labyrinths, kaleidoscopes, and the hopscotch court) is *figuras*, a word which suggests the seminal influence of Erich Auerbach's essay on figures and typology in the European tradition. In *Hopscotch,* as Lois Zamora suggests, "*Figuras* represent systems of relations, intuitive constellations of meaning in which people, events, places relate to each other across time and space in patterns that transcend discursive, diachronic reason" (83). Hence the focus on *figuras* in the novel serves as a means of superseding the dialectic with a trialectic "analogical consciousness" in which an "apocalyptic order opposes the historical moment and yet encompasses it, is limited by it yet transcends it" (Zamora, *Writing* 83).

Many of the characters in the novel are searching for a figure that will serve as a coagulant, so that "everything falls into its proper place and there taking shape you have a beautiful crystal with all its facets" (278). Gregorovius imagines "a tarot figure, something that has to resolve itself, a polyhedron in which every edge and every facet keeps its immediate sense, the false one, until the mediating sense is integrated" (142). This figure will be "A polyhedron, somewhat crystallized, which takes shape little by little in the darkness" (142). It can be a circle, a mandala, "the center of the crossroads," or "the hub of a wheel" (291). Paris itself "is a center, you understand, a mandala through which one must pass without dialectics, a labyrinth where pragmatic formulas are of no use except to get lost in" (427). Traveler uses alchemical metaphors to evoke "the rigorous crystallization of the system, like the mysterious *garden* in a sapphire, that mysterious spot in the gem that determines perhaps the coalescence of the system and which in sapphires irradiates its transparent celestial cross like a congealed energy in the heart of the stone" (505).

Cortázar implicates not only his characters, but also the reader in this apocalyptic search for a geometrical symbol. Morelli's meditation in Chapter 109 on the relationships between the central triad of writer–text–reader employs nearly all of the metaphorical *figurae* mentioned in the novel. In this chapter Morelli (speaking surely for Cortázar) tries to "justify his narrative incoherencies" as a way of placing the reader "in conditions ripe for taking a chance, for participating, almost, in the destiny of the characters" (468). This destiny is primarily an apocalyptic effort to unveil those patterns shaping the narrative which illuminate the reader's creation of meaning out of the fragments of the text: "The book would have to be something like those sketches proposed by Gestalt psychologists, and therefore certain lines would induce the observer to trace imaginatively the ones that would complete the figure" (469). Morelli then adopts the vocabulary of crystals and kaleidoscopes to delineate possible shapes of the figure. He "had hoped that the accumulation of fragments would quickly crystallize into a total reality;" but it will be "A crystallization in which nothing would remain subsumed, but where a lucid eye might peep into the kaleidoscope and understand the great polychromatic rose, understand it as figure, an *imago mundi*" (469). This conjunction of the quotidian and the sublime, and of chaos and creation is pure Cortázar, and constitutes a climactic synthesis of themes associated with apocalyptic revelation in the third section of the novel.

Another way of imagining these crystalline figures is as the fundamental elements of the creation; but the creation needs to be annihilated in order to reveal those elements. This aspect of apocalypse as annihilation and recreation suggest that the novel has been broken down into fragments in order that they may be recreated in a new order according to the combined poetic visions of author and reader. The end of the conventions of the old novel will lead to the creation of new forms, and destruction and creation will become two poles of a single process. Cortázar says early on in the book that Morelli "wanted his book to be a crystal ball in which the micro– and the macrocosm would come together in an annihilating vision" (25), and many of the chapters in section three imagine this apocalyptic *coincidentia oppositorum* as a reduction to elementals in order to create a new world.

The "*MORELLIANA*" recorded in Chapter 94, for example, discuss the way of "piece of prose can turn rotten like a side of beef," and by rotting be reduced to fundamental elements which can serve as the basis of new creation: "After all, rotting means the end of the impurities in the component parts and the return of rights to chemically pure sodium, magnesium, carbon. My prose is rotting syntactically and is heading—with so much work—towards simplicity" (429). The return to elementals is imagined here as an apocalyptic purgation, an "end of impurities" meant to make a new beginning possible. Morelli's effort is to "establish elements": "'When composition has reached its extreme limit, the territory of the elemental opens up. Establish them and if it is possible, be them'" (429). The sense that "Everything was breaking down into fragments which were in turn becoming fragmented" (456) then becomes a kind of trialectic by which a third new creation embraces without subsuming the dialectic of destruction and creation inherent to apocalyptic thinking. Hence, "the virtual self–destruction found in every fragment of his work was a kind of search for the noble metal among the slag" (535), Oliveira later muses, in a formulation that suggests an alchemical dimension of the apocalypse (similar to Márquez and Merrill)

In Chapter 124 Morelli refers to this self–destructive procedure as an "external and internal liquidation. But his fiction had ended up without words, without people, without things, and potentially, of course, without readers" (494). The purpose of the liquidation is to "drag himself out of the rut of the immanent and transcendental ethic in search of a nakedness that he called axial and sometimes called *the threshold*" (493). The imagery of the central axis of the mandala and of the doorway again surfaces here to figure a passage beyond the polemics of apocalypse: "the old dualism had become cracked in the face of the evidence of a common reduction of matter and spirit to notions of energy" (493). The reduction here goes beyond the chemical elements of the earlier passage to a pure realm of energy that Morelli elsewhere associates with the restored paradise (in Chapter 71). It is here figured as a means of superseding the old dualistic view of apocalypse by uniting spirit and matter in a third term.

In addition to these theoretical musings, Cortázar provides two extraordinarily dramatic instances of this apocalyptic rhythm of creation and destruction in the artistic process. In Chapter 64 Oliveira and Pola stop in the Latin Quarter to watch some artists use colored chalk to sketch such things as "an excellent reproduction of Chartres, and a little further on a mare and her foal in a green field" (365). Oliveira says "'They're using the Penelope system, but without unweaving first,'" because later that evening "'the women who sweep the streets will come and it's all over'" (365). Hence the colored chalk on the street, erased to be re–created for a profit the next day, becomes an "eschatological pattern" of annihilation and creation, every end circling back into a new beginning. Earlier, in the concluding chapter of section two of the novel, Oliveira had (or will, since Cortázar instructions for reading the novel make both possible: the circulation of time past and time future in time present is another characteristic of eschatological thinking which Cortázar shares with, say, Eliot and Mann), literally enact the Penelope principle by "constructing all manner of figures" (like "a huge transparent dodecahedron") out of colored threads, which he will then burn in a miniature conflagration, much to the chagrin of Gekrepten (327).

This focus on the moment of making and unmaking, on the apocalyptic rhythm of all creativity, and the task of reducing to pure elements is comparable to D.H. Lawrence's preoccupation with the "carbon identity" as a deeper mode of characterization in his novels, and to his efforts in *Apocalypse* to get back to the fundamental figures of mythic imagery which he sees beneath the superstructure of St. John's Revelation. Morelli's reduction to the basic elements of composition is also in line with much of Modernist painting: in the work of Mondrian, Klee, Kandinsky, Picasso, and many others (the first two are significantly juxtaposed early on in *Hopscotch*), we see precisely this annihilation of the external world as a subject of painting and a gradual revelation of the basic elements of painting (color fields, horizontal and vertical lines, intersecting planes, etc.) which can serve as the basis for the new kind of abstract painting that emerged after the war. Several of the works of these painters in fact bear titles associated with the apocalypse, such as Kandinsky's "Four Horsemen."[49]

All of these various strands in the web of apocalyptic imagery woven by Cortázar in the novel (the supercession of dualities, the annihilation of the external world, the reduction to the elements, and the revelation of the geometrical figures which give shape and significance to the "Great Work") come together in one final aspect of the myth: the nostalgic search for the restoration of the lost paradise. "Why have we had to invent Eden, to live submerged in the nostalgia of a lost paradise, to make up utopias, propose a future for ourselves?" (162) Oliveira asks early on in a novel much preoccupied with answering such questions. Gerald Martin, among others, has argued that such questions have characterized Latin American fiction and what he calls "Myths of the Mestizo Continent" ever since Columbus thought he had discovered the four rivers of Eden flowing into the Atlantic basin along South American shores.

But I would suggest that Cortázar was perhaps more driven towards this theme by the publication in Paris in 1957 of Mircea Eliade's *Mythes, Rêves, et Mystéres.*[50] Eliade's discussion, particularly in Chapter III: "Nostalgia for Paradise in the Primitive Traditions," contains a large number of motifs to be found in Cortázar's *Hopscotch*, published shortly afterwards in 1963. Among these motifs one might include Eliade's discussions of "an *axis mundi*—mountain, tree, or creeper—to be found at the *center of the world*, connecting Earth with Heaven" (60), and of the shamanic techniques of ascending this tree to recover the lost paradise and the secret languages that are spoken within it (61–66). "The most representative mystical experience of the archaic societies," Eliade writes, "that of shamanism, betrays the *Nostalgia for Paradise*" (66), and among the related motifs discussed within this connection (search for the center, return to origins, the flaming sword of the expulsion, a secret language of the animals, ascent of the central axis connecting Earth and Heaven, Columbus, etc.), nearly all are present in *Hopscotch.*

We find the nostalgia for paradise first in the ragtime and blues rhythms favored by the Club, particularly in Satchmo, who "brings them back into that obscure and forgotten central flame, clumsily and badly and precariously he delivers them back to a betrayed origin," to an "archetypal form" (70). The yearning also permeates Oliveira's musings, while the music plays, about a garden where the members of the Club could be "reconstituted outside their appearances among the Club, back to what they were, emerged, dawning, at best all might be just a nostalgic view of the earthly paradise" (73). Such longings dominate the climax of section one of the novel, when Oliveira suggests that his "Kibbutz of desire" is a "vehement nostalgia for a land where life could be babbled out according to other compasses and other names" (204), and when he discovers his kibbutz on the street level with the *clocharde* Emmanuéle: "Heaven was on the same level as Earth on the dirty sidewalk where you played the game," he says, as he imagines that "one day someone would see the true outline of the world, patterns pretty as can be, and perhaps pushing the stone along, you would end up entering the kibbutz" (216). This sense of the revelation of the "true outline of the world," of its archetypal "patterns" is central to Cortázar's adaptation of apocalypse.

Besides jazz, sex, and hopscotch, dreams also provide entrance points into the lost paradise in two important chapters of the third section of the novel, which begins with Oliveira waking up "with the remains of a paradise half–seen in dreams" lingering vividly in his mind, "hanging down over [him] like the hair on someone who's been drowned" (354). The most elaborately developed dream vision of paradise occurs in Chapter 123, when in an "imprecise zone" between waking and dreaming, Oliveira reenters his "childhood house" with "two windows that opened on the garden" (490). The room conjoins La Maga's room in Paris and Buenos Aires (the two principal opposing settings of sections one and two of the novel reconciled here): "in the effortless removal of contradiction there was the sensation of being where one should be, in the essential place" (490). This place is paradisiac; it is "*the place* of "inalienable belonging," and "in the dream it was necessary to choose the most peaceful spot in the place, the reason behind the dream seemed to be just that, choosing a peaceful place" (490). Oliveira senses the presence of his sister there as "a force with no visible manifestations, something that is or does through a presence that can do without appearances" (490), and together with his sister they choose the "living room that opened on the garden" as the most peaceful place, before Oliveira wakes up in La Maga's room (491).[51] This dream combines that sense of Edenic peace with the reconciliation of opposites characteristic of the myth of apocalypse, and gives the later pages of the novel as a whole a fine sense of closure.

If dreams can be imagined as providing a brief glimpse of paradise, waking can be conceived as a kind of fall: Oliveira remembers having dreamt "something marvelous and that in the end I felt as if expelled .... I don't know if I even closed a door behind me .... But I kept on sleeping, that business of expulsion and the door closing I also dreamed" (511). Note that the imagery of the doorway dividing the threshold between waking and sleeping, between the exile and the garden, persists in this passage, forging a coherent linkage between the mythic sub–texts of the *nekyia* and apocalypse; it is as if Oliveira prefers neither the exile nor the restoration of paradise, but the standing in the gateway, a place in between which brings the opposites together, negating neither, evoking both. It is this liminal moment spatialized in the imagery of the door that he is preoccupied with, as the passage continues: "A single and terrible certainty dominated that instant of transition within the dream: to know that irremediably that expulsion brought with it the complete forgetting of the previous marvel. I suppose that the feeling of a door closing was just that, fateful and instantaneous forgetting" (511).[52]

All of this dream experience is recalled in a café, the doors of which represent another variation on the imagery of the Eastward gate of Eden with its cherubic threshold guardians. As Oliveira's musings continue, he postulates an "Edenic root" for these processes of dream and waking, remembering and forgetting, restoration and expulsion: "Perhaps Eden, as some would see it, is the mythopoetic projection of good old fetal times that persist in the unconscious" (511), and perhaps the dream manifests its roots in "An Arcadia complex, the return to the great uterus, back to Adam" (377). Hence he continues in the present passage to suggest that awakening from the dream reenacts Masaccio's depiction of the expulsion at the gateway of Adam, who "covers his face to protect his vision, what had been his; he preserves in that small manual night the last landscape of his paradise" (511).[53] It is a paradise to be recovered in *Hopscotch* not only in dreams, but in cafés as well.

Cafés, Oliveira writes, "are the neutral territory for the stateless of the soul, the motionless center of the wheel from where one can reach himself in full career" (510). This center, as we will see, becomes one of the many figures for paradise regained in the novel; "excentration" refers to the expulsion from the little paradise of the café. In Chapter 78, Oliveira remembers "with timeless clarity the cafés in Buenos Aires where for several hours we would succeed in getting away from family and obligations" to enter the "*cielito lindo*' of the café, which offers "a kind of immortality" (390). Exiting the café into the street reenacts the "expulsion, always, the angel with the flaming sword directing traffic on Corrientes and San Martin" (392). The return homeward to those familial obligations is precisely the fall into time and human history which the members of the Club are attempting to escape in their quest for the apocalyptic recovery of the Earthly Paradise. For Oliveira, as for Morelli, the means of restoration are the narrative disruptions of those profane habits of reading, thinking, and writing that keep us locked outside the door of the garden, and which must be annihilated before the restoration occurs.

Such Morellian meditations on the millennial implications of creative writing and reading inform much of the third section of the novel, and are perhaps most fully developed in Chapter 71, which elaborates on Morelli's notion of what I would call Homo apocalypticus. For Cortazár, the artist becomes a special breed, one whose apparently shiftless escape from civic duties qualifies him for a purposeful quest for the "end" of human life, a restoration of paradise. It is an apocalypse to be achieved not at a literal end of time, but here and now, via those disruptions of the habitual modes of consciousness which inform our reading and writing, and indeed all other aspects of modern life. Chapter 71 brings together nearly all of the apocalyptic motifs which we have been discussing under the rubric of the restored paradise: the millennial return to Eden, threshold imagery, the uterine fantasy, etc.

"Basically, what is this story about finding a millenary kingdom, an Eden, another world?" the chapter begins (377). It proceeds to a dissection of all aspects of modern life as manifestations of an apocalyptic drive towards the millennium: "Everything written these days and worth reading is oriented towards nostalgia. An Arcadia complex, the return to the great uterus, back to Adam, *le bon sauvage* (and so it goes)" (377). Most interesting in this diagnosis of modern consciousness, is Morelli's reflection on the new physics of Planck and Heisenberg as the revelation of a realm of pure energy, beneath the phenomenal world of coffee cups, in which "everything vibrates and trembles and is like a cat about to take an enormous hydrogen or cobalt leap" (377). This underworld of quantum physics has behind it, Morelli remarks, the Arcadian nostalgia for "Paradise, the other world, trampled innocence which weeping darkly seeks the land of Hurqalyã" (377).[54] Furthermore, the notion of a "behind" or "beneath" which must be uncovered or unveiled (the root meaning of apocalypse) becomes, for Morelli, "the key idea of modern thought" (377), and hence the "key" idea to open all the doors of the novel. It is an archetypal idea visible, Morelli continues, in widely disparate realms of modern life: "the small escape, the little house in the suburbs, literary or scientific specialization, travel" and, more extremely, "drunkenness ... or mescaline, or homosexuality, anything magnificent and inane per se but stupidly elevated into a system, into a key to the kingdom" (379).

In fact, the use of the term "Hurqalyã" as a synonym for Paradise points towards the "specialization" of comparative religion. Hurqalyã is the Persian word for a particular kind of paradisal vision described by Henri Corbin in his books and articles on Islamic mysticism, many of which were published in Paris a little before and during the period in which *Hopscotch* was being written. Corbin's cartography of the Persian paradise may well have influenced Cortázar and been the source of the term Hurqalyã in the novel. Consider Henry Corbin's description of "an intermediary world, limiting and conjoining time and eternity, the spatial and the transspatial, just as its immaterial matter and its celestial Earthiness are, in themselves also a symbol of the *coincidentia oppositorum*, the conjunction of the sensible and of the intelligible in a pure space of the Archetypal Images" ("Terre Céleste" 163; my trans). This notion of the apocalyptic restoration of paradise as a conjunction of such opposites as time and eternity, Earth and Heaven, is central to Cortázar's thinking. In fact, Corbin's notion of a *mundus imaginalis* as a realm of archetypes generated by our creative imagination has much in common with Morelli's thoughts about how we gain access to paradise.

"Perhaps there is one way out," he continues in Chapter 71, "but that exit ought to be an entrance. Perhaps there is a millenary kingdom .... Until now this Century has been running away from all sorts of things, it has been looking for doorways" (379). The most significant key to these doorways, Morelli then suggests, is a peculiar activity of the creative imagination: the "millenary kingdom" does "not exist, one has to create it like the phoenix .... Let us say that the world is a figure, it has to be read. By read let us understand generated" (379). The "delicate alchemies" (379) which generate the apocalyptic vision of a Paradise within and behind the mundane world of suburban housing and cafés becomes, in a sense, the special privilege of poetry, which bypasses "an Orwellian or Huxleyan nightmare" to recover "a vestige of the forgotten kingdom" which eludes political control (380. It is this quest which informs, according to Morelli, the very essence of our imaginal being: "Everything can be killed," Chapter 71 concludes, "except nostalgia for the kingdom, we carry it in the color of our eyes, in every love affair, in everything that deeply torments and unites and tricks" (381). It is one of those central myths of postmodernism which we live, write, and read by.

Umberto Eco

Umberto Eco adds a curious range of geometrical figures revealed by apocalypse in his recent novel *Foucault's Pendulum*, a book which begins where it will end, and ends with its beginning scene: in the first and last chapters we watch the main character Casaubon hiding in the Conservatoire des Arts et Métiers in Paris, waiting to witness the secret meeting of an occult group which is seeking the key to an energy source which will give it power over the world. The Plan (as they call it) is itself apocalyptic, having been created by a mystical group of Templar Knights who arrange a sequence of seven meetings stretching over 666 years designed to achieve mastery of a mysterious underground power source variously identified with the philosopher's stone and the Holy Grail. The most recent meeting, scheduled for 1944, had been disrupted by World War II, so that we now find Casaubon waiting in Paris of the 1990's for the final meeting in which all secrets of the Plan are meant to be revealed. Eco divides his chapters using the ten Sephiroth of the cabalistic tree, which is also apocalyptic in that the fall of the divine light into the Creation in the beginning leads to the work of restoration and return to primordial origins known as *tikkun*. Hence, those basic forms giving shape and significance to life which are revealed in the beginning (of both the novel and the cabalistic Creation myth), are returned to at the end, when a cycle of re–creation begins. Like Pynchon, Merrill, and Lessing, Eco uses a diverse vocabulary (derived from the esoteric philosophies of alchemy, Gnosticism, and cabala and from the rather equally esoteric vocabularies of technology, mathematics, and physics) to establish the symbolism of these basic forms.

The first chapter is where the initial revelation of the fundamental forms governing life occurs. In the chapter named after Crown Sefirah known as Keter, Casaubon hides in the Museum contemplating the mysteries of the pendulum which he sees swinging from the ceiling, and to which the novel will gruesomely return at its end. The pendulum becomes a symbol of the origins of the Creation in the first emanation of the En–Sof, or God: Keter is "the beginning, the primal void. In the beginning He created a point, which became Thought, where all the figures were drawn .... He traced signs in the air; a dark light leapt from His most secret depth, like a colorless mist that gives form to formlessness" (18). Although His light streams down in exile to "illuminate the lower Sefiroth, and down, down to the Kingdom," there already exists, in the beginning, "the promise of return" (18). Alpha and Omega constitute a single figure, which Eco represents by the Pendulum hanging from the ceiling: it is the "Only fixed Point in the universe" (5), and the shape created by its swinging revolutions becomes the "single pattern" which forms the prototype of all the other figures in the novel: mandala, pentaculum, mystic rose, ellipse, or circle (4). Each of the first three chapters, all named after the initial world–creating trinity of the first three Sefirah, moves towards a revelation of the essence of the Plan of both world and novel, which will only be fully disclosed by the apocalypse of the end. In Hokhmah, "the Plan, the Universal Plot" of the Templar Knights, mentioned for the first time in Keter (6), begins to be revealed as Casaubon works to crack the code to the computer files his doomed friend Belbo kept. That what was covered or ciphered in the beginning must be uncovered or deciphered in the end is the essential idea of apocalypse (meaning to uncover or unveil). Hence, Hokhmah bears within itself the entirety of the as yet undisclosed creation, "wisdom, knowledge, the primordial thought that contains, as in a box, everything, all that will unfold in creation. Hokhmah holds the essence of all that will emanate from it" (41). It is the Aleph, you might say, a hologlyph, the Word which initiates the Creation, and which by extension becomes a metaphor for the way those novels which follow the Aristotelian conventions of complex plot begin (stating the problem that must be solved in the end). The basic plot of the novel, therefore, corresponds to the Plan of creation and the Form of human history, and it is fully disclosed by the time we finish the chapter called Binah. Binah is the Sefiroth in which "all forms are already formed" (158), corresponding to the "Thought, where all figures were drawn" of Keter (18), and "the essence of all that will emanate from it" of Hokhmah (41). The revelation of this fundamental "form," "Thought," or "essence" occurs when Colonel Ardenti shows up in the publishing office where Casaubon and Belbo work with a mysterious manuscript on parchment having to do with the Templar Plan to go underground for some 666 years until they emerge as "Masters of World control" (144). The parchment sets the pattern of seven meetings which the rest of the novel unfolds (in excessive detail).

As in Borges, Márquez, and Cortázar, apocalypse becomes then a matter of reading, a symbol of hermeneusis, of deciphering a text to force the revelation of its form and meaning. The characters create the plot of the novel they are in by interpreting the parchment Ardenti delivers, just as we the readers create interpretations of the novel which Eco delivers. As in Yeats, Cortázar, Pynchon, and Borges the revelation of the fundamental forms of poesis, hermeneusis, and genesis itself sometimes takes the form of hieroglyphic ideograms, like the cryptographs of Trithemius (134, 538), the esoteric glyphs of John Dee's Monas (418), Ardenti's runic map of the Plan (147), the binary networks of Kircher (473), the maps of the mystical cartographers (458), the transmission shaft of auto mechanics (377f.), the complex mathematical equations of physics (599), or indeed the tree of the Sephiroth itself (title page). These various ideograms are analogous to the ones found in Pound< Yeats, or James Merrill, and crystallize within themselves the eidola disclosed by apocalypse and the descent into Hades. As creators of these vast schemes of cosmic and aesthetic order, and as readers who interpret the texts which promise to disclose them, Eco compares us to the golem makers of cabalistic legend: the Plan itself becomes a golem, a creation of the readers in the text, which ends by destroying its creators, as the dying Diotallevi tells us (566). The scene in which Belbo dies by hanging at the end of the novel circles back to its beginning, and traces another geometrical ideogram on the pavement of the Museum. The intellectual climax of the novel comes with Diotallevi's evocation of the golem, that soulless man created by the recitation of the letters of the Torah in the ritual contexts of Hebraic mysticism. For Borges, all writers are golem makers, and themselves, ontologically speaking, golems created by God. For Broch, the golem was that primordial form which enclosed within itself all the mysteries of Creation. And for Eco, all readers are golem makers, devising forms by the manipulation of letters, forms which reveal the essence of our longing for apocalypse as a longing for meaning, at whatever cost.

James Merrill

James Merrill weaves many of the themes prevalent in the postmodernist apocalypse into his terrific trilogy, *The Changing Light at Sandover*. The threat of nuclear extinction naturally hangs over a poem devoted to question of humankind's survival of the 'great thinning' to come. And at least three Edens were destroyed in the poem's mythical past, with the nuclear cataclysm that destroyed Atlantis and the disastrous experiment in Thebes (when a crystalline capstone on the Great Pyramid at Giza exploded) receiving most attention. Along with the threat of annihilation, we have the polemos motif characteristic of the apocalyptic battle between the opposing forces of good and evil on the field of Armageddon; Merrill's polemic involves the "dichotomy" between positive and negative forces within the atom and the cell (461). More interesting, however, is Merrill's handling of the themes of ricorso and revelation, which have preoccupied writers in the modernist mode since Eliot, Mann, Broch, and Lawrence. In these writers, the return to the beginning at the end of time coincides with the revelation of that great design which makes renewal possible. What distinguishes Merrill's ricorso from these earlier modernist versions of the apocalypse, and what brings him closer to postmodernists like Thomas Pynchon, is his integration of science into the poem, thereby effecting a reconciliation with theology oddly reminiscent of Tennyson's great poem *In Memoriam*.

Ricorso is a predominant motif throughout *The Changing Light*, a poem which circles back to water as the first idea (241), to the first soul implanted in the hominids (236), to Akhenaton as the first individual, to Atlantis and Thebes as the first great civilizations, to the first dwellings of Homo sapiens in the caves and lakes of the Paleolithic, and, indeed, to dramatically extensive accounts of the genesis of the planet and its early life forms. Typically, ricorso leads both to revelation and renewal, so that the end becomes a new beginning, and the centripetal circle turns towards the centrifugal spiral of rebirth: for behind the apocalypse is, as the Daemmrichs put it, "the prospect that these reform circles will actually succeed in reshaping the larger outer circumference" (87). The goal of the Merrill's poem, and of its angelic pedagogy, is the restoration of the humanity's lost paradise (292–96), based on the construction of "A CHEMICAL SYSTEM FOR REACHIEVING / HIS IMMORTALITY" (439). This will be obtained through the reduction of the soul structure and the cell to those base elements which, refined over the centuries in the alchemical alembics of the R/Lab, can be modified to resist the radiation required to restore the lost Eden. The angel Gabriel calls this reconstituted Adam the "ALPHA MAN" (439), knowledge of whom Merrill wittily requests the Angels to withhold: "'My Lords, as to the Alpha men themselves / Accessorized with what new lobes, wings, valves, / And deathless like those characters in Shaw / Whose gifts amuse more often than they awe, / Spare us a full account'" (511).

What he seems more interested in is the revelation of that grand design which confers shape and significance upon life. Such a revelation constitutes a conventional climax of the apocalypse, which means to unveil, or uncover. Once the world is stripped of its vestments by the seven catastrophes, the invisible structures of soul, cell, and atom stand naked to view, like the skeleton revealed by the X–ray, or like a tree stripped of its leaves. Hence Merrill's preoccupation with the problem of design, an obsession expressed throughout *The Changing Light* in both its form and its content. The poem has already been hailed as a masterful encyclopedia of verse forms—blank verse, couplets, terza rime, sestets, septets, octaves, villanelles, canzone, and sonnets, of which there are some 40 or so, many of them examples of the technical fireworks all of Merrill's work is celebrated for. Merrill's handling of the sonnet form is dazzlingly playful (witness the Avebury and toy spyglass sonnets) in a manner generally characteristic of postmodernism (witness Borges, Nabokov, Cortázar, Cocteau). Also characteristically postmodern is Merrill's sometimes uneasily self–conscious awareness of the way these poetic forms impose order on what may ultimately be a chaotic reality. He remains, nevertheless, fundamentally serious in his concern with the Grand Design revealed to him by his dead friends, Ephraim, Mirabell, and the angels.

Angelic apparitions are, of course, natural to the literature of the Apocalypse, inspired by John's visions in The Book of Revelation. Their main role in Merrill's poem is pedagogic: they tell the stories of genesis, science, religion, and history to establish the shape and significance of the Creation and its future. In doing so, they rely on a vocabulary and iconography of form of the sort frequently found in Modernist and Postmodernist versions of the apocalypse, with the crucial addition of scientific terms to the lexicon. Mirabell is the first to identity God with Biology, and to address the problem of the "FATHER'S / GRAND DESIGN" (247–48). Mirabell is also the first to invoke the "NO ACCIDENT" clause, according to which the Creation (of poem and world) "FALLS INTO PLACE AS THEY HAVE PLANNED" (215). As Auden puts it earlier in the poem, during the lessons in "Mirabell," since "GOD BIOLOGY IS HISTORY," it follows that "NO SPARROW FALLS NOTHING / IN NATURE, NOTHING IN NATURE'S CHILD IS UNKNOWN TO HIM / THERE IS NO ACCIDENT" (187). Hence the numerous historical overviews throughout the trilogy, which chart the plan of divine Providence in a way critics don't like to think of as postmodernist. Nor would many postmodernist critics (predominately agnostic humanists) much care for the biblical plan of the Providence outlined by the angels and Mirabell, who says he sees "FAIR GREEN ATLANTEAN FIELDS" and a restored paradise of immortality in humankind's future (201).

Again, this "WORK OF EONS" (201) is to be achieved by a fusion of scientific and spiritual means. In addition to outlining the role of death, for example, in "OUR FATHER'S / GREAT DESIGN" (334), and in addition to delineating the duties of the archangels as they bend their "BACKS" to implement the "PLAN" of the grand 'ARCHITECT" (293), Gabriel and Michael also outline the role biology plays in God B's project. They criticize, for example, the "DRUDGE" whose "RESEARCH INTO THE LIVING CELL" neglects "THE IDEA OF A GRAND DESIGN" (375). They also praise Pythagoras and the "MATHEMATICIAN," whose numbers and formulas represent 'THE TRUE FORMS BEHIND" the art of creation (372). Ultimately, it is the intention of the angels and of Mother Nature (Psyche) to "EXPLAIN / ALL DEEP & DIRE THINGS! / AND IN THE EIGHTH FULL MOON, MY SIGN, / GIVE THEM OUR COMPLETE DESIGN" (410), a project which necessarily integrates quantum physics with theology, since the apocalyptic modifications "SOUL STRUCTURE" require radiation therapy in the R/Lab (417). In fact, the entire function of the angelic pedagogy is to make "THE LONG AND SHORT OF IT ... THE SUBSTANCE AND THE SENSE OF IT" (551), a comment which applies to the formation and purpose of the world and of the poem itself (form and content often provided by the angels).

This poetic fusion of theology and science is one of the poem's great achievements, as important to our era as Tennyson's similar marriage of the two was in *In Memoriam*. Like Tennyson, Merrill constructs a myth which unites evolutionary theory with biblical theology. For Tennyson, this involved combining the ideas about the evolution and extinction of the species (suggested by the fossil records discussed in Sir Charles Lyell's book, *On the Principles of Geology*) with the biblical paradigm of the apocalypse. Tennyson associated the higher man of the second coming (prefigured by his dead friend Arthur Hallam, for whom the poem was written) with that form towards which the human species is gradually evolving. Tennyson was perhaps less secular in this concern with the übermensch than Nietzsche was, though no less mythical. It has, in fact always been the role of the poet to create a new mythology appropriate to the intellectual, scientific, and spiritual climate of the era, and this task Merrill performs as brilliantly as Tennyson did. He does so by updating the scientific framework of the poem, and relating it to the biblical paradigm of genesis, fall, and redemption, which M.H. Abrams argued was the general task of the romantic poets and philosophers who preceded Tennyson. Hence, Merrill incorporates Darwinian theories about the evolution of Homo sapiens from the hominid line into his myth by suggesting that the entire process was inspired by the Angels infusing human densities into the monkey's soul. This was the origin of our species, which, according to Merrill's myth, will gradually evolve (through the mystical and biochemical experiments in the R/Lab) towards the Alpha men of the restored paradise. Hence, Auden instructs JM to ask about "THAT RACE / USING US, EVOLVING FROM US IN / THAT PARADISE ... NOW BEING READIED" (308).

The "Alpha man" is the higher species towards which all modern science and evolutionary development moves, guided, as in Tennyson, by a God of Biology who reconciles science and theology. As Psyche puts it in one of the lessons in the "Scripts for the Pageant," this marriage brings together "BLAKE'S FAITH, AND PHYSICS' LAW" (408) in an explosively creative fusion. Of all the other postmodernists, only Eco (in *Foucault's Pendulum*) and Pynchon (in *Gravity's Rainbow*) effect such a fusion. Eco and Pynchon, however, tend to focus on the paranoiac aspects of this apocalyptic fusion: both create international conspiracies to mastermind Armageddon. Merrill tends rather to focus on the fusion not as a symptom of paranoia, but as a symbol of poesis. For in Merrill's apocalypse, the composer, the scientist, and the scribe play an essentially positive role in the restoration of the lost paradise. Wagner appears during the pageant alongside Jesus, Buddha, and Mercury, and he announces the divine, priestly status of the composer by noting that "MUSIC'S RIVER GOLD STILL VEINS / A PEDESTAL THE GOD HAS TOPPLED FROM" (445). And Mercury appears next in the pageant to give the poet the alphabet, which Gabriel calls "THE NEW MATERIALS, YOUNG POET, FOR A NEW FAITH" (446). Merrill prepares us for such bold assertions of the apocalyptic function of the poet with earlier proclamations in the poem, such as that "The innate / Role of the Scribe must now be to supplant / Religion" (178). The rituals of the new religion will be the "RITES OF LANGUAGE," for "IF THERE ARE STILL 3 / MAJOR FAITHS THESE ARE NOW SCIENCE, POETRY & MUSIC" (239). The humanistic fusion of these three yields hope for the future of our species, endangered as it is by the fanatic controversies of religious fundamentalism.

Tennyson's symbol for the fusion of mind and nature, and of science and theology, like Merrill's, is the marriage ceremony of the lamb, derived from the Book of Revelation (19:7,9). The renewal of life and the thousand years of peace which that fusion makes possible is represented by the birth of the divine child (Rev. 12: 5). In Tennyson, this occurs in the famous section devoted to the marriage of his daughter, which is followed by the terrific evocation of the conception of her child during the wedding night by the sea. This passage from *In Memoriam* uses the Victorian notion that ontogeny recapitulates phylogeny to reconcile Darwinian notions of the evolution of the species with the apocalyptic prophecy of the higher man towards which that evolution moves, symbolized by the birth of the divine child. Like Tennyson, Merrill secularizes the biblical paradigm in his own marvelous conclusion by substituting a human for a divine child, ending his grand trilogy with the embryological development of the foetus that leads to the rebirth of Robert Morse. In each of the five ceremonies of the "Coda," one of the angels endows the foetus with one of the five senses, until it is ready to spiral down to earth—reminiscent of the role played by the Gnostic planetary deities in the rebirth of Charles Watkins in Doris Lessing's *Briefing for a Descent into Hell*. In *The Hearing Trumpet*, Leonora Carrington wreaks her own surrealistic havoc upon the apocalyptic theme of divine birth, and H.D. David Jones, and Gabriel Garcia Marquez conclude their fine apocalyptic works—*Trilogy*, *The Anathemata*, and *One Hundred Years of Solitude*—with the symbolism of marriage and birth. But they do not substitute a human for the Christ child. (Indeed, the existence of so many fine Nativity poems is one of the most surprising features of the literature of postmodernism, when one considers the agnostic and existential framework critics typically apply to the period).

The sacred marriage and birth at the end of time which makes its renewal possible occurs in *Revelation* in tandem with the descent of the Heavenly Jerusalem, a geometrical symbol of the restoration of divine symmetry. The biblical text devotes several verses to the architectonics of the city, which is basically a cube formed by four walls, of equal length and breadth, with three gates in each with three angels hovering them, the whole standing atop twelve steps made of precious stones. The twelve thousand furlongs of its measure and 144 (12x12) and cubits of the length, breadth, and height yield a cube based on the number 12, "according to the measure of man, that is, of the angel" (Rev. 21:17). Earlier in *Revelation* St. John provides another geometrical figuration of divine symmetry: the quincunx, formed by Jesus seated on a rainbow in the center of a square formed by the symbols of the four evangelists, with the 24 (2x12) elders seated on thrones round about. James Merrill's apocalyptic trilogy is saturated with this kind of mythical geometry, from the various squares and quincunxes of its hermetic and labyrinthine mathematics, to the ideogram with the "MINOAN WAIST" which the angels and God B inscribe upon the board at the climax to "Scripts for the Pageant."

Peter Weir

In Peter Weir's film, *The Last Wave*, we find an imaginative conflation of the myths of the apocalypse, the maze, and the underworld. A standard motif of the genre of the apocalypse—the ricorso, or circling back to the beginning of time at its end—governs the plot of the film, which revolves around the revelation of the archaic rituals of an aboriginal tribe practiced in the sewer system far beneath the traffic–clogged streets of modern Sydney. A young lawyer hired to defend an aboriginal boy accused of murder discovers the secrets of these rituals in the last sequence of the film, just before an apocalyptic wave annihilates the city. This last sequence in the film combines the motifs of the descent and the penetration of a maze with the apocalyptic motifs of revelation and destruction. It begins with the lawyer alone at home during a terrific storm which shatters the windows and inundates the house. The aboriginal boy mysteriously appears and guides the lawyer through the rain to a power station, where the descent begins. It proceeds, in a manner typical of the myths of the maze and the underworld, through a sequence of arches, doorways, stairways, corridors, canals, and caves.

The aborigine leads the lawyer first through a large stone arch into a corridor of the power station which ends at a fire door. Passing through the door, the pair descends a sequence of three meshwork metal stairways into the bifurcating canals of the sewer system beneath the station. The descent deepens as the pair climbs down an exposed manhole and crawls into a narrow rock passageway dripping with water. This passage opens into a large cavern with a Stonehenge-like post and lintel illuminated above in the distance. They pass through this threshold into a chamber littered with large ancestral heads sculpted in stone. The aboriginal boy explains that his dream and the lawyer's dream have brought them here; he then hands the lawyer the churinga stone with the spiral inscribed upon it, and directs him downwards, to the snake, beyond which he will find what he is looking for. Their movement is centripetal, from the present to the past; but it suggests the reciprocal revelations of the centrifugal spiral, from the human to the divine: as the Daemmrichs put it, "the spiral moving downward and inward toward a terminal point of closure and stasis in a closed circle carries a latent seed for potential regeneration" (319). The boy then disappears, saying that he is returning to his people, to the dreamtime, and the lawyer continues the descent, moving through a stone door with a snake painted on the lintel, to another stone lintel, through which he shines his flashlight, illuminating a large pair of spiraling eyes inscribed on the wall. All of these motifs—the passage through a sequence of doorways, the snake guarding the threshold, and the spiraling eyes within—evoke a long heritage of images associated with the maze and the underworld derived ultimately from Sumerian and Egyptian prototypes. In both, the penetration of the maze into the underworld is associated with the apocalyptic theme of revelation, whereby the fundamental forms of the mind which shape the world are manifested.

This occurs in the innermost chamber to the aboriginal sanctuary, the walls of which are painted with a prophetic calendar which predicts the rain, hail, and waves of the Australian apocalypse. There is also a kind of Minotaur in the midst of this maze—the ancient aborigine named Charlie, ritually painted and ominously waving a spear, whom the lawyer kills with the churinga stone when Charlie tries to prevent him from stealing a death mask and other treasures. The death mask is, mysteriously, of a white man, perhaps the lawyer's ancestor, but the mask is lost in the water as the lawyer struggles to make his way back out of the maze, running and stumbling back through the same sequence of caves, lintels, bifurcating canals, before which he pauses, runs up and back down the wrong one, and then up the correct one to the staircases, and corridors, only to collapse in front of the fire door of the power station, which has been locked. The lawyer then runs back down the corridors and staircases of the station to the bifurcating canals, turning down another dark canal which eventually leads to a long rounded tunnel leading up into the light of dawn on the beach. The lawyer crawls out of the sewer pipe and follows its stream to the sea, where he falls on his knees to wash his face. When he looks up, an enormous tidal wave curls towards Sydney and darkens his face with the shadow of the end.

Conclusion

Northrop Frye suggested that the use of such abstract figures in modernist painting as the point, the circle, the triangle, the square, and a variety of polygons is analogous to "the use of myth in Joyce or Cocteau, or the use of the folktale in Mann" (*Fables* 31). This remark points two ways, for it suggests that geometrical figures are the appropriate visual analogies to the use of myths in verbal narratives. The fundamental forms of visual structures are geometrical, and the fundamental forms of visual ones are mythic. Such figures are equally abundant in the literature, painting, and architecture of postmodernism, in which they become increasingly elaborate metaphors of poesis and hermeneutics. While modernists like Thomas Mann preferred the simple forms of the line and the sphere, postmodernists like Carrington and Eco move towards more intricate polygons in rather playful revisions of the mythical geometry of their precursors. At the same time, they tend to incorporate the imagery of science more thoroughly into their work. Pynchon, Lessing, Merrill, and Cortázar draw upon the language of the new physics (holography, quantum mechanics, and crystallography) in ways which indicate new developments in the relations between science, myth, and literature in postmodernism. And they often preserve in their work the kind of spirituality perhaps not seen in science since the "natural theology" of the Pre–Socratics.

A Mythical Geometry of Postmodernism

We find meditations on the point in "The Aleph," when Borges describes a speck of light revealed to him in the underworld of a basement as "one of the points in space that contains all other points" (*Borges* 159). The Aleph, that is to say, represents the ultimate source of all shape and significance. It is the part which contains the whole, a kind of holograph of the universe analogous to what the Hindu's called the *bindu*, that ineffable point in space where the divine energy roars into manifestation, creating the world of phenomenality. Umberto Eco begins *Foucault's Pendulum* with a similar epiphany of the point in space from which all figures of the Creation emanate. In the first and last chapters we watch the main character Casaubon contemplating the mysteries of the pendulum which he sees swinging from the ceiling of a museum. The pendulum becomes a symbol of the first emanation of Keter, "the beginning, the primal void. In the beginning He created a point, which became Thought, where all the figures were drawn" (18). It is the "Only fixed Point in the universe" (5), and the shape created by its swinging revolutions becomes the "single pattern" which forms the prototype of all other patterns, of mandala, pentaculum, mystic rose, ellipse, or circle (4). This pendulum point bears within itself, "as in a box, everything, all that will unfold in creation. Hokhmah holds the essence of all that will emanate from it" (41).

Emanating from the point we find, scattered throughout the literature of modernism and postmodernism, a variety of circles, spirals, cones, and vortices. In *A Vision*, Yeats used a intersecting pair of gyrating cones to represent the dynamic of incarnation and transfiguration which drives historical cycles, an image which Pound adapted in his notion of the vortex as a whirl of verbal figurations emanating from a central node of meaning. James Merrill has humorously adapted these ideograms to form a reflecting pair of cones formed by X's and triangles in *The Changing Light at Sandover* (474–75). At the end of Thomas Mann's *Joseph and His Brothers* we have the "ingenious and remarkable dance" ('kunstreichen und wirklich sehenswerten Fakeltanz') into which the marriage procession of Joseph and Asenath breaks up in the fountain court. The dancers move "in a ninefold spiral" ('in neunfacher Spirale') to the left around a fountain, while tossing flaming torches back and forth (1005; 1131). In *Doctor Faustus*, Mann represents those "fundamental types of emotional significance" distilled and crystallized by Adrian's music (488) in the form of the circle. Adrian's apocalyptic technique, the narrator Zeitblom says, rests upon "the curvature of the world, which makes the last return unto the first" (376). This notion of cyclical refiguration also becomes a central political, aesthetic, and mythological motive in Mann's novel. In *Joseph and His Brothers*, Mann uses the sphere instead of the circle as a metaphor of narrative structure (124). In "The God's Script" Borges turns to the wheel instead of a spiral radiating out from the central axis of the point. Borges confers upon his prisoner in the underworld a vision of Ezekiel's Wheel, a compound of water and fire which contains the "total fabric," "the intimate designs," and the "origins" of the universe (172–73).

There are numerous instances of the alchemical problem of squaring the circle, with the help of a triangle, in postmodernism. In the story by Borges called "Death and the Compass," the detective Lönnrot expects to discover that "Secret Name" of the cabbalists, in which the "immediate knowledge of all things that will be, which are and which have been in the universe" is encoded (78). This refers to the "Tetragrammaton—the name of God, JHVH" (86) which Scharlach has used as the clue to the sequence of murders executed to lure Lönnrot to his death. Scharlach uses the secret mysteries of names and the four letters to lay four murders out on a quadrangular grid connecting the four quarters of Paris. Borges evokes a variety of related polygons at the climax of this story. The quaternity was also explored by D. H. Lawrence in his last book, *Apocalypse*. Lawrence interprets John's vision of Jesus surrounded by the "four beasts full of eyes before and behind," each with six wings "full of eyes within" (Rev. 4: 6–10), as the "four Creatures of the four quarters of the heavens, winged and starry," derived from Anaximander's wheels, the star lore of Chaldean cosmology (31), and the Greek theory of the "Four Elements" (93). The squaring of the circle combines the two figures with the triangle. In Mann's *Magic Mountain*, a patient expends countless hours and reams of paper in his efforts to square the circle or to ascertain the exact value of pi. The union of the square and the circle also emerges in the climactic moment of H.D.'s *Trilogy*, when Kaspar sees a speck of light in Mary Magdalen's hair evolve into a magnificent epiphany of a gemstone (598). This stone radiates from a circle of blue, purple, and violet gems cut in squares. Like the Aleph, wheel, or hexagonal labyrinth in Borges; like the many geometrical figurations in Cortázar's work; or like the meditations upon the line, the circle, and the sphere in Mann's *Joseph* novels, the stone contains within itself all possible forms, seen from all angles (599), and its revelation is hence an alchemical archetype of poesis. The circle and the square also occur in the works of Leonora Carrington and Doris Lessing. At the climax of *Down Below*, the heroine finds the "triangle" formed by three "rectangular" tanks attached to the "circular" walls of a special room in the mental hospital to which she has been committed. In *Briefing for a Descent into Hell*, Doris Lessing has her protagonist, Charles Watkins, hallucinate a mysteriously potent "circle in the square" of the island city to which his psychotic journey brings him, and he sets about clearing it of carnage in preparation for a space landing on the next full moon (54). The revelation of the squared circle also forms the climax of Umberto Eco's novel, *Foucault's Pendulum*. Surrounding the central axis of the pendulum's circle (to which Belbo is tied), Eco places three mediums on chairs, who are then surrounded by four dervishes who whirl through the ritual at each of the four corners. This gives us seven hierophants and the circle, triangle, and square of alchemical computations, forming a mathematical figure much like the ones that so preoccupied Lawrence, Mann, H.D., Carrington, Borges, and Cortázar. In *The Anathemata*, David Jones also prefers the symbolism of the square: he associates the Welsh urn–burial of Branwen with a cist laid out "four square" (80), the lay out of the primordial cities of the Po Valley with the "trapezoidal platforms" and "the Quadrilateral Plan" celebrated by Virgil (81). For Jones, these are abstract representations of the archetypal forms upon which all human "poeisis" is based (79).

In many other postmodernist works the simple forms of the point, the circle, the square, and the triangle exfoliate into an elaborate array of polygons, often in affiliation with the maze. The narrator of "The Immortals" by Borges journeys through a desert, where, after being "lacerated by a Cretan arrow," he falls asleep within sight of the "pyramids and towers" of the Immortal City (107). The next day he descends a stairway in a cave to a "vast circular chamber" beneath a mountainous and elaborately wrought city: "there were nine doors in this cellar; eight led to a labyrinth that treacherously returned to the same chamber; the ninth (through another labyrinth) led to a second circular chamber equal to the first," and so on through a vast "stone network" that the narrator eventually escapes climbing up a ladder (109–10). Borges uses geometrical polygons to represent the text and the world again in "The Library of Babel," in which the universe is compared to a library composed of "an indefinite and perhaps infinite number of hexagonal galleries," with a spiral stairway, and a mirror in the hallways, which replicates the infinite network of galleries and chambers (51). "Death and the Compass" is saturated with geometrical figures: the "equilateral triangle" sent to Treviranus; the four cardinal points of the compass on the paint shop sign where the first murder occurs; the "pointless symmetries" and "maniacal repetitions" of the villa (83); the fourth point of the "perfect rhomb" where a "punctual death" awaits Lönnrot (86); and the "diamonds" of yellow, green, and red which divide the sky above the villa (86). All of these figures are meant to suggest that symmetry in time and space (82) which comprises the universal order encoded in the Secret Name, which, like the Aleph and like Ts'ui Pên's labyrinthine novel, is a holograph, a part which contains the whole, and which is revealed to Lönnrot just before his death in an abandoned villa, belonging to the King of Sadness, Red Scharlach, Mafioso Lord of an industrial underworld.

Like Borges, Umberto Eco takes considerable pains to portray the exact geometrical configuration of the sequence of rooms in his own library in *The Name of the Rose*. William and Adso become lost in a bewildering succession of "quadrangular or vaguely trapezoidal rooms, each with one window, arranged around a windowless heptagonal room to which the stairway leads" (170). The plan of the library is later revealed by writing down the first letters of the scriptural verses inscribed on the scrolls above the arched doorways of each of the sixteen rooms of the bifurcated octagonal wings of the central axis of the library, and of the seven rooms which surround the central heptagonal chambers of each of the four towers of the library. H.D. raises similar questions about the "shape" of the Holy City of the Apocalypse; in "Tribute to the Angels," the second poem of the *Trilogy*, she rejects the idea that the walls of "transparent glass" sitting upon the "twelve foundations" are "four–square," suggesting instead (like Eco) that the "octahedron" is the appropriate mythical figure of Revelation (548). Elsewhere in the poem, H.D. evokes the "geometric pattern" of a "blue gentian" reflected in an "ice–floe", which she contrasts with the "geometry on the wing" of migratory snow geese and the "flower–cone" of a "lily / folded like a pyramid" (585). Although she warns us not to "be beguiled / by the geometry of perfection" (577), these figures serve to elaborate her vocabulary of poesis in the *Trilogy*.

One of the most elaborate assortment of polygons is to be found in Leonora Carrington's novels. The room where the revelations occur in *Down Below* is in a building with three storeys with a doorway open in each. In the tower at the top, she finds "a circular room lighted by five bull's eye windows" (42), which revolve around a column serving as an axis which passes through a pentagonal table in the center of the room (43). During the protracted descent in Hades in Carrington's *The Stone Door,* the King of the underworld gives the dream woman, Air, "a small wooden wheel in the center of which was a spider," and then explains that "The eight legs of the spider are love and death. The eight spokes of the wheel are triumph, movement, and life" (22). The "stream of beings" in the underworld appear in diverse geometrical configurations: some are "joined like siamese twins in two's or three's or in greater numbers, forming geometrical shapes and objects such as five–, six–, eight–, nine–, or twelve–sided polygons, triangles, squares, circles" (24). Then there is the "small white child who stood frail and luminous in the road" with a five–pronged crown of root and bone on his forehead, who announces that "All the colors on Earth have made me white; all the animals under the sky have made my body" (27). This divine homunculus is holographic, a small part which contains within itself the entire creation, all its colors and all its animals. The white child leads the woman to six horsemen, who hold aloft an eight–spoked wheel with the eight–legged spider in the middle.

In the last chapters of the novel, Carrington continues to combine the journey to the underworld with a splendid variety of geometrical figures curiously transformed by her unique breed of surrealism. Zacharias sees his dream "sister" slit a goat's throat with a black triangular stone in the center of circle filled with polygons which the 'sister' draws while chanting a litany of the four elements (66–67). Old "Böles Kilary" lies dead in a tavern on a "sexagonal bier" wearing a "long black shirt exquisitely embroidered with scarlet letters, circles, and polygons" (98). The huge stones of the tavern where he lies are "squashed into a great cube" (100) like the one Dürer's Melancholy sits beside. The stones of the tavern are holographic, each part containing the whole universe, since encoded in them is all the "old mineral knowledge from the nine planets" (100).

Julio Cortázar's *Hopscotch* is also much concerned with the revelation of geometrical figures. In the "Orphic hymn" near the end of the novel, Cortázar evokes "the hub of the wheel of origins [where] the initial and final figures are sketched" (542). The novel often evokes geometrical symbols for that ultimate pattern of reconciliation revealed by apocalypse. Author, character, and reader are all searching for such a "figure, an *imago mundi*"" (469), imagined variously as a hopscotch court and kaleidoscope; a crystal taking shape (278); "a tarot figure" or "a polyhedron in which every edge and every facet keeps its immediate sense" (142); "the center of the crossroads" or the "hub of a wheel" (291); "a mandala through which one must pass without dialectics, a labyrinth where pragmatic formulas are of no use except to get lost in" (427); fundamental elements like "chemically pure sodium, magnesium, carbon" (429); the text itself, imagined as one of "those sketches proposed by Gestalt psychologists" in which certain lines would induce the observer to trace imaginatively the ones that would complete the figure" (469); a Rorschach blot or polychromatic rose (469); or finally as "the mysterious *garden* in a sapphire, that mysterious spot in the gem that determines perhaps the coalescence of the system and which in sapphires irradiates its transparent celestial cross like a congealed energy in the heart of the stone" (505). Several dramatic images of artistic creation in the novel also evoke the notion of the *figuras*, as when Oliveira amuses himself in Buenas Aires by "constructing all manner of figures" out of colored threads, as for example "a huge transparent dodecahedron," which he then burns, much to the chagrin of Gekrepten (327).

Postmodernist Painting and Architecture

The revelation of such mathematical and geometrical figures in conjunction with the mythical method is, therefore, typical of much of the literature in the postmodernist mode. The same might be said of modernist and postmodernist painting and architecture: we have masters of the circle (Wassily Kandinsky, Kenneth Noland), of the square and rectangle (Joseph Albers, Piet Mondrian, Frank Stella), of the cube (Cezanne, Picasso, and Braque), of the spiral (M. C. Escher), and of the pure line (Paul Klee and Josef Albers) and stripe (Gene

Davis and Barnett Newman). These geometrical forms become the most fundamental elements of composition, and therefore lend themselves to works which become, in essence, allegories of Creation.

Josef Albers, for example, who devoted his life to the study of color squares in various arrangements and proportions, ended his career with a series of three screen prints specially designed for the three parts of the Oxford Edition of the Washburn College Bible, published in 1979. The first of these, called "Introitus," precedes Part 1, from Genesis to Nehemiah. The white rectangles receding into the yellow background suggest the light of Genesis 1 and the interior nave of a Gothic Cathedral (Foreword xiii). One might add that the rectangle effectively anticipates the importance of the quaternity in the Bible as a whole, from the four rivers radiating from Eden out to the four cardinal points of the compass in Genesis, to the intersecting horizontal and vertical angles of the Cross, to the four sides of the heavenly city in Revelation. Albers called his frontispiece to Part 2 of the Washburn Bible "Seclusion," a "mazelike pattern" of silver lines radiating out from two squares on a black background meant to suggest "in graphic terms the melancholy wanderings of the tribes" (Foreword xiii). Finally, the third print of the series (the frontispiece for Part 3: Matthew to Revelation) is called "Ascension," a "radiant cloud of linear forms" (Foreword xii) created by a twisting interlace of rectangular orange lines on a luminous red ground. The impenetrable maze of the diaspora has yielded to the inscrutable maze of the divine revelation. To further exploit the potentialities of geometrical metaphors of the Creation, the producers of the Washburn Bible use a design from the mosaics of Santa Constanza, a mausoleum built in 350 A.D. for Constantine's daughter. The design is composed of a central cross with four octagons circumscribing four circles at each axis, and four hexagonal lozenges in between. The motif was adapted by Borromini for the dome of San Carlo alle Quattre Fontane in Rome, 1638–41, and since then has become a standard device of ecclesiastical architecture (Foreword xii–xiii). The octagon, which became the figure of choice for Baptistries and fonts, is secularized by postmodernist architects like Graham Gund, designer of the Fernbank Natural History Museum in Atlanta (see below), but it still retains its sacred connotations, since the museum houses a permanent overview of the creation and evolution of the world.

The three screen prints Albers chose for the Washburn Bible were selected from an earlier sequence of graphic tectonics, figures constructed entirely of horizontal and vertical lines of varying thicknesses. Albers tells us that the lines "perform space and volume illusions of multiple images, thereby inducing several interpretations," beguiling the eye with shifting perceptions of the fragmentary forms of Euclidean geometry, which are destroyed as soon as they are perceived by the movement of the angle of vision (Bucher 11, 24). Francois Bucher refers to the series as a "labyrinth which discipline built to channel human perception," and suggests that the geometrical forms created by the interplay of lines change "with every turn of the wheel" (17). It is as if the philosophical and hermeneutic issues at stake raised by the mythical geometry in the literary works of Borges, Eco, Marquez, and Cortázar have been translated into the most rudimentary of visual terms. Albers simultaneously tempts and frustrates the eye's natural tendency to interpret the text, i.e., to perceive Euclidean shapes of symbolic significance which the image simultaneously evokes and denies. In the Washburn sequence, for example, one notes the recurrence of the numbers twelve and four in the rectangles and squares created by the lines: there are twelve rectangles perfectly inscribing each other in the "Introitus," and two sets of twelve meandering lines, which twist around a central group of three hermetically sealed six–sided rectangular shapes, to form the complex locutions of the twenty four twisted polygons which comprise the whole. The number three suggests the trinity of the New Testament (which the figure introduces as a frontispiece), and the number twelve anticipates the Book of Revelation (the number of foundations steps and doorways of the Heavenly Jerusalem, and the number of tribes). These, however, are the twelve tribes lost in the maze of the diaspora evoked by the middle print, "Seclusion," in which two large squares frame an inner figure inscribing two smaller symmetrically situated squares with an upper and lower set of five meandering lines that generate intertwining rectangles. One is tempted to note the appropriate simplicity of the twelve hermetically sealed rectangles of the "Introitus" introducing Genesis, in contrast with the labyrinthine tangle of the solemn "Seclusion" print, which uses a mythical geometry to express the notion of the scattering of the tribes after the fall from the Garden. But the complexity of the figures eludes any single perspective or interpretation, and hence raises hermeneutic questions about the perception of order in a chaotic universe (of text or world).

The incorporation of such fundamental geometrical figures is as characteristic of postmodernist painting and architecture, as it is of postmodernist bookmaking and literature. These geometrical forms are archetypal symbols of those images which give a shape and significance to art, which is contrasted by the chaos of daily life. M. C. Escher's "Order and Chaos" of 1950 depicts a pair of interlocking five pointed stars enclosed within a sphere, the center of which they share. Each tip of the stars rises from a pentagonal base to create a five–sided pyramid. Surrounding this elaborate figure of geometrical "Order" we see some fifteen broken objects (a pipe, a bottle, a sardine can, an egg, some crumpled paper, some string, etc.), all of which we suppose represent "Chaos," until we realize that the geometrical figure is so madly ornate as to suggest chaos, and that the objects are all broken or crumpled in orderly, predictable ways. The viewer is forced to ask the same kinds of questions the reader of postmodernist texts is confronted with: is the world orderly or chaotic, are the patterns in the text random or purposeful, artificial or natural, created by the author, or by me?

It all depends, perhaps, on the reader's perspective, which is itself constantly shifting, a problem posed eloquently by another postmodernist painting, now hanging in the Hirschorn Museum. Yaacov Agam's "Double Metamorphosis" of 1968 (Lucie–Smith Pls. 241–42) presents the viewer standing directly in front of its surface with a chaotic multitude of tiny colored squares and rectangles scattered a sequence of numerous vertical ridges. As one moves towards the right side of the painting, however, the innumerable little color squares begin to converge into larger rectangles of one color containing smaller rectangles of another (as if several Albers squares had been put on one canvas). As one continues moving to the right, these larger rectangles gradually extend to form three differently colored horizontal bands interspersed by three horizontal black bands. When one returns front and center, this illusion of order dissolves once again into to the chaos of infinitely colored rectangles. But as one continues moving off to the left of the painting, these minutely scattered rectangles once again coalesce to form Albers like rectangles of color containing smaller rectangles of another color, and then to stretch out into three bands of vertical color separated by three black areas interspersed between them.

A more eloquent and playful statement of the viewer's participation in the act of perceiving patterns of order within chaos is hardly to be found, though Frank Stella used a somewhat simpler geometry to make a similar point. His early 'Black Period' canvases of 1958 and 59 show us what at first appear to be flat surfaces with thin white lines painted on a black background to create a sequence of narrow rectangles enclosing or adjacent to each other. "Tomlinson Court Park," for example, is composed of narrow, horizontally oriented rectangles emanating out from the small rectangle in the center of the canvas to the larger rectangles approaching the frame. The surface appears flat, but the steady gaze produces first an illusion of depth (rectangles receding within rectangles into the center of the canvas), and then an illusion of height (rectangles within rectangles protruding outward toward the viewer, so that the smallest internal rectangle forms the apex of a pyramid). These two illusions begin to alternate with the illusion of flatness, until a kind of optical vibration is formed. "The Marriage of Reason and Squalor" complicates the pattern by juxtaposing two sets of narrow, vertically oriented sequences of enclosing rectangles, and "'Die Fahne Hoch'" goes a step farther by dividing the canvas exactly into quadrants, each of which contains receding sequences of rectangles (the upper two receding along an axis lined up with the floor upon which the viewer stands, and the lower two receding along an axis defined by the ceiling).

The labyrinthine effect of these painting recalls the mazes of Eco and Borges, and raises similar hermeneutic questions about the role the reader plays in the interpretation of the text. It is an effect intensified by Stella's addition of color in later works, like "Jasper's Dilemma" of 1962–63, in which a canvas is divided into halves, one composed of twisting bands of grey and white, and the other of brilliantly colored twisting bands. Both halves are inscribed by thin white lines that divide each half into four slightly asymmetrical triangles, which, after the illusion of flatness diminishes, seem, alternately, to protrude into the form of a "fictive ziggurat" or to recede into a pair of "scintillating" labyrinths (Rosenblum 30). A variation occurs in "Rabat" of 1964, in which a thin white diagonal line (lower left to upper right) bifurcates two areas of yellow and blue color bands into a receding hall (from one perspective), or the two sides of the edge of a pyramid (from the other). The intensity of these "vertiginous mazes" of color creates, under the steady gaze, an illusion of pulsating light which the later geometrical complexities of the protractor series of the late 1960's foregoes. These later paintings, based on the arc and the semi–circle, create the kind of kaleidoscopic labyrinth of geometrical form that Julio Cortázar attempted to embody in the structure of *Hopscotch*. Rosenblum compares the "labyrinthine bewilderment of these arced interlaces" to the "abstract geometries of Islamic art" and to the "prodigious linear intertwinings" of the Book of Kells (48).

It is curious to note that during the years when Frank Stella was at Princeton, the Bollingen Foundation copyrighted its edition of Jung's work on mandala symbolism (in 1959). One of the first mandalas in the sequence corresponds almost exactly to the plan of Stella's painting, "Jasper's Dilemma," the right half of which is composed of color bands of red, green, yellow, and blue spiraling around a central point to create a receding hallway of squares. Figure 4 of Jung's *Mandala Symbolism* is likewise composed of a square spiral "painted in the typical colors, red, green, yellow, and blue" (78). It was painted by a middle–aged woman in such a way as to combine the circle and the square, four bands of each color consistently twisting around in the shape of a square. Generally speaking, Jung associates the mandala with the Self, the totality of the psyche (conscious and unconscious, male and female). He argues that the mandalas drawn by his patients involve a "new kind of centering" with the purpose of "reducing the confusion" caused by "chaotic psychic states of disorientation" to some semblance of order, wholeness, and harmony (76). To the extent to which the mandalas achieve their purpose, they exert a "magical" influence on the unconscious (77). The geometrical forms, that is to say, serve a creative function, magically restoring harmony during periods of crisis, and laying the foundation for future growth and development. Certainly some sense of the magical and creative power of these forms is suggested by the Post–Modernists in whose work they appear, works in which "a new kind of centering was at work" as the artists broke away from their precursors.

The importance of geometrical forms in postmodernism is to be found in architecture as well as in painting. The Fernbank Museum of Natural History (to choose one example among many) is a kind of spatial mandala which incorporates such basic forms as the arch, the pyramid, the octagon, the circle, the pillar, and the column. All of these fundamental elements are combined into a "playful simulation of the architecture of the past," to create a work which is both "monumental and playful." These are adjectives which might as well be applied to the paintings of Frank Stella, as to the novels of Cortázar and Carrington. The "playfully inflated formality of the Fernbank's public façade" (Robert Campbell 3), for example, has an oversized arch in the center (a large semi–circle rather like Stella's protractor paintings), flanked by two large spheres at either base of the arch, and a line of three rectangular windows to either side, interspersed by four "hey–look–at–me–I'm–not holding–anything–up columns across the front" (Robert Campbell 3). These free–standing columns are reminiscent of the archaic pillars of Egypt, as for example those enormous pillars standing free in the great entrance hall of the Temple of Luxor. The Egyptian motif is echoed at the Fernbank by the pyramids atop the Great Hall in the middle of the building, and atop the IMAX theater and Discovery Room Exhibit Hall at either end. The Great Hall of the interior is a marvelous mélange of postmodernist geometry. It is a huge octagon stretching from the floor to the glass roofing of the building, with the three floors of exhibit halls, dining area, offices, gift shop, and IMAX radiating out from the center in a sprawl of cubic, rhomboidal, and semi–circular chambers set playfully askew to balance the strict symmetry of the façade. The four steel columns that support the glass pyramid on the ceiling and the eight brick sides of the octagon form a square set in the middle of the Hall floor in such a way that the corners of the square bisect the sides of the octagon, forming a diamond. These four steel columns "exfoliate into trusses that support" the glass roof, five flying buttresses radiating out from each column very much in the manner of the columned vaultings in the nave of a Gothic Cathedral. The apertures which puncture the walls of the three floors radiating out from the Hall use three different motifs: three Roman arches on each of the eight sides of the bottom floor; three rectangular window–apertures on each of the eight sides of the ground level floor; and three circles on six of the eight sides of the third floor, with a variation of two circles flanking two narrow rectangles on the two sides the third floor which contain a window on the one hand, and the attached staircase on the other. A lovely spiral staircase connects the bottom and ground level floors. The play of light and shadow created in the Great Hall by the fusion of Egyptian, Roman, and Gothic elements is also reminiscent of "the great glass–topped halls of Victorian museums" (Robert Campbell 3).

The overall impact of the architecture is characteristically postmodern in its playful fusion of the fundamental forms of the past, with the purpose of creating a public edifice which combines the sacred and the civic, the ludic and the solemn, the present and the past. It is my belief that at least some of the power of the geometrical figures in postmodernist texts, architecture, and paintings comes from the sacred font of the mythical and literary past, with its well of archetypal images which emerge spontaneously in the mind of the poet, painter, and architect as symbols of the orderly cosmos of his or her creation. But these images also emerge spontaneously in the mind of the reader and critic, as symbols of the orderly cosmos towards which the hermeneutic process naturally tends. We speak of the "point" of a poem, for example, suggesting a central meaning round which a circumference of images and figures of speech revolves. J. Hillis Miller favors the line as an image of narrative (in *Ariadne's Thread*), while Northrop Frye and Georges Poulet prefer the circle. Frye uses the circle to describe the Bible's insistent rhythms of Incarnation, Descent, and Resurrection. He then elongates the circle into the form of a narrowing parabolic sine wave to represent the mythoi of Biblical narrative as a whole (*Code* 171–75). Indeed, such geometrical figurations as the embedded circles used to outline the syntactical Gestalt of metaphor seem irresistible to Frye (*Code* 57). And then of course we have that vast skeleton key to world mythology which Joseph Campbell called the monomyth and illustrated with two circles (*Hero* 30, 245).

Contrary to the dogmatic assertions of contemporary theory, these figures are elementary, archetypal, and spiritually charged, transcendent of gender and culture differences. As Samuel Edgerton argues in his recent book on Giotto, the geometricization of space is an innate aspect of the human mind which cannot be reduced either to an instrument of patriarchy or of postcolonialism (5–10). To risk another heretical assertion: contemporary theory and definitions of the postmodern tend to deny any spiritual or religious content to its products. Critics like Ihab Hassan, for example, have focused on the Orphic encounter with the void and the consequent nihilistic strain in postmodernist works. But the truth is that much of postmodernism represents a polemic against the secularization of the modern world, which Robert Lowell refers to as a "sublunar secular sprawl." Even Beckett's work (in a play like *Endgame*, for example) is laced with Biblical allusions (to John's Apocalypse) which go far beyond the ironic subversion of spirituality typically attributed to the playwright. I agree with Leon Surette when he points out that "Although skepticism and relativism are undoubtedly the two definitional dogmas of modern enlightened academic humanism, it is far from obvious that they are the guiding principles of modernism" (161). Christine de Lailhacar similarly suggests that writers like "Blanchot and Borges sacralize writing," and she uses the phrase "religious atheists" to describe the paradoxical aspects of their modernist spirituality (86). We have seen in the chapters above a consistent concern with spiritual issues in works by Borges, Eco, Carrington, Cortázar, H. D., Merrill, and Lessing which suggests something like a reversal of secularization: in fact, one is tempted to use the word sacralization to characterize the process by which myths are revived and geometrical figures given a new spiritual significance. Mark Rothko's majesterially solemn black paintings for his Chapel in Houston, Joseph Albers's last prints for the Washburn Bible, H. D.'s crown of gems in Mary Magdalen's hair, James Merrill's conversations with the angelic hierarchies, Marquez's apocalyptic paradigm of Latin American history, Borges's and H. D.'s long obsession with the metaphysical issues of the cabbalah and hermeticism, Cocteau's contrast between belief (croire) and understanding (comprendre), the current fascination with angels in the pop culture and on Broadway: all suggest a spiritual dimension of postmodernism frequently obscured by critics who refuse to acknowledge its presence, because it doesn't fit their theory.

The sacralization of postmodernism is perhaps most evident in a work which combines architecture and painting: the Rothko Chapel in Houston, originally to have been the chapel at St. Thomas University, a project later affiliated with the Institute for Religion and Human Development, and finally independently incorporated as a broadly ecumenical place of worship (Barnes 105–08). Like so many of the monuments of postmodernism (literary, painterly, architectural), the Rothko Chapel employs a sacred geometry based on the octagon and the rectangle. The architectural plan for the Chapel was originally formulated by Phillip Johnson, and eventually taken over by Howard Barnstone and Eugene Aubry. The final design is of an octagonal building with an octagonal skylight to enclose Rothko's eight large rectangular canvases: all solemn mixtures of deep black and purple, five panels and three triptych's hanging from the eight walls of the interior (Barnes 66). Barnett Newman's sculpture, "Broken Obelisk," which stands in a reflecting pool to the south of the Chapel, on an axis with the main entrance, incorporates the cube, the square, and the pyramid, geometrical forms which are fused to form an inverted broken obelisk, the downward pointing tip of which stands on top of the pinnacle of the pyramid sitting in the pool on its square base (Barnes 94). Since 1971, the Chapel and grounds of this postmodernist masterpiece have served as "a place of worship and meditation, a forum for the advancement of human rights in the world, and living proof of mutual religious understanding and the common humanity in which we share" (Barnes 108).

Barnett Newman's painting also addresses the dialectic between secularization and sacralization in postmodernism. The titles of his large canvases were frequently drawn from the Old and New Testaments: titles like "The Word," "Genesis—The Break," " Covenant," "Abraham," "The Promise," "Eve,", "Adam," "Joshua," "Jericho," and, of course, "The Stations of the Cross: Lema Sabachthani." All of these titles evoke biblical contexts which the compositions themselves seem to belie: most combine one or two stripes of color on an intense monochrome field, though the Cross sequence uses mainly black lines on a white field, precisely positioned a large canvases, the Pythagorean proportions of which have suggested cabbalistic number symbolism to some critics. And indeed, there is something awesome, metaphysical, infinite, and spiritual about these works, which, although not strictly religious in the orthodox sense, nevertheless powerfully evoke the sacred space (Makom) with which Newman was explicitly concerned. Newman writes of a "fundamental spiritual dimension" in his painting, and that a genuine sense of the "sacred" depends on the "quality of the work of art, on its uniqueness, on its rigor" (qtd. Rosenberg 246). Newman seems here to agree with another pioneer of American minimalism, Ad Reinhardt, who said that the "creative process" is a "sacred procedure" (qtd. Hughes 15). In this sense, the paintings imply a kind of ecumenical spirituality, transcendent of sectarian creeds (whether Buddhist, Hindu, Jewish, Christian, or Muslim), the kind of spirituality which geometry and myth are eminently more qualified to express than pictures with representational and overtly religious content. In fact, Robert Hughes has suggested that much of the sacred energy mysteriously present in postmodernist painting may have its "prophetic" roots in the "august and austerely geometrical" quilts of the Amish women (34), whose work combine a dazzling array of colors with forms like the squared circle, bars and stripes, and interlocking diamonds.

Hieroglyphs and Holographs

Ultimately, the mythical geometry of postmodernism involves a quest for unity, for the one figure which contains a multiplicity of all shapes in potential. Let me therefore risk a third heretical assertion: postmodernism seriously involves itself in a quest for unity, for that single figure of thought unifying all opposites which can reverse the secular tendency towards nihilism and fragmentation, so often glibly assumed to be the last word on the subject. Admittedly, it is a quest for what Shakespeare called "an union in partition" (*Dream*), for the kind of ternary logic, espoused by Julio Cortázar, which would subsume without annihilating the opposites. Hence the complexity of the polygons favored by the postmodernists; of single figures which embrace and create a multiplicity of figures, like Solomon's seal, in which two large triangles inscribe a central hexagon, with six smaller triangles based on each of its sides. The quest for this kind of union in partition, symbolized by geometrical forms, has its roots far back in the modernism of Kandinsky and Mondrian, Mann and Lawrence.

Ezra Pound and H.D., for example, were much concerned with the notion of a fundamental network of mythological symbols which formed the essence of what Eliot called the "Tradition." Pound's "Ur–myth" was the descent into

Hades, with which he begins the *Cantos*. He used the term "vortex" and "ideogram" to refer those such fundamental forms of the mythic and literary imagination which Frye would call later call *The Stubborn Structure.* In 1912, Pound compared words to "electrified cones, charged with 'the power of tradition, of centuries of race consciousness, of agreement, of association'" (Kenner 238), and in 1914 he defined the vortex as "a radiant node or cluster ... from which, and into which, ideas are constantly rushing" (Kenner 146). Kenner calls the vortex "a patterned integrity" informing the work of the poet and of the age (147), and Guy Davenport suggests a parallel between the vortex and the Homeric oral–formulae of Lord and Parry: in Pound, the vortex is composed of "words shaped by the masters" which become "the formulaic gists of ideas in maximum verbal focus" (58). The vortex is therefore analogous to Pound's notion of the Image as "an intellectual and emotional complex in an instant of time" and of the Ideogram as a "complex word" (Davenport 58) or "vibrating field of force" gathering together all of the particulars of language and symbol into a single icon (Kenner 160).

H.D. used the word "hieroglyph" for such an "image," "ideogram," or "complex," which embraces the whole within a single unit. She found the connection between these terms during her analysis with Freud, who approached the imagery of the dream as a "hieroglyph of the unconscious" (*Tribute* 93). Hieroglyphs are "fundamental truths" represented pictorially, "visual epiphanies" (Friedman 64) comparable to Joyce's notion of a "sudden spiritual manifestation" in the ordinary events of daily life, or to moments of being in Proust or Virginia Woolf which seem to embrace all of time in a single instant. H.D.'s discovery of the hieroglyph was clearly related to Freud's notion that dream images bear within themselves the vestigial forms of primitive thinking which Jung called the archetypes. For the hieroglyph contains within itself all of time and all of history, so that, in the words of Joseph Riddell, H.D.'s poetic breakthrough was the discovery that she bears "'within herself ... the whole race and relives in her own consciousness the recurrent and hence real experience of all history'" (qtd. Friedman 83). As Friedman puts it, the use of the hieroglyph in Trilogy urges H.D.'s discovery that "the ultimate reality of any single moment in history is contained in a pattern of essential experiences which inform all time" (103). H.D. referred to this essential pattern when she spoke of the Grimms tales as making "a group, a constellation ... a groove or pattern, into which or upon which other patterns fit" (*Tribute* 28–9), while Joseph Riddel called this essential pattern, recorded in the hieroglyphic constellations of H.D.'s own work, the "Ur–myth," "Ur–form," "Ur–pattern," or "formula" which structures "the past, orders the present, and will shape the future" (qtd. Friedman 113).

H.D. found parallels to the poetic and psychoanalytic notions of the hieroglyph in the cabbalistic notion of the En–Sof as "the infinite One, the pure potentiality that encompasses all possibility" (Friedman 280). Like the Aleph in Borges, the En–Sof symbolizes the mystery of the "Divine One" which contains and encompasses the entire multitude of the Creation (Borges 175). And like the image of Ezekiel's Wheel at the climax of "The God's Script," H.D. turned to an astronomical symbol to embody the notion of the part which contains the whole. In *Helen in Egypt*, Helen comes to see the "One that incorporates all the manifestations of the created world" in the seven planets of the "'*Zodiac hieroglyph*'" which embraces the opposites of Love and Death (qtd. in Friedman 293). This notion of the hieroglyph as the part which contains the whole comes out strongly in H.D.'s in her definition of the "determinative" as that picture "that is used in the actual hieroglyph ... that contains the whole series of pictures in itself" (*Tribute* 56). This is the kind of mythological image (like the lily, seed grain in Mary Magdalen's hair) around which H.D. structures her late poetry, and which all of the postmodernists attempted to develop a set of formal terms and symbols to describe.

The idea of a single part which can serve to contain the whole has, in fact, a long history, from the Platonic notion of the realm of form to recent scientific interest in the holographic paradigm. Plato's concept of God as the single author of those pure spiritual forms of the divine intellect from which all creation proceeds was later adapted by the Neoplatonists of the Renaissance, who saw the many contained in the one, and the one present in the many, as the essential paradox of their philosophy (Wind 133). One finds similar notions in Medieval scholasticism, according to which the many things of the world bear the signature of the one God, so that Stephen Dedalus can say in *Ulysses* "Signatures of all things I am here to read." The scholastic notion that "the beauty of the cosmos derives not only from unity in variety, but also from variety in unity," as William of Baskerville puts it in Eco's *The Name of the Rose* (16), also implies that the part contains the whole. In the 17th century, Leibniz developed the idea of the monads, each one of which mirrors not only itself, but the entirety of the universe (Ross 94): the whole, that is to say, is in each part. Coleridge revived this notion in his understanding of a symbol as that which expresses "the omnipresence of all in each," or the "aweful omneity in unity" (qtd. in Warnock 80, 82). William Blake's doctrine of "minute particulars" which somehow contain within themselves the entire Creation was expressed famously in the line "To see the world in a grain of sand." Similarly, in the "Spring" Chapter of *Walden*, Thoreau comes to see a thawing sand bank as "hieroglyphic" that "illustrated the principle of all the operations of Nature" (568), which he demonstrates by comparing the circulatory and skeletal systems of the human body to the vegetal patterns of leaves, rivers, and the sandbank. Since many of the modernist notions regarding mythological symbols evolved directly out of the Romanticism of the 19th century, it is perhaps not surprising to notice such parallels in the mutual search for an Ur–myth, Urbild, proto–form, or hieroglyph which contains all subsequent symbols within itself.

What is more surprising is to find recent scientific work which suggests that the notion of a single form which contains the information and potential energy of the whole system may in fact be an important fact about the physical world. The development of postmodernism in literature and the arts has, of course, coincided with radical changes in the scientific views of reality, from the relativity theories of Einstein in 1905, to the quantum mechanics of Niels Bohr and Werner Heisenberg during the 1920's, and on to the so–called holographic paradigm in the physics of David Bohm. Bohm, who was Einstein's student, has been particularly important in pursuing his master's quest for the unified field. His theory of the implicate order has taken physics far beyond Heisenberg's uncertainty and Einstein's relativity, making a refigured notion of wholeness a respectable aspect of the New Physics. The idea of the implicate order is based on holographic photography, in which any single part of the image contains the whole within itself, so that when one illuminates any single piece of a hologram with a laser beam, the entire image is revealed (Wilbur 2): the part is in the whole, yet the whole is in each part, like the world in Blake's grain of sand, or like the "whole scope and plan" of civilization within H.D.'s grain of light refracted from Mary Magdalen's hair. A holographic parallel from the world of myth can be found in the "Indian image of the 'Net of Gems,' where in every gem of the net all the others are reflected" (Campbell, *Inner Reaches* 111). The postmodernist quest for the pure forms of myth which contain the whole within the part must therefore be seen in a scientific as well as a mythological context. This is not often the case, given the predominance of structuralist and psychoanalytic views in our understanding of the postmodernist use of myth. Most critics have ignored the spiritual implications of the emerging paradigms of the New Physics, largely because they take the notions of nihilism, alienation, and fragmentation (conventionally attributed to literature in the postmodernist mode) as axiomatic. A notable exception is the work of Katherine Hayles, who has usefully addressed the importance of field theory for such authors as Lawrence, Nabokov, Borges, and Pynchon, without, however, incorporating more recent developments in holography.

I would suggest that the vocabulary, iconography, and mythology of form developed in postmodernism represents a precise and intuitive anticipation of the holographic paradigm shift in science, and, in Cortázar's case, a direct application of the new scientific ideas of Einstein, Heisenberg, and others to literature. The overall cultural importance of this development has to do with the reconciliation between the scientific and the spiritual realms of human life, a reconciliation reflected in the religious dimensions of the postmodernist use of myths, and holding out the promise of a new sort of Renaissance culture, one which can combine "the sensate, the ideational, and the idealistic," Pitrim Sorokin's terms for "the three basic value systems that underlie all manifestations of a culture" (Capra 31). The search for myth, then, is ultimately holographic: as the alchemists put it, it is a search for the one "Figure conteyning all the secrets of the Treatise both great and small" (Fabricius, fig. 382).

Notes

Introduction

[1]I have analyzed the presence of these myths in modernist texts, and the vocabulary of form which goes with them, in my previous books and articles, referenced in the Works Cited. This book focuses entirely on texts of the postmodernist period, written since the closing years of the Second World War, and it develops a new methodology for interpreting the interrelations of myth and geometric form found in them.

Chapter 1: Forthrights and Meanders

[2]See various publications by Evans: "Excavations at Knossos," *Annals of the British School at Athens*, Vol VIII, 1902; "Mycenaean Tree and Pillar Cult," *Journal of Hellenic Studies*, Vol. XXI, 1901; "The Tomb of the Double Axes at Knossos," *Archaeologica*, Vol. LXV, 1914; and then his sequence of volumes entitled *The Palace of Minos*, published from 1921-1935.

[3]Guy Davenport's fine essay "The House That Jack Built" starts with Ruskin and moves up to Pound and Joyce. Frances Yates shows the importance of the maze gardens of the *Hortus Palatinus* at Heidelberg Castle in relation to Shakespeare's *The Tempest* (*Rosicrucian*, plate 5), and Janet Bord provides several illustrations of garden mazes all the way up to the present.

[4]See Lawrence di Stasi's *Mal Occhio* for a fascinating discussion of the eye Goddess and for a stunning sequence of images documenting the continuity of eye symbolism from Sumer to Egypt (95-110).

[5]J. Hillis Miller also reverts to the myth of the maze as the archetype of narrative in his recent study, *Ariadne's Thread: Story Lines*.

Chapter 2: Our Lady of the Honeycomb

[6]Walter Burkert cites a line of scholarly interest in the Great Goddess from Frazer and Evans around 1900, to J. Leipoldt's *Sterbende und auferstehende Götter* of 1923 and L. Franz's "Muttergöttin im Vorderen Orient und in Europa"

of 1937, and on up to J. Przyluski's *La grande déese* of 1950 and E. O. James' *The Cult of the Mother Goddess* of 1959 (*Structure* 187).

[7]The literature on the mysteries is extensive, beginning with Frazer and Harrison, and continuing all through the postmodernist period up to the present: a representative selection would include Kerényi (whose studies of 1939f. directing influenced Mann), Campbell, Meyer, Burkert and many others.

[8]Diller does not suggest any sources for the Goddess imagery in Grass, but we should note that *Die Blechtrommel* (*The Tin Drum*) was published in 1959, and that two important studies of the imagery of the Great Goddess (including her Cretan avatar, so important in the novel) had appeared in German shortly before: Erich Neumann's *The Great Mother* (in English translation in 1955), and Martin Nilsson's classic study of the Minoan backgrounds of Greek mythology, *Geschichte der grieschischen Religion* (1955). Furthermore, the deciphering of the Cretan Linear B script in 1953 opened up an exciting new access to Minoan mythology.

[9]See Mary Haskins for a fine overview of the myth of Mary Magdalene, which, however, neglects both Carrington and H.D.

[10]The cup, the Grail, and the cauldron are universal archetypes of world mythology. The Chinese sacrificial vessels are splendid if terrifying examples (Campbell, *Mythic Image* 124f. and *Treasures of the Bronze Age of China*). A wide range of images can be found in *The Grail*, by John Matthews.

[11]Janice Robinson would no doubt see the allusion to the phoenix as further evidence of her theories about H.D.'s relationship with Lawrence. This section of the poem in fact could be seen as a disguised confession regarding the conception of Perdita. But I intend to avoid the personal in lieu of the mythological dimension of H.D.'s work.

[12]In the "Dora" case study, for example, Freud focuses on purses and satchels as symbols of the womb, curiously not mentioning Pandora's box or jar as a mythological prototype.

Chapter 3: Squaring the Circle

[13]Karl Preisendanz (ed.), *Papyri Grecae magicae*, 2 vols. (Leipzig and Berlin, 1928-31). Richard Reitzenstein, "Alchemistische Lehrschriften und Märchen bei den Araben," in *Heliodori carmina quattor* (Religionsgeschichtliche Versuche und Vorarbeiten, XIX, 2.) (Giessen, 1923); *Die hellenistischen Mysterienreligionen* (Leipzig, 1910); *Poimandres: Studien zur griechisch-ägyptischen und frühchristlichen Literatur* (Leipzig, 1904). Julius Ruska, *Tabula smaragdina: ein Beitrag zur Geschichte der hermetischen Literatur* (Heidelberg, 1926); *Turba Philosophorum: ein Beitrag zur Geschichte der Alchemie* (Quellen und Studien zur Geschichte der Naturwissenschaften und der Medizin, 1.) (Berlin, 1931). Walter Scott, (ed.), *Hermetica: The Ancient Greek and Latin Writings Which Contain Religious or Philosophical Teachings Ascribed to Hermes Trismegistus*, 1924-1936, 4 vols. (Boulder: Hermes House, 1982). Herbert Silberer, *Probleme der Mystik und ihrer Symbolik* (Vienna,

1914). Karl Sudhoff and Wilhelm Matthiessen (eds.), *Theophrast von Hohenheim gennant Paracelsus Sämliche Werke*, 14 vols. (Munich and Berlin, 1922-1933). Arthur Waite, *The Hermetic Museum Restored and Enlarged*, 2 vols. (London, 1893).

[14]Mann speaks of "an alchemistic, hermetic pedagogy" and the initiatory rites of "Freemasonry" in his afterword, "The Making of the Magic Mountain," *The Magic Mountain* (New York: Alfred Knopf, 1966), 728. For the line of transmission, see Dame Frances Yates, *Giordano Bruno and the Hermetic Tradition*, Midway Reprint, (Chicago: The University of Chicago Press, 1979). Yates begins the process of charting the line of transmission at the end of *The Rosicrucian Enlightenment* (Boulder: Shambhala, 1978), 231-32, leaving the task of filling in the links in the genealogical chain to others.

[15]The *Eranos-Jahrbuch*, Band IX, (Zürich: Rhein-Verlag, 1942) focused on "The Hermetic Principle in Mythology, Gnosis, and Alchemy," and Jung's first great compendium of hermetic lore, *Psychology and Alchemy*, Trans. R.F.C. Hull, Bollingen Series XX, Second Edition (Princeton: Princeton UP, 1968) was first published the next year, in 1944, at the peak of a second great flowering of Modernism.

[16]Qtd. in Janice Robinson, *H.D.: The Life and Work of an American Poet* (Boston: Houghton Mifflin Company, 1982), 304. H.D.'s hermeticism is discussed by Susan Stanford Friedman in *Psyche Reborn: The Emergence of H.D.*, A Midland Book, Bloomington: Indiana UP, 1981). Friedman cites Denis de Rougemont, *L'Amour et l'occident* (Paris, 1939), Jean Chaboseau, *Le Tarot* (Paris: Éditions Niclaus, 1946), and Robert Ambelain, *Dans l'ombre des cathédrales*, (Paris, Éditions Adyar, 1939), *Adam, dieu rouge* (Paris: Éditions Niclaus, 1941), *Le Martinisme* (Paris: Éditions Niclaus, 1946), and *La Kabbale practique* (Paris: Éditions Niclaus, 1951), 171-72.

[17]Anna Balakian, *André Breton: Magus of Surrealism* (New York: Oxford UP, 1971), and Gloria Orenstein, *The Theater of the Marvelous* (New York: New York UP, 1975). The most notable exception is Leon Surette's *The Birth of Modernism*, which, however, addresses only the Anglo-American tradition.

[18]For a discussion of the myths of alchemy, the apocalypse, the goddess, the maze, and the underworld, see my *Ricorso and Revelation: An Archetypal Poetics of Modernism*, Columbia, SC: Camden House, 1995. Several of Merrill's critics acknowledge the general importance of myth in Merrill's work, without, however exploring that assertion in any detail: Galassi notes "the complex mythology of his personal experience" (182); Helen Vendler calls Merrill's work "a poetry of exuberant mythology ... a defiant mythology ... which must couch itself in scientific terms," and she compares Merrill's development to the typical modernist movement from the short lyric to "large mythological outlines" (90-91). John Hollander remarks that Merrill "adduces new mythologies in explanation of older ones" (122), and Charles Berger adds that he "recapitulates past myths" and "rearranges "known elements within the sacred storehouse of myths" ("Conservative Epic" 182-83). Stephen Yenser compares the angelic cosmogony of the trilogy to a "New World myth, one more variation on a venerable theme"

(309). Finally, J.D. McClatchy agrees that "Merrill's private anxieties are manifest in familiar and recurring mythic formulas," without specifying which ("Monsters Wrapped in Silk" 141). Richard Sáez ("Oedipal" 39), J.D. McClatchy (139), and Helen Vendler (93) touch fleetingly upon hermetic aspects of Merrill's myth, but no one delves into its specific alchemical motifs.

[19]Charles Berger calls Merrill an "apocalyptic scribe," using Frank Kermode's *Sense of an Ending* to contrast Merrill and Pynchon's "late modernism" to the "early modernism" of Joyce ("Merrill and Pynchon" 282-97).

[20]Merrill's words in response to C.A. Buckley's questions (429, 431).

[21]Although some critics still want to use variations on the dialectic between Classicism and Romanticism to discuss his place, Merrill himself frequently evokes the forms of the musical baroque in his poems, and in fact uses the word "baroque" in response to Maria's evocation of the first epiphany of the angel Emmanuel (302). Richard Sáez uses a contrast between renaissance stasis and "mannerist tension" in his discussion of Merrill's poem, "The Broken Home" ("Oedipal Fire" 46).

[22]See Scholem, "*Die Vorstellung vom Golem*" for a detailed account of the ritual creation of the Golem. All translations of Scholem's article are my own.

[23]For images of the Creative Word see Maclagan as follows: Book of Kells for John's "In the beginning was the Word" (64); Dogon signs of Egg of Amma ("The Belly of the World's Signs") from which the world is created with four segments as four elements with two character signs for each, and from thence a total of 11, 616 signs for all the creation (76); the *Red Book of Delaware Indians*, in which the world is a syntax of fundamental forms which can be variously combined (79). For the Oriental imagery see Mookerjee: the seed syllable *Aum* (*Yoga Art* Plate 10); and temple sculpture of *Sabda* (Word) unfolding into a mandala field (an image which corresponds to the image of Christ as the Logos surrounded by the four corners of the world represented by the Evangelists) (*Tantric* 85). For Kali, see Mookerjee (*Tantric* Plate 3) and Campbell *The Mythic Image* (Plate 323).

[24]See Mookerjee (154-156) or Joseph Campbell's *The Mythic Image* (Plates 312-14; 332-34) for pictures of the chakras and the letters associated with each.

[25]Sylvia Brinton Perera bases a profound study of the psychology of women at mid-life on the story of Inanna.

[26]For a rather stunning collection of images of the androgyne as a symbol of the reconciliation of male and female in alchemy, religion, literature, and myth, see Elémire Zolla.

[27]See also the beautiful crucifixion from the Psalter of Robert de Lindesey of 1220 (Marks and Morgan Plate 3).

[28]Harold Bloom, Ed., "Introduction" (*James Merrill* 7). Stephen Yenser hails the trilogy as "one of the most ambitious, original, and variously brilliant works written by an American," and celebrates its "sustained and varied excellence" (217). J.D. McClatchy calls Merrill "a poet in the tradition of greatness," and praises him for the "virtuosity of his diction," his mastery of "verse technique," and for the "exuberance" of his "exquisite disciplines" ("Lost Paradises"

305). Jonathan Galassi calls the "Book of Ephraim" "brilliant," and suggests that its style is "the most elaborate in contemporary American poetry" (305). Peter Sacks calls Merrill "our greatest poet of serious and far-reaching solace," and contrasts his elegiac brightness with the sombre cast of other modernist poets of the long poem (Eliot, Williams, Berryman, Pound, Lowell) (159).

[29]J.D. McClatchy associates Hermes with mirrors and the child, a mercurial psychopomp who appears throughout Merrill's work (Bloom 139).

[30]David Lehman, Willard Spiegelman, and Tim Materer have followed Bloom's lead in focusing on Gnostic and Kabbalistic elements in Merrill's poem. Lehman discusses the shattering of vessels (*shevirah hakelim*) in relation to Merrill's manipulation of traditional verse forms ("Elemental Bravery" 33). Spiegelman connects Bloom's discussion of the breaking of vessels to the "breakups, interruptions, and disruptions" that persistently punctuate *The Changing Light* (186-210). Materer takes Jung as his starting point for a discussion of such Gnostic motifs as the return of the dead, "the Call, the reconciliation through the feminine, and the expectation of a perfected race" (79). I prefer to focus on the Kabbalistic strategies of *gematria*, *notarikon*, and *temura* (manipulating letters and numbers), and I prefer Scholem to Bloom as a source, particularly Scholem's article, "Die Vorstellung vom Golem."

[31]Richard Sáez focuses on the symbolism of fire in Merrill's work, which he associates with alchemical apparatus as an image of poesis ("Oedipal Fire" 38). Stephen Yenser chooses water as the primary element of reverie, and uses Jung's image of God as "an eternally flowing current" as a concluding point (240).

[32]Stephen Yenser uses both Leibniz's concept of the monad, and the Buddhist allegory of Indra's Net, in which every gem contains the reflected relations of every other, throughout the universe, to describe the marvelous unity of Merrill's work, in which every lyric reflects themes of the epic as a whole (217, 312).

[33]Several critics have discussed the presence of Yeats in *The Changing Light*: see the indexed references in Harold Bloom, ed., *James Merrill*.

[34]Richard Sáez evokes the cooling process of metallurgical operations as an alchemical image of poesis in Merrill's work (40, 55).

[35]I discuss these and other writers in my article, "Alchemy and Modernism," *Cauda Pavonis: Studies in Hermeticism*, 13:1 (Spring 1994): 11-18.

[36]Robert Lamm uses the phrase to distinguish the mannerist style of the later 16th century from the formality of the High Renaissance (304). Richard Sáez proposes and rejects the term "camp" to describe Merrill's mannerism, using instead Huizinga's notion of the ludic to outline the "lyric theodicy" of the poem. Sáez also suggests affinities between Merrill and the Baroque when he writes of "the kinship of Merrill's epic to Calderón's religious masques" (214-16, 243).

Chapter 4: Voices From the Well

[37]See Samuel Noah Kramer's commentary in *Inanna: Queen of Heaven and Earth*, and Joseph Campbell's plates and captions in the *Historical Atlas*, Vol. 2, Part 1 (80-83) for details on the Sumerian material, and Sir Wallis Budge's *The Gods of the Egyptians*, Vol. 1 for plates and commentary on "The Book of Pylons" and the "Book of the Tuat" (174-262). Of the importance of Frobenius, who may have been to the German Modernists what Frazer and Harrison were to the English, Joseph Campbell notes that *Paideuma*, "an anthropologically documented study in historic depth of the psyche and its symbolic forms," appeared in 1921, one year before *Ulysses* and three before *The Magic Mountain* (*Creative Myth* 644).

[38]Guy Davenport devotes two fine essays to the figure of Persephone in Pound and Eudora Welty: "Persephone's Ezra" and "That Faire Field of Enna," a title which acknowledges Milton's correlation of Eve and Persephone in *Paradise Lost*.

[39]See the "Introduction" to *Rape and Revelation* on the four chambers of the underworld (temenos, crypt, granay, and inferno). The phrase "patchwork of quotations" comes from Aizenberg's paraphrase of Kristeva (73), but long before Kristeva's "mosaic of citations," intertextuality, or Bloom's precursor and ephebe, we had Eliot's "Tradition and the Individual Talent," Joyce's *Ulysses*, and Pound's *Cantos*.

[40]On the cabbalah in Borges, see Edna Aizenberg's article, and her edited anthology of essays on Borges, with sections on film and painting.

[41]The Sumerian word for underworld, *kur*, also means mountain (see Wolkstein and Kramer). Gilgamesh reaches the Land of the Living, where the immortal Utnapishtim lives, via a journey through the twelve leagues of darkness beneath the mountains. In Egyptian myth, the sun god Ra begins his journey with a descent into the mountains of the west (the tombs of the Pharaohs are on the west side of the Nile, in the Valley of the Kings, up in the mountains) (see Budge).

[42]John Matthews notes the affiliation between the cups of the Classical mysteries, Celtic cauldrons, Christian Grails and three types of alchemical vessel: the crucible, the flask, and the still.

[43]Though the symbolism usually involves the circle, the square, and the triangle, more elaborate figures like interlocking spirals (Godwin Fig. 75) and vortices inscibed with a numerical system of "simple numbers, their squares and cubes" derived from Pythagoras, Plato, and Pico della Mirandola are also common (Godwin 21). Dürer drew also from this line of hermetic speculation, linking melancholy, Masonic mysteries, and the understanding of the artistic temperament with the help of his reading of Marsilio Ficino's *De Vita Triplici*, translated into German in 1505 (Schoch 312).

[44]See my discussion of Jung's use of the Tibetan Book of the Dead and his relationship to literary Modernists whose works are informed by the descent to

the underworld in "Jung and His Brothers: The Descent to the Underworld" (Princeton UP).

[45]It is odd and interesting that this suggests about seven layers of clothing, just as Inanna is wearing seven articles of clothing during her descent through the seven gateways into the underworld, at each of which gateways an article of clothing is stripped from her until she stand naked in the presence of her sister, Ereshkigal, the Goddess of Death (see Wolkstein and Kramer, *Inanna: Queen of Heaven and Earth*.

[46]See *The Road to Eleusis* for the data suggesting the use of an hallucinogen derived from the ergot of wheat in the mysteries, and *Die Nacht* for a thorough analysis of the Greek affiliation of Night, Sleep, and Death.

[47]On the net of gems, see the last chapter of Joseph Campbell's *Inner Reaches of Outer Space*, and on the holographic paradigm, see Ken Wilbur.

Chapter 5: Re-Figuring Revelation

[48]As Gerald Martin notes, "a world of successively unfolding dualities" in the novel originating in "the male-female axis" and blossoming to include the "Europe-America axis," and such others as "culture-nature, civilization-barbarism, and their familiar echoes" (202). I would add the polemic between Mondrian and Klee in Chapter 9, and the fusion of waking and sleeping in the penultimate Chapter 56, with its confrontation between Oliveira and Traveler and with its "end" which leads simply to the new beginning in section three.

[49]See Chapter 7 of *Rape and Revelation* for a more detailed discussion of this connection between Modernist painting and literature.

[50]Translated into English by Philip Mairet as *Myths, Dreams, and Mysteries: The Encounter Between Contemporary Faiths and Archaic Realities.* It is interesting to note here that Octavio Paz, whose *Labyrinth of Solitude,* published in 1950 and another influence on Cortázar, footnotes Eliade's *Histoire des Religions* of 1949 on the page where he discusses the nostalgia for paradise: "The feeling of solitude, which is a nostalgic longing for the body from which we were cast out, is a longing for a place. According to an ancient belief, held by virtually all peoples, that place is the center of the world, the navel of the universe. Sometimes it is identified with paradise, and both of these with the group's real or mythical place of origin" (208). Lois Zamora, in her study *Writing the Apocalypse*, also suggests the influence of Paz on Cortázar's notion of the "special nature of the new world created by the artist" as indicative of a "nostalgia for paradise" (81).

[51]One thinks of Jung's discussion of the *soror mystica* in his *Psychology of the Transference,* in which the image of the alchemical sister serves as an anima figure leading the adept to the consummation of the Great Work, which in essence is a restoration of Paradise.

[52]It is interesting to note that Regina Schwartz attempts to replace Frye's notion of type and anti-type with the terms forgetting and remembering in her

analysis of the Joseph story in Genesis.as a type for the loss and restoration of paradise (114-124).

[53]This description of Adam 'covering' his face at the moment of exile bears a curious resemblance to the image of Hester Prynne leaving the prison doorway in Hawthorne's *The Scarlet Letter,* which, as I have shown in my article "Re-Figuring Revelation," is structured throughout by the biblical rhythm of covering and uncovering associated with apocalypse.

[54]For a discussion of the related metaphor of the world of quantum physics as an underworld, and of the importance of this metaphor for Modernist art and literature, see *Rape and Revelation*, Chapter 7. See also Katherine Hayles for a general discussion of the impact of the new physics on Modernism.

Works Cited

Aizenberg, Edna. *The Aleph Weaver: Biblical, Kabbalistic, and Judaic Elements in Borges.* Potomac, MD: Scripta Humanistica, 1984.

---, ed. *Borges and His Successors: The Borgesian Impact on Literature and the Arts.* Columbia: University of Missouri Press, 1990.

Albers, Josef and François Bucher. *Josef Albers: Despite Straight Lines.* Revised Edition. Cambridge: MIT Press, 1977.

Alexandrov, Vladimir E. *Nabokov's Otherworld.* Princeton: Princeton UP, 1991.

Apuleius. *The Golden Ass*. Trans. Jack Lindsay. Bloomington: Indiana UP, 1960.

Athanassakis, Apostolos N. *The Homeric Hymns.* Baltimore: Johns Hopkins UP, 1976.

Auerbach, Erich. "Figura." *Scenes from the Drama of European Literature* New York: Meridian, 1959. 11-76.

Bachelard, Gaston. *Water and Dreams: An Essay on the Imagination of Matter.* Trans. Edith Farrell. Dallas: The Pegasus Foundation, 1983.

Bachofen, J.J. *Das Mutterrecht: Eine Untersuchung über die Gynokratie der alten Welt nach ihrer religiösen und rechtlichen Natur*. Stuttgart, 1861. Reprinted, Basel, 1897.

---, *Myth, Religion, and Mother Right: Selected Writings of J.J. Bachofen*. Trans. Ralph Mannheim. Bollingen Series LXXXIV. Princeton: Princeton UP, 1967.

Barnes, Susan J. *The Rothko Chapel: An Act of Faith.* Austin: A Rothko Chapel Book, 1989.

Berger, Charles. "Merrill and Pynchon: Our Apocalyptic Scribes." *James Merrill: Essays in Criticism.* Ed. David Lehman and Charles Berger. Ithaca and London: Cornell UP, 1983: 282-97.

---, "*Mirabell*: Conservative Epic." *James Merrill*. Modern Critical Views. Harold Bloom, Ed. New York: Chelsea House, 1985.

Biedermann, Hans. *Dictionary of Symbolism: Cultural Icons and the Meaning Behind Them.* Trans. James Hulbert. New York: Facts on File, 1992.

Blamires, David. *David Jones: Artist and Writer.* Toronto: University of Toronto Press, 1972.

Bloom, Harold, ed., "Introduction." *James Merrill*: Modern Critical Views. New York: Chelsea House, 1985.

Bonnefoy, Yves, ed. *American, African, and Old European Mythologies.* Trans. Wendy Doniger. Chicago: The University of Chicago Press,

Bord, Janet. *Mazes and Labyrinths of the World.* New York: E.P. Dutton and Company, 1975.

Borges, Jorge Luis. *Borges: A Reader.* Ed. Emir Rodriguez Monegal and Alastair Reid. New York: E.P. Dutton, 1981.

---, "The Garden of Forking Paths." *Labyrinths: Selected Stories and Other Writings.* Ed. Donald A. Yates and James E. Irby. New York: New Directions Books, 1964.

---, *Labyrinths: Selected Stories and Other Writings.* Ed. Donald A. Yates and James E. Irby. New York: New Directions Books, 1964.

---, *Obras Completas.* Buenas Aires: Emecé Editores, 1957. Vol. 3.

Broch, Hermann. *The Death of Virgil.* Trans. Jean Starr Untermeyer. San Francisco: North Point Press, 1983.

Browne, Sir Thomas. *Selected Writings.* Ed. Sir Geoffrey Keynes. Chicago: University of Chicago Press, 1968.

Bucher, François and Josef Albers. *Josef Albers: Despite Straight Lines.* Revised Edition. Cambridge: MIT Press, 1977.

Buckley, C.A. "Exploring *The Changing Light at Sandover*: An Interview with James Merrill." *Twentieth Century Literature.* Winter (1992): 415-35.

Budge, E.A. Wallis. *The Gods of the Egyptians, or Studies in Egyptian Mythology.* Vol.1. (1904). New York: Dover Publications, 1969.

Burkert, Walter. *Ancient Mystery Cults.* Boston: Harvard UP, 1987.

---, *Structure and History in Greek Mythology and Ritual.* Berkeley: The University of California Press, 1979.

Campbell, Joseph. *The Flight of the Wild Gander.* New York: The Viking Press, 1969.

---, *The Hero With a Thousand Faces.* Princeton NJ: Princeton UP, 1949.

---, *Historical Atlas of World Mythology.* 2 Vols. New York: Harper and Row, 1988.

---, Introduction. *Myth, Religion, and Mother Right: Selected Writings of J.J. Bachofen.* Trans. Ralph Mannheim. Bollingen Series LXXXIV. Princeton: Princeton UP, 1973.

---, *The Inner Reaches of Outer Space: Metaphor as Myth and as Religion.* New York: Alfred van der Marck Editions, 1985.

---, "Joseph Campbell on the Great Goddess." *Parabola* 5 (1980): 74-85.

---, *The Masks of God: Creative Mythology.* Penguin Books, 1968.

---, *The Masks of God: Occidental Mythology.* New York: Viking Press, 1964.

---, *The Mythic Image.* Bollingen Series C. Princeton: Princeton UP, 1974.

---, "Myths and Mysteries of the Great Goddess." Seminar. The Human Relations Institute: April 6-8, 1983.

---, *Myths to Live By.* New York: Bantom Books, 1978.

---, "Thomas Mann and James Joyce." Seminar. C.G. Jung Institute of San Francisco. 1982.

Campbell, Robert. "Architectural Record." Atlanta: Fernbank Museum of Natural History, 1993.

Capra, Fritjof. *The Turning Point: Science, Society, and the Rising Culture.* New York: Bantam Books, 1982.

Carrington, Leonora. *Down Below*. (1944). Chicago: Black Swan Press, 1983.

---, *The Hearing Trumpet.* (1974). San Francisco: City Lights Books, 1976.

---, *The Stone Door*. (1976). New York: St. Martin's Press, 1977.

Cirlot, J.E. *A Dictionary of Symbols.* Second Edition. New York: Philosophical Library, 1962.

Clark, Raymond. *Catabasis: Vergil and the Wisdom-Tradition.* Amsterdam: B.R. Gruner, 1979.

Clark, R.T. Rundle. *Myth and Symbol in Ancient Egypt.* London: Thames and Hudson, 1959.

Coomaraswamy, Ananda. "The One Thread." *Parabola: The Magazine of Myth and Tradition.* 22.2 (1992): 26-33.

Corbin, Henry. "Pour une Morphologie de la Spiritualité Shîite." *Eranos-Jahrbuch 1960: Mensch und Gestaltung*. Vol. 29. Ed. Olga Fröbe-Kapteyn. Zürich: Rhein Verlag, 1961.

---, *Spiritual Body and Celestial Earth: From Mazdean Iran to Shi'te Iran*. Trans. Nancy Pearson. Bollingen Series XCI: 2. Princeton: Princeton UP, 1977.

---, "Terre Céleste et Corps de Résurrection d'après quelques Traditions Iraniennes." *Eranos-Jahrbuch 1953: Mensch und Erde.* Vol. 22. Ed. Olga Fröbe-Kapteyn. Zürich: Rhein-Verlag, 1954.

Cortázar, Julio. *Hopscotch*. Trans. Gregory Rabassa. New York: Pantheon Books, 1966.

Craft, Robert. Program Notes. *Igor Stravinsky: The Composer*. Vol. 1. Compact Disc. Music Masters (Classics): Amerco Inc., 1991.

Cross, Richard. *Malcolm Lowry: A Preface to His Fiction.* London: The Athlone Press, 1980.

Crossley-Holland, Kevin. *The Norse Myths.* New York: Pantheon Books, 1980.

Cunliffe, Barry. *The Celtic World.* New York: McGraw-Hill Book Company, 1979.

Daemmrich, Horst S. and Ingrd G. *Spirals and Circles: A Key to Thematic Patterns in Classicism and Realism.* Vol. II. New York: Peter Lang, 1994.

Davenport, Guy. *The Geography of the Imagination: Forty Essays by Guy Davenport.* San Francisco: North Point Press, 1981.

Davidson, H.R. Ellis. "Odin: Grim Lord of Valhalla." *Man, Myth and Magic: An Illustrated Encylopedia of the Supernatural.* Ed. Richard Cavendish, et. al. New York: Marshall Cavendish Corporation, 1970.

---, *Scandinavian Mythology*. London: Paul Hamlyn, 1969.

Derrida, Jacques. *D'un ton apocalyptique adopté naguère en philosophie*. Paris: Éditions Galilée, 1983.

Diller, Edward. *A Mythic Journey: Günter Grass's Tin Drum.* Lexington: The University of Kentucky Press, 1974.

Dobbs, Betty Jo Teeter. *The Foundations of Newton's Alchemy, or "The Hunting of the Green Lyon*." Cambridge: Cambridge UP, 1975.

Dodds, E.R. *The Greeks and the Irrational.* Berkeley: University of California Press, 1951.

Doob, Penelope Reed. *The Idea of the Labyrinth: From Classical Antiquity to the Middle Ages*. Ithaka: Cornell UP, 1990.

Doolittle, Hilda. *H.D.: Collected Poems 1912-1944*. Ed. Louis Martz. New York: New Directions, 1983.

---, *Hermetic Definition.* New York: New Directions, 1972.

Doty, William G. *Mythography: The Study of Myths and Rituals.* University: The University of Alabama Press, 1986.

Drucker, Johanna. *The Alphabetic Labyrinth: The Letters in History and Imagination*. London, Thames and Hudson, 1995.

Eco, Umberto. *Foucault's Pendulum.* Trans. William Weaver. San Diego, New York, London: Harcourt Brace Jovanovich, 1989.

---, *The Name of the Rose*. Trans. William Weaver. San Diego, New York, London: Harcourt Brace Jovanovich, 1983.

Edgerton, Samuel Y. Jr. *The Heritage of Giotto's Geometry: Art and Science on the Eve of Scientific Revolution*. Ithaca and London: Cornell UP, 1991.

Edinger, Edward. *Anatomy of the Psyche: Alchemical Symbolism in Psychotherapy.* La Salle: Open Court, 1985.

---, *Moby-Dick: A Jungian Commentary: An American Nekyia.* New York: New Directions, 1978.

Eliade, Mircea. *The Forge and the Crucible: The Origins and Structure of Alchemy*. 2end Ed. Trans. Stephen Corrin. Chicago and London: The University of Chicago Press, 1978.

---, *Myths, Dreams, and Mysteries: The Encounter Between Contemporary Faiths and Archaic Realities.* New York: Harper and Row, 1960.

---, *Shamanism: Archaic Techiniques of Ecstasy.* Princeton: Princeton UP, 1964.

---, *Symbolism, the Sacred, and the Arts.* Ed. Diane Apostolos-Cappadona. New York: Crossroad, 1985.

---, "La Terre-Mère et les Hiérogamies Cosmiques." *Eranos-Jahrbuch (1953): Mensch und Erde*. Vol. 22. Ed. Olga Fröbe-Kapteyn. Zürich: Rhein Verlag, 1954.

Eliot, T.S. "*Ulysses*, Order and Myth." (1923). *The Modern Tradition.* Ed. Richard Ellmann and Charles Feidelson. New York: Oxford UP, 1965.

Ellmann, Richard and Charles Feidelson, Jr. *The Modern Tradition: Backgrounds of Modern Literature.* New York: Oxford UP, 1965.

Emerson, Ralph Waldo. "Circles." *Ralph Waldo Emerson: Essays and Lectures*. Ed. Joel Porte. New York: The Library of America, 1983.

Evans, Sir Arthur. *The Palace of Minos*. 4 Vols. London: Macmillan and Company, 1921 and 1934.

Fabricius, Johannes. *Alchemy: The Medieval Alchemists and Their Royal Art.* Copenhagen: Rosenkilde and Bagger, 1976.

Faivre, Antoine. *The Golden Fleece and Alchemy*. Albany: State University of New York Press, 1993.

Fowler, Douglas. *A Reader's Guide to Gravity's Rainbow*. Ann Arbor: Ardis, 1980.

von Franz, Marie-Louise. *Alchemy: An Introduction to the Symbolism and the Psychology*. Toronto: Inner City Books, 1980.

---, *An Interpretation of Apuleius' Golden Ass.* Dallas: Spring Publications, 1980.

---, *On Dreams and Death: A Jungian Interpretation.* Boulder and London: Shambhala, 1984.

---, *Projection and Re-Collection in Jungian Psychology: Reflections of the Soul.* La Salle: Open Court, 1980.

---, *Puer Aeternus.* 2end Ed. Santa Monica: Sigo Press, 1981.

Friedman, Susan. *Psyche Reborn: The Emergence of H.D.* Indiana UP, 1981.

Frobenius, Leo. *Das Zeitalter des Sonnengottes.* Berlin: 1904.

Frye, Northrop. *Fables of Identity: Studies in Poetic Mythology.* New York: Harcourt Brace Jovanovich, 1963.

---, *The Great Code: The Bible and Literature.* New York: Harcourt Brace Jovanovich, 1982.

Galassi, John. "Lost Paradises." *Parnassus: Poetry in Review.* 5:1 (1976): 305-20.

van Gennep, Arnold. *The Rites of Passage.* Trans. Monika B. Vizedom and Gabrielle L. Caffee. Chicago: The University of Chicago Press, 1960.

Gide, André. *Two Legends: Oedipus and Theseus.* Trans. John Russell. New York: Vintage Books (Random House), 1950.

Gimbutas, Marija. *The Language of the Goddess.* San Francisco: Harper and Row, 1989.

Godwin, Jocelyn. *Athanasius Kircher: A Renaissance Man and the Quest for Knowledge.* London: Thames and Hudson, 1979.

Grass, Günter. *The Tin Drum.* (1959). Trans. Ralph Mannheim. New York: Vintage Books, 1990.

Gray, Ronald D. *Goethe the Alchemist.* Cambridge: Cambridge UP, 1952.

Graves, Robert. *The White Goddess.* Amended and Enlarged Edition. New York: Farar, Straus and Giroux, 1948.

Green, Miranda J. *Dictionary of Celtic Myth and Legend.* London: Thames and Hudson, 1992.

Grof, Stanislav and Christina Grof. *Beyond Death: The Gates of Consciousness.* London: Thames and Hudson, 1980.

Grof, Stanislav. "East and West: Ancient Wisdom and Modern Science." *Journal of Transpersonal Psychology* 15 (1983): 13-36.

---, *Beyond the Brain: Birth, Death, and Transcendence in Psychotherapy.* Albany: State University of New York Press, 1985.

---, *Realms of the Human Unconscious: Observations from LSD Research.* New York: Viking Press, 1975.

Hagstrum, Jean H. *Esteem Enlivened by Desire: The Couple from Homer to Shakespeare.* Chicago: The University of Chicago Press, 1992.

Halifax, Joan. *Shamanic Voices: A Survey of Visionary Narratives.* New York: E.P. Dutton,. 1979.

Harrison, Jane. *Prolegomena to the Study of Greek Religion.* (1903). London: Merlin Press, 1962.

Hart, Mickey. *Drumming at the Edge of Magic: A Journey into the Spirit of Percussion.* With Jay Stevens. San Francisco: HarperSanFrancisco, 1990.

Hayles, N. Katherine. *The Cosmic Web.* Ithaca: Cornell UP, 1984.

Hillman, James. "Anima Mundi: The Return of Soul to the World." *Spring* 1982: 71-93.

---, *Archetypal Psychology*. Dallas: Spring, 1983.

---, *The Dream and the Underworld*. New York: Harper and Row, 1979.

---, ed. *Facing the Gods*. Dallas: Spring, 1980.

---, *Healing Fiction*. Station Hill, 1983.

---, *Loose Ends: Primary Papers in Archetypal Psychology*. Dallas: Spring, 1978.

---, *The Myth of Analysis*. Evanston: Northwestern UP, 1972.

---, *Pan and the Nightmare*. Zürich: Spring, 1972.

---, "Puer Wounds and Ulysses' Scar." 1977. *Puer Papers*. Dallas: Spring, 1979.

---, *Re-Visioning Psychology*. New York: Harper and Row, 1975.

---, "Salt: A Chapter in Alchemical Psychologizing." *Images of the Untouched*. Ed. Joanne Stroud and Gail Thomas. Dallas: Spring, 1982.

---, "The Thought of the Heart." *Eranos Lectures 2.* Dallas: Spring, 1981.

Hoggard, James. "Tornado's Eye." *Two Gulls, One Hawk.* Fort Worth: Prickly Pear Press, 1983.

Hollander, John. "Mirror." *James Merrill*. Modern Critical Views. Harold Bloom, Ed. New York: Chelsea House, 1985.

Homer. *The Odyssey*. Trans. Robert Fitzgerald. New York: Anchor Books, 1963.

The Hours of Catherine of Cleves. Ed. John Plummer. New York: George Braziller, 1975.

Hughes, Robert. *Amish: The Art of the Quilt*. Julie Silber (Plate Commetary). New York: Alfred A. Knopf, 1993.

Jaffé, Aniela, ed. *C.G. Jung: Word and Image*. Bollingen Series XCVII: 2. Princeton: Princeton UP, 1979.

Janson, H.W. *History of Art*. New York: Prentice-Hall and Harry N. Abrams, 1967.

Jonas, Hans. *The Gnostic Religion*. Second Edition. Boston: Beacon Press, 1963.

Jones, David. *The Anathemata*. London: Faber and Faber, 1952.

Josipovici, Gabriel. *The Book of God: A Response to the Bible*. New Haven and London: Yale UP, 1988.

Jung, Carl Gustav. *Alchemical Studies*. Princeton NJ: Princeton UP, 1969.

---, *Four Archetypes*. Princeton: Princeton UP, 1969.

---, *Mandala Symbolism*. (1959). Trans. R.F.C. Hull. Princeton: Princeton UP, 1972.

---, *Memories Dreams Reflections*. Ed. Aniela Jaffe. New York: Random House, 1965.

---, *Modern Man in Search of a Soul.* Trans. W. S. Dell and Cary F. Baynes. New York: HBJ, 1933.

---, *Mysterium Coniunctionus*. Princeton: Princeton UP, 1963.

---, "On the Psychology of the Trickster Figure." *The Trickster: A Study in American Indian Mythology*. Paul Radin. New York: Schoken Books, 1972.

---, "A Psychological Commentary on The Tibetan Book of the Dead." 1935. *Psychology and Religion: West and East*. New York: Pantheon Books, 1958.

---, *Psychology and Alchemy*. Princeton NJ: Princeton UP, 1968.

---, *Psychology of the Transference*. Princeton NJ: Princeton UP, 1966.

---, *Word and Image*. Ed. Aniela Jaffé. Princeton: Princeton UP, 1979.

Kaufman, Walter, ed. *The Portable Nietzsche*. New York: The Viking Press, 1968.

Kazantzakis, Nikos. *The Odyssey: A Modern Sequel*. Trans. Kimon Friar. New York: Simon and Schuster, 1958.

Kenner, Hugh. *The Pound Era*. Berkeley: University of California Press, 1971.

Kerényi, Karl. *Eleusis: Archetypal Image of Mother and Daughter*. Trans. Ralph Manheim. Princeton, NJ: Princeton UP, 1967.

---, *Essays on a Science of Mythology: The Myth of the Divine Child and the Mysteries of Eleusis*. Trans. R.F.C. Hull. Bollingen Series XXII. Princeton: Princeton UP, 1963.

---, *The Gods of the Greeks*. London: Thames and Hudson, 1979.

---, *Hermes: Guide of Souls*. Zürich: Spring, 1976.

---, *The Heroes of the Greeks*. London: Thames and Hudson, 1959.

---, Preface. *Mythology and Humanism: The Correspondence of Thomas Mann and Karl Kerenyi*. Trans. Alexander Gelley. Ithaca: Cornell UP, 1975.

Knapp, Bettina L. *Dream and Image*. Troy, New York: Whitson Publishing Company, 1977.

---, *Theatre and Alchemy*. Detroit: Wayne State UP, 1980.

Lailhacar, Christine de, trans. "The Third Tiger; or From Blanchot to Borges." *Borges and His Successors: The Borgesian Impact on Literature and the Arts*. Ed. Edna Aizenberg. Columbia: University of Missouri Press, 1990.

Lamm, Robert. *The Humanities in Western Culture*. 4th Brief Edition. London: Brown and Benchmark Publishers, 1996.

Lauf, Detlef-I. Captions and Graphic Essays. *Myths*. Alexander Eliot, et. al. New York: McGraw-Hill, 1976.

Lavin, Marilyn Aronberg. *Piero Della Francesca*. New York: Harry N. Abrams, Inc., Publishers, 1992.

Lawrence, D.H. *Apocalypse*. Ed. Mara Kalnins. New York: Viking Press, 1982.

Leeming, David. *Mythology*. New York: Newsweek Books, 1979.

Lehman, David. "Elemental Bravery." *James Merrill: Essays in Criticism*, David Lehman and Charles Berger, eds. Ithaca and London: Cornell UP, 1983.

Leisegang, Hans. "The Mystery of the Serpent." (1939). *The Mysteries: Papers From the Eranos Yearbooks*. Ed. Joseph Campbell. Bollingen Series XXV. Princeton: Princeton UP, 1955.

Lessing, Doris. *Briefing For a Descent Into Hell*. New York: Random House, 1981.

Lowery, Philip. "A Letter." *Agenda: David Jones Special Issue*. 12 (1): 32-34. London: 1974.

Lucente, Gregory L. *The Narrative of Realism and Myth: Verga, Lawrence, Faulkner, Pavese*. Baltimore: Johns Hopkins UP, 1981.

Lucie-Smith, Edward. *Art Now: From Abstract Expressionism to Superrealism*. New York: William Morrow, 1976.

MacDonald, Ronald R. *The Burial Places of Memory: Epic Underworlds in Vergil, Dante, and Milton*. Amherst: The University of Massachusetts Press, 1987.

Maclagan, David. *Creation Myths*. New York: Crossroad, 1979.

Mann, Thomas. *Doctor Faustus: The Life of the German Composer Adrian Leverkühn as Told by a Friend*. New York: Alfred Knopf, 1948.

---, *Doktor Faustus: Das Leben des deustschen Tonsetzers Adrian Leverkühn erzählt von einem Freunde*. *Gesammelte Werke* 12 Vols. Oldenburg: S. Fischer Verlag, 1960. Vol. 6.

---, "Einführung in den *Zauberberg*." *Rede und Antwort: Über Eigene Werke, Huldigungen, und Kränze: Über Freunde, Weggefährten, und Zeitgenossen*. Nachwort von Helmut Koopman. Frankfurt am Main: S. Fischer Verlag, 1984.

---, *Joseph and His Brothers*. New York: Alfred Knopf, 1976.

---, *Joseph und Seine Brüder*. Frankfurt am Main: Fischer Verlag, 1964.

---, *Thomas Mann: Diaries 1918-1939*. Selection and Foreword by Hermann Kesten. Trans. Richard and Clara Winston. New York: Harry N. Abrams, Inc., Publishers, 1982.

Merivale, Patricia. "The Flaunting of Artifice in Vladimir Nabokov and Jorge Luis Borges." *Critical Essays on Jorge Luis Borges*. Ed. Jaime Alazraki. Boston: G.K. Hall & Co., 1987: 141-52.

Marks, Richard and Nigel Morgan. *The Golden Age of English Manuscript Painting: 1200-1500.* New York: George Braziller, 1981.

Marlowe, Christopher. *Doctor Faustus*. *The Literature of Renaissance England*. Ed. John Hollander and Frank Kermode. New York and London: Oxford UP, 1973.

Martin, Gerald. *Journeys Through the Labyrinth: Latin American Fiction in the Twentieth Century.* New York: Verso, 1989.

Márquez, Gabriel García. *One Hundred Years of Solitude*. Trans. Gregory Rabassa. New York: Harper and Row, 1970.

Materer, Tim. "The Error of His Ways: James Merrill and the Fall into Myth." *American Poetry* 7: 3 (Spring 1990).

Matthews, John. *The Grail: Quest for the Eternal*. New York: Crossroad, 1981.

Matthews, W.H. *Mazes and Labyrinths: Their History and Development.* (1921). New York: Dover Books, 1970.

McClatchy, J.D. "Monsters Wrapped in Silk: *The Country of a Thousand Years of Peace*." *James Merrill*. Modern Critical Views. Harold Bloom, Ed. New York: Chelsea House, 1985.

---, "Lost Paradises." *Parnassus: Poetry in Review*. 5:1 (1976): 305-20.

McGuinn, Bernard. *Visions of the End: Apocalyptic Tradition in the Middle Ages.*

McGuire, William. *Bollingen: An Adventure in Collecting the Past.* Bollingen Series. Princeton: Princeton UP, 1982.

Meer, Frederick van der. *Apocalypse: Visions from the Book of Revelation in Western Art.*

Merrill, James. *The Changing Light at Sandover.* New York: Atheneum, 1982.

Meyer, Marvin, ed. *The Ancient Mysteries, A Sourcebook: Sacred Texts of the Mystery Religions of the Ancient Mediterranean World.* New York: Harper and Row, 1987.

Michell, John. *The Earth Spirit: Its Shrines and Mysteries.* New York: Crossroad, 1975.

Miller, J. Hillis. *Ariadne's Thread: Story Lines.* New Haven: Yale UP, 1992.

Milton, John. *Complete Poems and Major Prose*. Ed. Merritt Y. Hughes. Indianapolis: The Odyssey Press (Bobbs Merrill Educational Publishing), 1957.

Nabokov, Vladimir. *Ada, or Ardor: A Family Chronicle.* New York: McGraw Hill, 1969.

---, *Pale Fire.* (1962). New York: Vintage International, 1989.

---, *Pnin*. New York: (Vintage International), 1989.

Neumann, Erich. "Die Bedeutung des Erdarchetyps für den Neuzeit." *Eranos-Jahrbuch 1953: Mensch und Erde*. Vol. 22. Ed. Olga Fröbe-Kapteyn. Zürich: Rhein Verlag, 1954

---, *The Great Mother: An Analysis of the Archetype*. Princeton: Bollingen Series XLVII, Princeton University Press, 1963.

Nietzsche, Friedrich. *The Birth of Tragedy and The Case of Wagner.* Trans. Walter Kaufmann. New York: Vintage Books, 1967.

---, *The Will to Power*. Trans. Walter Kaufmann and R.J. Hollingdale. Ed. Walter Kaufmann. New York: Vintage Books, 1967.

Orenstein, Gloria. *The Theater of the Marvelous*. New York: New York UP, 1975.

Owen, D.D.R. *The Vision of Hell: Infernal Journeys in Medieval French Literature*. Edinburgh: Scottish Academic Press, 1970.

The Oxford Classical Dictionary. Second Edition. Ed. N.G.L. Hammond and H.H. Scullard. Oxford: Oxford UP, 1970.

Patch, Howard Rollin. *The Other World: According to Descriptions in Medieval Literature*. Cambridge: Harvard UP, 1950.

Patrides, C.A. and Joseph Wittreich. *The Apocalypse in English Renaissance Thought and Literature: Patterns, Antecedents, and Repercussions*. Ithaca: Cornell UP, 1984.

Paz, Octavio. *The Labyrinth of Solitude: Life and Thought in Mexico.* Trans. Lysander Kemp. New York: Grove Press, 1961.

Perry, John Weir. *Lord of the Four Quarters: Myths of the Royal Father.* New York: George Braziller, 1966.

Phillips, K. J. *Dying Gods in Twentieth Century Fiction*. Lewisburg: Bucknell UP, 1990.

Poncé, Charles. *Kabbalah: An Introduction and Illumination For the World Today*. Wheaton: Quest Books, 1973.

Pynchon, Thomas. *The Crying of Lot 49*. 1965. London: Picador, 1979.

---, *Gravity's Rainbow*. New York: Viking Press, 1973.

Quinones, Ricardo J. *Mapping Literary Modernism: Time and Development*. Princeton NJ: Princeton UP, 1985.

Quispel, Gilles. "*Der Gnostische Anthropos und Die Jüdische Tradition*." *Eranos-Jahrbuch (1953): Mensch und Erde*. Vol. XXII. Ed. Olga Fröbe-Kapteyn. Zürich: Rhein Verlag, 1954.

Raine, Kathleen. *Blake and Antiquity*. Bollingen Series. Princeton: Princeton UP, 1977.

---, *William Blake*. New York: Praeger Publishers, 1970.

Raphael, Alice. *Goethe and the Philosopher's Stone: Symbolical Patterns in "The Parable" and the Second Part of Faust*. New York: Garrett Publications, 1965.

Reed, Bika. *Rebel in the Soul: A Sacred Text of Ancient Egypt*. New York: Inner Traditions International, 1969.

Reitzenstein, Richard. "Alchemistische Lehrschriften und Märchen bei den Arabern." *Heliodori carmina quattor*. (Religionsgeschichtliche Versuche und Vorarbeiten, XIX, 2.) Giessen, 1923.

---, *Die hellenistischen Mysterienreligionen*. Leipzig, 1910.

---, *Poimandres: Studien zur griechisch-ägyptischen und frühchristlichen Literatur*. Leipzig, 1904.

Robbe-Grillet, Alain. *Dans le Labyrinth*. Paris: Les Editions de Minuit, 1959.

---, *In the Labyrinth*. Trans. Richard Howard. New York: Grove Press, 1960.

Roberts, Gareth. *The Mirror of Alchemy: Alchemical Ideas and Images in Manuscripts and Books From Antiquity to the Seventeenth Century*. Toronto and Buffalo: The University of Toronto Press, 1994.

Robinson, Douglas. *American Apocalypses: The Image of the End of the World in American Literature*. Baltimore: The Johns Hopkins UP, 1985.

Robinson, Janice. *H.D.: The Life and Work of an American Poet*. Boston: Houghton Mifflin Company, 1982.

Rosenberg, Harold. *Barnett Newman*. New York: Harry N. Abrams, 1978.

Rosenblum, Robert. *Frank Stella*. Penguin New Art 1. London: Penguin Books, 1971.

Rubin, William S. *Dada, Surrealism, and Their Heritage*. New York: The Museum of Modern Art, 1968.

Sacks, Peter. "The Divine Translation: Elegiac Aspects of *The Changing Light at Sandover*. *James Merrill: Essays in Criticism*. Ed. David Lehman and Charles Berger. Ithaca and London: Cornell UP, 1983.

Sáez, Richard. "'At the Salon Level:' Merrill's Apocalyptic Epic." *James Merrill: Essays in Criticism*, David Lehman and Charles Berger, eds. Ithaca and London: Cornell UP, 1983.

---, "James Merrill's Oedipal Fire." *James Merrill*. Modern Critical Views. Harold Bloom, ed. New York: Chelsea House, 1985.

Schoch, Rainer. "Albrecht Dürer: Melencolia I." *Gothic and Renaissance Art in Nuremburg: 1300-1550*. Munich: Prestel Verlag and The Metropolitan Museum of Art, 1986.

Scholem, Gershom. *Kabbalah*. New York: New American Library, 1974.

---, "Die Vorstellung vom Golem in ihren tellurischen und magischen Beziehungen." *Eranos Jahrbuch 1953: Mensch und Erde*. Vol. 22. Ed. Olga Fröbe-Kapteyn. Zürich: Rhein-Verlag, 1954.

Schopenhauer, Arthur. *The World as Will and Representation.* Vol.1. Trans. E.F.J. Payne. New York: Dover Publications, 1969.

Schwartz, Regina M. "Joseph's Bones and the Resurrection of the Text: Remembering in the Bible." *PMLA* 103 (1988): 114-124.

Scott, Walter. Ed. and Trans. *Hermetica: The Ancient Greek and Latin Writings Which Contain Religious or Philosophical Teachings Ascribed to Hermes Trismegistus*. (1924). Vol. 1. Boulder: Hermes House, 1982.

Shakespeare, William. *A Midsummer Night's Dream.* Ed. Madeleine Doran. *William Shakespeare: The Complete Works.* Ed. Alfred Harbage. Baltimore: Penguin Books, 1969.

---, *The Tempest*. Ed. Louis B. Wright and Virginia A. Lamar. The Folger Library Shakespeare. New York: Washington Square Press, 1961.

Sheldrake, Rupert. *A New Science of Life: The Hypothesis of Formative Causation.* Los Angeles: J.P. Tarcher Inc., 1981.

Silberer, Herbert. *Probleme der Mystik und Ihrer Symbolik.* Vienna, 1914.

Smith, Evans Lansing. "Alchemy and Modernism." *Cauda Pavonis: Studies in Hermeticism.* New Series. 13 (1994): 11-18.

---, "Apocalypse and Modernism." Paper. Special Session. MLA: December, 1992.

---, "The Arthurian Underworld of Modernism: Thomas Mann, Thomas Pynchon, Robertson Davies." *Arthurian Interpretations.* Spring, 1990. 4 (2): 50-64.

---, "The Descent to the Underworld in Borges and Cortázar." *Yearbook of Comparative and General LIterature*. 1992 (40): 105-115.

---, "The Descent to the Underworld: Jung and His Brothers." *C.G. Jung and the Humanities: Towards a Hermeutics of Culture*. Ed. Karin Barnaby and Pellegrino D'Acierno. Princeton: Princeton, UP. 1990.

---, "Framing the Underworld: Threshold Imagery in the Films of Murnau, Cocteau, and Bergman." *Literature / Film Quarterly.* Forthcoming.

---, "The Golem and the Garland of Letters." *Journal of the Fantastic in the Arts*. Special Issue. Forthcoming.

---, *The Hero Journey in Literature: Parables of Poesis*. Lanham: University of America Press, Forthcoming (Fall 1996).

---, *Rape and Revelation: The Descent to the Underworld in Modernism*. Lanham: The University Press of America, 1990.

---, "Re-Figuring Revelation: Nathaniel Hawthorne's *The Scarlet Letter." The American Transcendental Quarterly.* June, 1990. 4 (2): 91-104.

---, "Re-figuring Revelation: D.H. Lawrence, Thomas Mann, and Hermann Broch." *Faculty Papers: Midwestern State University*. Series 3. 12 (1992-94): 113-127.

---, *Ricorso and Revelation: An Archetypal Poetics of Modernism*. Greenville: Camden House, 1995.

Spengler, Oswald. *Der Untergang des Abendlandes.* Munich: C.H. Beck, 1923.

Spiegelman, Williard. "Breaking the Mirror: Interuruption in Merrill's Trilogy." *James Merrill: Essays in Criticism.* David Lehman and Charles Berger, eds. Ithaca and London: Cornell UP, 1983.

Stasi, Lawrence di. *Mal Occhio {Evil-Eye}: The Underside of Vision.* San Francisco: North Point Press, 1981.

Strauss, Walter A. *Descent and Return: The Orphic Theme in Modern Literature*. Cambridge: Harvard UP, 1971.

Surette, Leon. *The Birth of Modernism: Ezra Pound, T. S. Eliot, W. B. Yeats and the Occult*. Montreal: McGill-Queen's UP, 1993.

Taylor, Thomas. *The Eleusinian and Bacchic Mysteries: A Dissertation*. Ed. Alexander Wilder, M.D. New York: J.W. Boulton, 1875 (Third Edition) and 1891 (Fourth Edition).

Thoreau, Henry David. *Walden*. Ed. Robert Sayre. The Library of America. New York: Literary Classics of the United States, Inc., 1985

Tindall, William York. *Forces in Modern British Literature: 1885-1956.* New York: Random House, 1956.

Treasures From the Bronze Age of China. New York: The Metropolitan Museum of Art and Ballantine Books, 1980.

Trungpa, Chögyam. "Commentary." *The Tibetan Book of the Dead*. Trans. Francesca Fremantle and Chögyam Trungpa. Boulder and London: Shambhala, 1975.

Vendler, Helen. "James Merrill: 'Braving the Elements.'" Harold Bloom, Ed., *James Merrill*: Modern Critical Views. New York: Chelsea House, 1985.

Virgil. *The Aeneid of Virgil*. Trans. Allen Mandelbaum. Berkeley: University of California Press, 1982.

Waite, Arthur Edward. *The Hermetic Museum Restored and Enlarged.* 2. Vols. (1893). Reprinted, London: 1953.

Walcott, Derek. *Omeros*. New York: Farrar, Straus, and Giroux, 1990.

Walker, Barbara. *The Woman's Dictionary of Symbols and Sacred Objects.* San Francisco: HarperSanFrancisco, 1988.

---, *The Woman's Encyclopedia of Myths and Secrets.* New York: Harper and Row, 1983.

Warnock, Mary. *Imagination*. Berkeley: University of California Press, 1989.

The Washburn College Bible. Designed by Bradbury Thompson. New York: Oxford UP, 1979.

Wasson, Gordon, Albert Hofmann, Carl A.P. Ruck. *The Road to Eleusis: Unveiling the Secret of the Mysteries.* New York: Harcourt, Brace Jovanovich, Inc., 1978.

Wilbur, Ken. *The Holographic Paradigm and Other Paradoxes: Exploring the Leading Edge of Science*. Boulder: Shambhala, 1982.

Wilkinson, Richard H. *Reading Egyptian Art: A Hieroglyphic Guide to Ancient Egyptian Painting and Sculpture.* London: Thames and Hudson, 1992.

Wind, Edgar. *Pagan Mysteries in the Renaissance*. (1958). Revised and Enlarged Edition. New York: W. W. Norton and Company, 1968.

Wolkstein, Diane and Samuel Noah Kramer. *Innana: Queen of Heaven and Earth: Her Stories and Hymns from Sumer*. New York: Harper and Row, 1983.

Woodroffe, Sir John. *The Garland of Letters: Studies in the Mantra-S'Astra.* Pondicherry: Ganesh and Company, 1979.

Wooley, Sir Charles Leonard. *Publications of the Joint Expedition of the British Museum and of the Museum of the University of Pennsylvania to Mesopotamia.* 2 vols. London: Oxford University Press, 1934.

---, *Ur of the Chaldees*. London: Ernest Benn, Ltd., 1929.

Wosien, Gabriele Maria. *Sacred Dance: Encounter with the Gods.* London: Thames and Hudson, 1974.

Yates, Frances A. *Giordano Bruno and the Hermetic Tradition.* (1964). Midway Reprint. Chicago: The University of Chicago Press, 1979.

---, *Majesty and Magic in Shakespeare's Last Plays: A New Approach to Cymbeline, Henry VIII, and The Tempest*. Boulder: Shambhala, 1978.

---, *The Occult Philosophy in the Elizabethan Age*. London and Boston: (Routledge and Kegan Paul) Ark Paperbacks, 1983.

---, *The Rosicrucian Enlightenment*. (1972). Boulder: Shambhala, 1978.

Yeats, W.B. *The Poems of W.B. Yeats*. Ed. Richard J. Finneran. New York: Macmillan Publishing Company, 1983.

---, *A Vision*. 1937. New York: Collier Books, 1966.

Yenser, Stephen. *The Consuming Myth: The Work of James Merrill*. Cambridge: Harvard UP, 1987.

Zaleski, Carol. *Otherworld Journeys: Accounts of Near-Death Experience in Medieval and Modern Times*. New York: Oxford UP, 1987.

Zamora, Lois Parkinson. "The Myth of Apocalypse and the American Literary Imagination." *The Apocalyptic Vision in America: Interdisciplinary Essays on Myth and Culture*. Ed. Lois Parkinson Zamora. Bowling Green: Bowling Green University Popular Press, 1983.

---, *Writing the Apocalypse: Historical Vision in Contemporary U.S. and Latin American Fiction.* Cambridge: Cambridge UP, 1989.

Zimmer, Heinrich. *The King and the Corpse*. Princeton: Princeton UP, 1957.

---, *Philosophies of India*. Ed. Joseph Campbell. Bollingen Series XXVI. Princeton: Princeton UP, 1953.

Zolla, Elémire. *The Androgyne: Reconciliation of Male and Female*. New York: Crossroad, 1981.

Studies on Themes and Motifs in Literature

The series is designed to advance the publication of research pertaining to themes and motifs in literature. The studies cover cross-cultural patterns as well as the entire range of national literatures. They trace the development and use of themes and motifs over extended periods, elucidate the significance of specific themes or motifs for the formation of period styles, and analyze the unique structural function of themes and motifs. By examining themes or motifs in the work of an author or period, the studies point to the impulses authors received from literary tradition, the choices made, and the creative transformation of the cultural heritage. The series will include publications of colloquia and theoretical studies that contribute to a greater understanding of literature.

For more information, contact:

Peter Lang Publishing, Inc.
Acquisitions Department
275 Seventh Avenue, 28th floor
New York, New York 10001